GREAT DAYS *in* TEST CRICKET

Published by ABC Books for the
AUSTRALIAN BROADCASTING CORPORATION
GPO Box 9994 Sydney NSW 2001

First published 1996

ISBN 0 7333 0536 9

Designed by Deborah Brash, Brash Design Pty Ltd
Set in 10/13½ Sabon by Brash Design Pty Ltd, Sydney
Colour separations by First Media, Adelaide
Printed and bound in Australia by Allwest Print, Perth

5 4 3 2 1

GREAT DAYS *in* TEST CRICKET

RICK SMITH

an
ABC
BOOK

Contents

Acknowledgments

The author owes a debt of gratitude to all of the following. Without their assistance and cooperation this work could not have been produced.

First, thanks to the following players who so willingly answered questions about these great days: David Allen, Richie Benaud, David Boon, Sir Donald Bradman, Bhagwat Chandrasekhar, Asantha de Mel, Richard Dumbrill, Andy Flower, Grant Flower, David Gilbert, Sir Richard Hadlee, John Hampshire, Jack Kerr, Justin Langer, Dennis Lillee, Greg Matthews, Duleep Mendis, Arthur Morris, Geoff Rabone, Derek Shackleton, Bob Simpson, Maninder Singh, Heath Streak, Raman Subba Row, Bert Sutcliffe, 'Billy' Wade, John Waite, Ajit Wadekar, Doug Walters and John Wright.

Ron Williams for his assistance in researching and proofreading material.

Ric Finlay for helping with statistics and proofreading.

David Parsons (New Zealand), Pete Martin (South Africa) and Rohan Wijeyaratne (Sri Lanka) for their help in interviewing players and researching games played in their own countries.

Khadim 'Kim' Baloch and Kersi Meher-Homji for their help and advice regarding Pakistani and Indian Test cricket.

Jena Pullman, the Library staff at the Melbourne Cricket Club and the Club itself for their assistance and permission to reproduce photographs from their collection.

Don Wigan for interrupting his holiday to interview players in South Africa and Zimbabwe, and for assisting with proofreading.

The Advertiser (Adelaide), *The Age* (Melbourne), *The Evening Post* (Wellington), Brian Bassano, Maurice Blunden, Doug Crampton, Patrick Eagar, Moss Seigert, Gordon Vidler and Nicholas Wilson for permission to reproduce photos from their collections.

Unless quoted otherwise photographs come from the author's collection. Every effort has been made to contact the copyright owners of the photographs, and I hope any errors or omissions will be excused.

RICK SMITH
Prospect, Tasmania, 1996

Introduction

LOVERS OF CRICKET argue endlessly about the game. They debate all manner of things from the relative merits of players, to the vagaries of selectors, to the eyesight of umpires. Discussion can be endless and answers elusive. Is Shane Warne the best leg spinner of them all? Who was the best left-handed batsman? Was Gary Sobers a better all-rounder than Ian Botham? Who was the best keeper, the best fast bowler? It could go on and on.

One thing all will agree on, however, is that Test cricket is a special game. While it can occasionally fail to excite, it can also create matches and moments that will live forever in the minds of those who witnessed them—just ask those who were lucky enough to be at the Gabba in Brisbane on the last day of the Tied Test.

Because of the amount of time over which it is played, a Test match is broken into segments of days and sessions, each of which can stand on its own.

While books have been written about Test matches, looking at a game in its entirety, this work concentrates on the segments, in particular those days which will live in the memory long after the rest of the match has been forgotten.

These are the days when the spectators walk out knowing they have been privileged to see something special. These are days of gripping finishes, when the tension mounts over hours to reach almost unbearable proportions. They are days of astonishing performances when the game's finest players are at their brilliant best, but they are also times when some lesser-knowns secure their piece of immortality.

There are, too, those very rare days—like Boxing Day, Ellis Park, Johannesburg, 1953, when Bert Sutcliffe and Bob Blair showed different kinds of courage, and in the process lifted cricket to something way beyond a mere game. I defy anyone to read the account of that most dramatic of days and not be moved by it.

In all Test history there are many days which could qualify for inclusion in this book, but space has limited the final choice. While many will argue that other days deserve a mention, they would be hard put to leave out any of those chosen. The best... the fastest... the greatest? The answers will always be elusive—but then, that's part of Test cricket's endless fascination and the reason it remains the greatest of games.

For my son David —
may your days be great ones.

The Beginning

ENGLAND v AUSTRALIA

Melbourne Cricket Ground
15 March, 1877 – Day One

THERE HAVE BEEN more interesting and exciting days in Test cricket than this, but none is more important, because this is the day when it all began. On this day a combined Australian team met the English tourists of James Lillywhite on even terms for the first time. On previous visits to Australia, matches had always been against odds, with the locals not being considered good enough to meet the tourists on even terms.

In the period between the first visit of an English team to Australia in 1861–62 and the fourth tour in 1876–77, colonial cricket had improved to such an extent that the coming game was approached with some confidence, despite the fact that earlier in the tour the Englishmen had comfortably defeated a New South Wales XI.

Lillywhite's team was composed entirely of professionals, and was not representative of the full strength of English cricket. Despite the absence of amateur talent and some of the best professionals, there were still some very

James Lillywhite captained England in the first Test. (Maurice Blunden)

1

The Melbourne Cricket Ground at the time of the first Test. (Melbourne Cricket Club)

good players. The attack led by the captain contained Alfred Shaw and James Southerton, all steady and experienced; George Ulyett was a top class all-rounder and a number of others could 'turn their arms over' to good advantage.

While the batting was not as strong, Harry Jupp, Tom Armitage and Andrew Greenwood were all solid players, and with Ulyett made a good core of talent.

The team did, however, have one or two disadvantages to overcome. It had just completed the New Zealand segment of its tour, and had only just arrived back in Australia. It had no chance to warm up with a game or two before the big match.

The other handicap was the absence of the wicketkeeper, Ted Pooley, who had been arrested in New Zealand. While in Christchurch Pooley bet a gullible spectator £1 to 1s that he could predict the score of every local batsman. He then said that each would score nought, a fairly common occurrence in such games. When 11 of them scored ducks, Pooley claimed £11 less the 33 shillings for those who scored. On realising that he had been tricked the punter refused to pay, and the resulting fight saw Pooley arrested and charged with assault and maliciously damaging property. He was forced to remain in New Zealand awaiting trial, and although he was subsequently cleared, he could not rejoin his team in time for the game. As there were no other specialist keepers in the team, Pooley's absence could prove costly.

This match was not premeditated in any way. It had not been part of the original itinerary, and had been added partly as a compliment to the improvement of the locals, and as an opportunity to increase profits, as all of these early tours were financial speculations by the promoters, rather than visits sponsored by cricketing authorities.

If the Englishmen were not at full strength, then neither were their opponents. Three of their best bowlers, Frank Allan, Edwin Evans and Fred Spofforth, were missing—the last named as a protest against the selection of

The England team which toured Australia and New Zealand in 1876–77. *Standing:* H. Jupp, T. Emmett, A. Hogben, A. Hill, T. Armitage. *Seated:* E. Pooley, J. Southerton, J. Lillywhite (capt.), A. Shaw. G. Ulyett, A. Greenwood. *In front:* H.R.J. Charlwood, J. Selby.

Victorian keeper John McCarthy Blackham ahead of New South Welshman W.L. Murdoch. Spofforth, the country's best bowler, considered that Blackham was incapable of keeping to his bowling. One Melbourne paper commented that as Murdoch could not be selected, 'this modest gentleman (Spofforth) had to be left behind'. Throughout his career Edwin Evans showed a reluctance to travel away from Sydney, and Allan was a late withdrawal when he said he could not find the time to play. Apparently he had arranged to meet friends at a local fair. This was roundly condemned by cricket followers and in the press. *The Argus* stated: 'The defection of Allan was a topic universally commented on, and not one word anywhere was heard in his favour'. His reasons for not playing were described as 'inadequate'.

Their replacements to share the attack with 18-year-old New South Wales all-rounder Tom Garrett were left arm spinner Tom Kendall, all-rounder Billy Midwinter (who bowled medium pace) and John Hodges. Of these, Hodges could have been called the luckiest man in the country. He began the season playing for a minor club called the Capulets, but his left arm round-arm bowling attracted the attention of the Richmond club. He had done well enough to earn the notice of the selectors. Like Kendall, this game was to be Hodges's first class debut.

At half-past twelve on a fine autumn Thursday there were about a thousand people present when Dave Gregory, captain of the Grand Combined

Left: Bearded Dave Gregory led the Australians. (Maurice Blunden) *Right:* Charles Bannerman, whose batting dominated Test cricket's first day. (Maurice Blunden)

Melbourne and Sydney XI, won the toss and decided to bat. The new stand was sparsely filled, but the lawns and embankment had a good sprinkling of spectators. *The Argus*, commenting on this 'Grand Combination Match', thought that the crowd was far more moderate than the occasion deserved.

Right on one o'clock Charles Bannerman and Nat Thomson, both of New South Wales, came out to open the innings. Jack Selby of Nottinghamshire took Pooley's place behind the stumps as Alfred Shaw got ready to deliver the first ball in Test cricket to Bannerman. At the time many believed the right arm medium-paced Shaw to be the best bowler in the game, and well capable of destroying the colonials' batting.

Lillywhite set what was a standard field for the time. In addition to Selby behind the stumps, they were placed as follows: James Southerton at short slip, Allen Hill cover point, Tom Emmett point, Lillywhite short leg, Jupp mid-off, Armitage mid-on, Henry Charlwood deep square leg, Ulyett long-on, Greenwood 'over the bowler's head' (straight hit?).

Bannerman began with a cut past point for a single off the second ball, then the fast round arm Hill, who opened from the other end, commenced with a maiden. The veteran Thomson, who had been a New South Wales representative since 1858, took a single off Hill, but was clean bowled in Hill's second over.

The new batsman was Tom Horan, born in Ireland, and as 'Felix' of *The Australasian*, later to become one of Australia's greatest cricket writers. He scored the first boundary of the innings, edging Hill through the slips.

Bannerman, however, settled in and began batting with great confidence. Horan played defensively and fed his partner as much of the bowling as possible. The score had reached 30 when Lillywhite decided to switch ends with his bowlers. Ten runs later he was rewarded when Horan played back to a short-pitched delivery from Shaw and the ball clipped his glove and lobbed to Hill at short slip. This gave Hill the first catch, as well as the first wicket in Tests.

The Australian captain, Dave Gregory, came in for a brief stay. He scored a single off Hill, then was run out by a throw from Jupp. It was

Jack Selby took over behind the stumps when regular keeper, Ted Pooley, was detained in a New Zealand gaol. (Maurice Blunden)

largely his own fault. *The Argus* could only conclude that Gregory must have thought the fieldsman was asleep.

With the score at 3/41, and Australia teetering on the brink of disaster, lunch was taken. There was to be no tea break, with play scheduled to finish at five o'clock.

After the adjournment, which lasted 40 rather than the stated 30 minutes, Bannerman was joined by Bransby Beauchamp Cooper. Born in England, he was the most experienced player in the side, having represented Kent, Middlesex and the Gentlemen. In 1869 he had enjoyed making 101 in an opening partnership of 283 with W. G. Grace for the Gentlemen against the Players.

In a crucial situation Cooper used his experience to great effect, wisely allowing Bannerman to have his head. The New South Welshman, on the other hand, continued to score freely and easily. He was particularly severe on Alfred Shaw, striking the famous 'length bowler' for two fours in an over.

Such an attack forced Lillywhite to replace Shaw with the slow lob bowling of Armitage, while at the other end, Southerton—to this day the oldest man to make his Test debut—came on for Ulyett.

With the score reaching 3/100 England needed a breakthrough, and Armitage tried to oblige with his underhand slows, producing a variety of deliveries. In one over he sent a full toss over Bannerman's head, and then one which rolled along the ground. This was followed by a further full toss, which cleared both batsman and keeper. It failed to bother the Australian, who scored from almost every ball, although the reporter for the Melbourne *Age* called it 'such rubbish... as has probably never been seen on the ground'.

Left: England fast bowler Allen Hill took the first wicket, and later, the first catch in Tests. (Maurice Blunden) *Right:* Tommy Armitage, whose lob bowling was derided by the crowd and enjoyed by the batsmen. (Maurice Blunden)

According to *The Argus*, 'He (Armitage) has brought no small reputation to Australia, but seems to have thrown his skill overboard on the passage out'.

Lillywhite quickly removed Armitage after just three overs, bringing himself into the attack. But it was Southerton who made the break, clean bowling Cooper for a patient and valuable 15. He had suffered one uncomfortable moment when a rising ball from Hill struck him on the hand. The blow forced him to call for a batting glove. The pair had added 77 for the fourth wicket to take the Australians out of immediate danger. Bannerman had moved smoothly to 86 in two hours.

Midwinter was the new batsman. He was to have a unique career. Born in England, he remains the only man to represent both England and Australia in matches between the two countries. As his career progressed he made regular journeys between England and Australia—the first globetrotting professional.

On this day, however, he was not at all comfortable. Lillywhite caused him considerable trouble, which he attempted to solve with some big hitting. After collecting a four and a one, he was caught by Ulyett on the fence, trying to smash Southerton out of the ground. Had it been just a fraction higher it might have succeeded. He had stayed long enough, however, to see Bannerman past a famous century, which he achieved by driving Southerton for a single. This event was received with loud cheering by the crowd.

Five for 142 quickly became 6/143 when veteran Ned Gregory, elder brother of Dave, drove a Lillywhite delivery into Greenwood's hands at long-on. The stroke gave him a piece of unwanted immortality: the first duck in Test cricket.

The English fielding had been most impressive, providing the bowlers with plenty of support.

Wicketkeeper Blackham now came to the crease. He was not a great batsman, but he was a fighter and could be difficult to remove. Adopting the supporting role used successfully by Cooper earlier in the day, the bearded Victorian let Bannerman continue on his merry way.

There were no further wickets for the Englishmen, and the Australians went to stumps at 6/166. Incredibly, Bannerman was 126 not out. It was the first Test century and one of the greatest, particularly considering the lack of support he received from the other batsmen. The 25-year-old, playing in his seventh first-class match, gave only one chance, an ankle-high catch to Shaw at mid-off when he was in the nineties. Without Bannerman's effort, the visitors would have certainly had the match in their keeping. *The Argus* called it 'the grandest display of batting by a colonial player'.

The Englishmen thought it was the best innings they had seen, and Lillywhite believed that only W. G. Grace himself could have rivalled it.

The next day Bannerman moved on to 165 before a ball from Ulyett split the index finger on his right hand and forced him to retire. His score remains the highest made by an Australian in his first Test innings, and it was the major factor in Australia's 245. No one else made 20. In all he batted 290 minutes and struck 18 fours.

Midwinter took 5/78 to restrict the Englishmen to 196, conceding a useful lead of 49. Jupp made 63, Charlwood 36 and Hill 35 not out.

Bannerman could not repeat his heroics of the first innings. No doubt handicapped by his injury, he was bowled by Ulyett for four. Horan top-scored with 20 in a disappointing total of 104. Left 154 to win, the visitors must have thought they had a chance, but they reckoned without the left arm spin of Kendall. Born in England, he had grown up in Victoria, and this was his finest moment. In 33.1 overs he took 7/55 to give his team a 45 run win. Kendall later moved to Tasmania, where he continued to play for many years. He was a talented but wayward character, and Australian cricket should have seen more of him.

In spite of Kendall's brilliant bowling, this Test—like its historic first day—will be remembered for Charlie Bannerman's batting. The star of Test cricket's first day toured England in 1878, and played against Lord Harris's team in 1878–79, the last of his three Tests. He was thought to be the best Australian batsman of the time. Like Kendall, he was something of a character, and did not make the most of his ability. Regardless of that, his single prodigious feat ensured his fame will last as long as Test cricket is played.

AUSTRALIA v ENGLAND

Played at Melbourne Cricket Ground on 15, 16, 17, 19 March, 1877.
Toss: Australia.

AUSTRALIA

C. Bannerman	retired hurt	165	b Ulyett	4
N. F. D. Thomson	b Hill	1	c Emmett b Shaw	7
T. P. Horan	c Hill b Shaw	12	c Selby b Hill	20
D. W. Gregory *	run out (Jupp)	1	(9) b Shaw	3
B. B. Cooper	b Southerton	15	b Shaw	3
W. E. Midwinter	c Ulyett b Southerton	5	c Southerton b Ulyett	17
E. J. Gregory	c Greenwood b Lillywhite	0	c Emmett b Ulyett	11
J. M. Blackham +	b Southerton	17	lbw b Shaw	6
T. W. Garrett	not out	18	(4) c Emmett b Shaw	0
T. K. Kendall	c Southerton b Shaw	3	not out	17
J. R. Hodges	b Shaw	0	b Lillywhite	8
Extras	(B 4, LB 2, W 2)	8	(B 5, LB 3)	8
Total		**245**		**104**

Fall: 2, 40, 41, 118, 142, 143, 197, 243, 245.

7, 27, 31, 31, 35, 58, 71, 75, 75, 104.

Bowling

First Innings: Shaw 55.3–34–51–3, Hill 23–10–42–1, Ulyett 25–12–36–0, Southerton 37–17–61–3, Armitage 3–0–15–0, Lillywhite 14–5–19–1, Emmett 12–7–13–0.
Second Innings: Shaw 34–16–38–5, Ulyett 19–7–39–3, Hill 14–6–18–1, Lillywhite 1–0–1–1.

ENGLAND

H. Jupp	lbw b Garrett	63	(3) lbw b Midwinter	4
J. Selby +	c Cooper b Hodges	7	(5) c Horan b Hodges	38
H. R. J. Charlwood	c Blackham b Midwinter	36	(4) b Kendall	13
G. Ulyett	lbw b Thomson	10	(6) b Kendall	24
A. Greenwood	c E. Gregory b Midwinter	1	(2) c Midwinter b Kendall	5
T. Armitage	c Blackham b Midwinter	9	(8) c Blackham b Kendall	3
A. Shaw	b Midwinter	10	st Blackham b Kendall	2
T. Emmett	b Midwinter	8	(9) b Kendall	9
A. Hill	not out	35	(1) c Thomson b Kendall	0
J. Lillywhite *	c & b Kendall	10	b Hodges	4
J. Southerton	c Cooper b Garrett	6	not out	1
Extras	(LB1)	1	(B 4, LB 1)	5
Total		**196**		**108**

Fall: 23, 79, 98, 109, 121, 135, 145, 145, 168, 196.

0, 7, 20, 22, 62, 68, 92, 93, 100, 108.

Bowling

First Innings: Hodges 9–0–27–1, Garrett 18.1–10–22–2, Kendall 38–16–54–1, Midwinter 54–23–78–5, Thomson 17–10–14–1.
Second Innings: Kendall 33.1–12–55–7, Midwinter 19–7–23–1, D. Gregory 5–1–9–0, Garrett 2–0–9–0, Hodges 7–5–7–2.

Australia won by 45 runs

2

The Demon Creates the Ashes

The Oval
29 August, 1882 – Day Two

CRICKET'S HOLY GRAIL is not an item like a gold cup which breathes wealth and importance. It is a small, rather cheap-looking terracotta urn, with its accompanying velvet bag. It was created as a joke by a group of young ladies and presented to the Hon. Ivo Bligh at Rupertswood, Victoria during his team's tour of Australia in 1882–83. Bligh, on his arrival in Australia, had laughingly said that he had come to bring back the Ashes, in reference to an event which had taken place at London's Kennington Oval earlier in the year.

The events of that late August day inspired a legend, giving Test cricket's oldest protagonists a focus for their rivalry. 'To win the Ashes' is a dream to fire any cricket-loving boy, and a reality given to a very few. Even fewer still were involved in its creation on this day of high drama.

The Australian team, captained by W. L. Murdoch, had been enjoying a successful tour of England, after beating a strong English side during the 1881–82 season. Virtually the same team was involved in defeating nearly all comers during its progress around the countryside. Before the Test it had won 14 games and lost only three. The England selectors, Lord Harris, I. D.

The Australian team which toured England in 1882. *Standing:* H. H. Massie, G. J. Bonner, S. P. Jones, F. R. Spofforth. *Seated:* C. W. Beal, J. M. Blackham, G. Giffen, W. L. Murdoch (capt.), A. Bannerman, P. S. McDonnell, H. F. Boyle. *Front:* G. E. Palmer, T. W. Garrett. *Absent:* T. P. Horan. (Melbourne Cricket Club)

and V. E. Walker and F. R. Burbidge, knew that their chosen combination would certainly be in for a fight. Most thought that the skills of the locals would ultimately triumph.

The selectors picked a strong team. Led by A. N. Hornby, the side comprised W. G. Grace, R. G. Barlow, G. Ulyett, A. P. Lucas, Hon. A. Lyttelton, C. T. Studd, J. M. Read, W. Barnes A. G. Steel and E. Peate. Almost without exception this was the best side England could field.

To oppose them the Australians fielded, in batting order, a team of A. C. Bannerman, H. H. Massie, W. L. Murdoch, G. J. Bonnor, T. P. Horan, G. Giffen, J. M. Blackham, T. W. Garrett, H. F. Boyle, S. P. Jones and F. R. Spofforth. This, too, was a strong combination, with plenty of depth and variety in the batting, and in Spofforth they had the best bowler in the game.

The Oval pitch for this match was not a good one. Murdoch won the toss and elected to bat, but left arm medium-pacer Barlow (5/19) and left arm spinner Peate (4/31) bowled them out for 63. Only Blackham (17), Murdoch (13) and Garrett (10) reached double figures.

England did only a little better in its first innings. Spofforth was irresistible, taking 7/46 in a total of 101. Ulyett (26), Read (19), Steel (14) and Barlow (11) reached double figures.

Under such conditions, the lead of 38 runs could prove vital, and the

Left: Billy Murdoch led Australia superbly and scored a vital 29 in his side's second innings. (Maurice Blunden) *Right:* Hugh Massie, who hit 55 in difficult conditions in the second innings. (Maurice Blunden)

Englishmen were confident that they would be chasing only a small total in the second innings. But 29 August was a day when almost nothing would go to plan.

The second day dawned dull, and in spite of heavy rain in the morning, a large crowd, which grew to 25,000 during the day, was present. Play was due to start at 11.30, but the weather meant that there was a delay of 35 minutes before the Australians could begin their second innings. Although there was little rain during the remainder of the day, the weather was bitterly cold and the sky overcast. Charles Frederick Pardon, in his account of the tour, believed that the wet conditions initially hampered the bowlers and compensated the Australians for their deficit of 38.

The openers, Bannerman and Massie, were as different as any pair could be. 'Alick', brother of first Test century maker Charlie, was one of the game's great stonewallers. A small man with endless patience, he was the sheet anchor of the Australian batting. Hugh Massie, on the other hand, was a very aggressive player, always seeking to dominate the bowling.

Bannerman cut the first ball of the innings for two, but soon reverted to more natural and dour methods, while Massie played his own game. It was evident that apart from one or two deliveries, the pitch lacked the movement of the previous day. The bowling of Barlow and Ulyett could make no

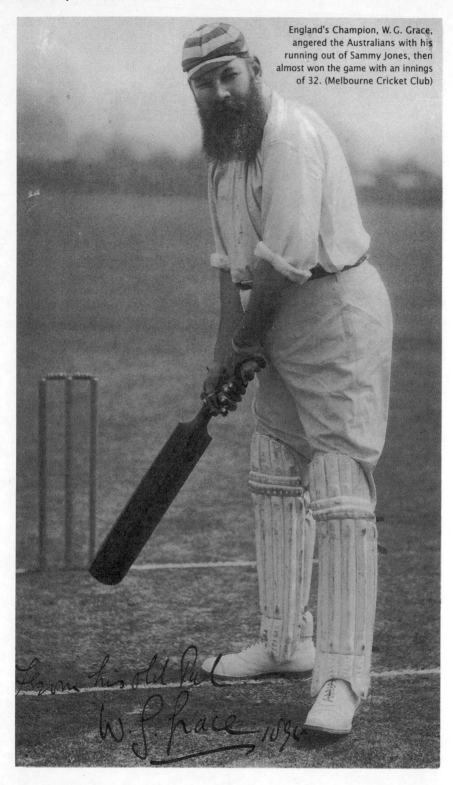

England's Champion, W. G. Grace, angered the Australians with his running out of Sammy Jones, then almost won the game with an innings of 32. (Melbourne Cricket Club)

impression, and they were replaced by Peate and Studd. Massie on-drove both to the boundary, and after 40 minutes' play the first innings deficit was erased without loss.

The Australians now had an excellent opportunity to build a sizeable lead and put pressure on the home side.

Barnes was brought on to replace Studd, and Massie on 38 hit the first ball hard and high to Lucas, who got both hands to it, but dropped it. Enjoying his reprieve, the batsman continued to hit out, reaching an invaluable 50. Massie had made 55 out of 66 when Peate bowled him, securing the break. Massie had hit nine fours in the innings of his life.

Eager to keep the tactic of a hitter and a stonewaller going, Murdoch changed the order and sent in the giant George Bonnor. Hornby countered by bringing back Ulyett, who knocked the slogger's middle stump out of the ground with the addition of only four more runs.

With the score still not advanced beyond 70, Bannerman's defiant innings came to an end, when he was caught at cover point by Studd off Barnes for 13 after 70 minutes of concentration.

The two quick wickets brought the crowd to life, and it was up to Murdoch and Tom Horan to restore the situation. The Australian captain hit Peate to the boundary, but the left armer responded by dismissing Horan (2) and Giffen (0), both caught at point by Grace from successive deliveries. After such a good start five wickets had fallen for only 13 runs, and the lead was just 49.

Blackham avoided the hat-trick by hitting his first ball, a long hop, for four, and in Peate's next over Murdoch almost played on. Lyttelton then missed a delivery which went for four byes, and the score moved into the nineties.

With the total on 99 a shower of rain sent the players from the field to an early lunch.

Play was resumed at 2.45 and Blackham was immediately dismissed, caught by keeper Lyttelton off Peate. Murdoch scored a single to bring up the 100, and the new batsman Sammy Jones cut Barlow for a two and a four.

Steel quickly replaced Barlow, as Hornby was concerned at the possibility of having to chase too many runs in the second innings. Steel's advent to the bowling crease soon saw a controversy which gave the game an edge. From the second delivery a single was scored. Lyttelton had moved to field the ball and return it over the stumps to a fieldsman. This player fumbled the ball and it fell to the ground.

Jones considered that all was safe, and moved out of his ground to prod the pitch. Grace collected the ball and broke the stumps, appealing for a run out. The umpire, Bob Thoms, had no option but to uphold the appeal as the ball was technically not dead, and Australia slumped to 7/114. This act of gamesmanship on the part of Grace incensed the Australians. Murdoch

Fred Spofforth, the demon bowler, whose 14 wickets created a famous victory and the legend of the Ashes. Note the resemblance to Dennis Lillee. (Maurice Blunden)

openly expressed his disapproval, and there were comments about 'dirty cricket' and 'sharp practice'.

Grace's behaviour was particularly annoying to Spofforth, who could have done the same thing to Hornby the day before, but declined to do so. The English champion's action was within the law, but not the spirit, of the game. Charles Pardon expressed the view in his account of the tour that Grace's action was 'legal and fair', but he did not approve of it. *Wisden*, however, commented that Jones ought to thank Grace for teaching him something.

Spofforth stayed with Murdoch while three more runs were added, before he was bowled middle stump by Peate for nought. Joined by Garrett, Murdoch off-drove the ball past Hornby and set off for two, as he believed the English captain had an injured throwing arm. Showing great presence of mind, Hornby flicked the ball to Studd, who returned it in time to beat Murdoch home. Australia was 9/122 and the captain had made a valuable 29.

The innings ended without further addition when Steel bowled Boyle, and England had to make 85 to win. Most considered this well within their capabilities, and felt the Australians had squandered a good start. They also believed that the visitors would fight every inch of the way.

Hornby and Grace opened the innings and Spofforth began bowling very rapidly, still angry at W. G.'s behaviour. In the pavilion he had spurred on his fellows by telling them in no uncertain terms that the game could be won. There was no immediate breakthrough, as runs came in singles until Hornby cut Spofforth to the boundary. Revenge came quickly when the Australian flattened his off stump for nine, and then Barlow played on to his first ball.

At 2/15 there was a glimmer of hope, but this appeared to be snuffed out immediately by Ulyett, who refused to be flustered by the situation and began to support Grace in a good partnership.

Grace hit Spofforth for four and three, and with 30 on the board, Murdoch had his star bowler change ends. As the score mounted Spofforth cut down his run to nine paces and started to 'get some work on the ball'.

The score slowly mounted in spite of some good Australian fielding and the 50 was reached after 55 minutes. Harry Boyle had come on to partner Spofforth, and one run later he made the break, having Ulyett caught low down on the off side by Blackham for 11, after a stand of 36.

Two runs later Boyle did it again when he claimed the prize wicket of Grace for 32. The English champion tried to drive and was caught by Bannerman at mid-off. The Australians must have seen a glimmer of hope, but with six wickets in hand and only 32 runs needed, the odds were still very much in England's favour.

With Lyttelton and Lucas together

Harry Boyle's medium-pace bowling provided excellent support for Spofforth. (Maurice Blunden)

the pressure seemed to be starting to tell on the batsmen. One delivery nearly bowled Lyttelton, but resulted in three runs. Lucas almost played a ball to Murdoch, but when he hit Boyle for two and followed it with a boundary off Spofforth, the scales seemed to be tilting towards England.

The tension, which had been building steadily all day, reached unbearable proportions as 12 maiden overs in succession were delivered by Spofforth and Boyle. The run supply simply dried up, and the batsmen and spectators began to wonder where those few necessary runs would come from. In an effort to break the deadlock, Spofforth suggested deliberately misfielding a ball in order to give the batsmen a single and make them change ends. This was done, and after another four maidens it showed success.

At 5.15, and with the total on 66, Lyttelton was bowled by Spofforth for 12, bringing Steel to the crease. Five wickets remained to score 19 runs, and logic favoured England. But cricket has not always dealt in logic.

Lucas played a ball through the slips for four, leaving 15 to get. Steel was unable to help, as Spofforth caught and bowled him from a 'wretched stroke' before he could open his account. In the same over he bowled Read second ball for nought to reduce England to 7/70.

Barnes was the new batsman, and a very good one to have at number nine. Only the previous season he had scored over a thousand runs in first-class cricket. No doubt the Englishmen were hoping that his aggression could finish matters before much more damage was done. When he on-drove

15

a two, which was followed by three byes, the scales began tilting back towards England once more.

On a day when his nickname of 'the Demon' was truly earned, Spofforth struck again when Lucas played on for five.

In the dressing room the next man, C. T. Studd, a fine batsman, was suffering so badly from nerves that he was shivering under a blanket. Spofforth had Barnes taken off his glove by Murdoch at point, and in the next over from Boyle, Peate—who was a true tailender—hit two and then was bowled to end the match. Studd, who did not receive a ball, remained not out. Australia had won an immortal victory by seven runs. The cream of English batting had lost eight wickets for just 26.

When asked why he tried to hit the winning runs himself, Peate is reputed to have replied, 'Ah couldn't trust Master Studd'.

Whatever was said, it was Spofforth's game; 7/44 gave him 14/90 in the match. In all the Tests to come, few would produce anything to rival or exceed the demon bowler's effort. Spofforth was carried into the pavilion by his admirers. Interviewed years later, he said he reached the pavilion almost without a shirt on his back. He made a speech standing on a table, but later confessed that he could never remember what he said. There were also cries for the other victorious players to come forward.

The crowd broke into excited cheering as the tension was finally over. But for one man it had all been too much. Mr George Ebor Spondler of Brooke Street, Kennington collapsed after complaining that he was unwell, and died in the pavilion. Another spectator became so engrossed that he chewed through the handle of his umbrella without realising it. The pressure also got to the scorer, who wrote 'Geese' instead of 'Peate' in his book.

With such an unexpected result—from England's point of view anyway— many questions were asked. The most popular answer was that, apart from Grace, the English batting had lost its nerve. Many critics believed the batsmen's tactics were faulty. While most admitted that Spofforth was difficult to attack, Boyle was another matter. His bowling was very straight, and perhaps some aggression may have worked against him. But hindsight is a wonderful thing. It took some time for the obvious answer to sink in: that Australia might just have had the better side. Certainly, they had Spofforth, and England had nothing to compare with him. It was the classic case of bowlers winning matches.

In spite of this, complaints were uttered about the decline of English cricket—words that still have a familiar ring.

One supporter, Reginald Brooks, believed the country's cricket had declined so much that he was moved to print the following notice in *The Sporting Times*.

IN AFFECTIONATE
REMEMBRANCE
OF
ENGLISH CRICKET
WHICH DIED AT THE OVAL
ON

29th August 1882

Deeply lamented by a large circle of
sorrowing friends and acquaintances.

R.I.P.

N.B. The body will be cremated,
and the ashes taken
to Australia.

In that little joke lay the birth of a sporting legend and a contest that has
kept England and Australia locked in combat ever since. For that they have
to thank a bowler of extraordinary skill, who chose the moment to produce
his greatest display and to create another legend, that of 'the Demon Bowler'.

ENGLAND v AUSTRALIA

Played at Kennington Oval, London on 28, 29 August, 1882.
Toss: Australia.

AUSTRALIA

A. C. Bannerman	c Grace b Peate	9	c Studd b Barnes	13
H. H. Massie	b Ulyett	1	b Steel	55
W. L. Murdoch *	b Peate	13	(4) run out	29
G. J. Bonnor	b Barlow	1	(3) b Ulyett	2
T. P. Horan	b Barlow	3	c Grace b Peate	2
G. Giffen	b Peate	2	c Grace b Peate	0
J. M. Blackham +	c Grace b Barlow	17	c Lyttelton b Peate	7
T. W. Garrett	c Read b Peate	10	(10) not out	2
H. F. Boyle	b Barlow	2	(11) b Steel	0
S. P. Jones	c Barnes b Barlow	0	(8) run out	6
F. R. Spofforth	not out	4	(9) b Peate	0
Extras	(B 1)	1	(B 6)	6
Total		**63**		**122**

Fall: 6, 21, 22, 26, 30, 30, 48, 53, 59, 63.

66, 70, 70, 79, 79, 99, 114, 117, 122, 122.

Bowling
First Innings: Peate 38–24–31–4, Ulyett 9–5–11–1, Barlow 31–22–19–5, Steel 2–1–1–0.
Second Innings: Peate 21–9–40–4, Ulyett 6–2–10–1, Barlow 13–5–27–0, Steel 7–0–15–2, Barnes 12–5–15–1, Studd 4–1–9–0.

ENGLAND

R. G. Barlow	c Bannerman b Spofforth	11	(3) b Spofforth	0
W. G. Grace	b Spofforth	4	(1) c Bannerman b Boyle	32
G. Ulyett	st Blackham b Spofforth	26	(4) c Blackham b Spofforth	11
A. P. Lucas	c Blackham b Boyle	9	(5) b Spofforth	5
Hon. A. Lyttelton +	c Blackham b Spofforth	2	(6) b Spofforth	12
C. T. Studd	b Spofforth	0	(10) not out	0
J. M. Read	not out	19	(8) b Spofforth	0
W. Barnes	b Boyle	5	(9) c Murdoch b Boyle	2
A. G. Steel	b Garrett	14	(7) c & b Spofforth	0
A. N. Hornby *	b Spofforth	2	(2) b Spofforth	9
E. Peate	c Boyle b Spofforth	0	b Boyle	2
Extras	(B 6, LB 2, NB 1)	9	(B 3, NB 1)	4
Total		**101**		**77**

Fall: 13, 18, 57, 59, 60, 63, 70, 96, 101, 101.

15, 15, 51, 53, 66, 70, 70, 75, 75, 77.

Bowling
First Innings: Spofforth 36.3–18–46–7, Garrett 16–7–22–1, Boyle 19–7–24–2.
Second Innings: Spofforth 28–15–44–7, Garrett 7–2–10–0, Boyle 20–11–19–3.

Australia won by 7 runs

3

Jessop's Match

ENGLAND v AUSTRALIA

The Oval
13 August, 1902 – Day Three

AUSTRALIA'S TOUR of England in 1902 provided two of Test cricket's closest results. The visitors, led by Joe Darling, brought a strong and competitive side, the star player being the legendary Victor Trumper in his finest season. In an incredibly wet summer, Trumper dazzled spectators by reeling off one century after another, frequently in conditions all in favour of the bowlers.

While Trumper received, and deserved, top billing, there were plenty of others capable of producing outstanding performances: Batsmen Reggie Duff; Clem Hill and Syd Gregory; all-rounders Monty Noble, Warwick Armstrong and Bert Hopkins; and a capable keeper in J. J. Kelly. If there was a weakness it lay in the bowling. Tall Hugh Trumble, who bowled off–cutters at medium pace, could destroy a batting line-up, but his only support came from left-armer Saunders and the all-rounders. Fast bowler Ernie Jones was in the side, but the pace of former tours had gone and he played no part in the series after the first two Tests.

Opposed to the Australians was an equally strong English team. Because the series was being played in England the home side could select from all its talent, including players who were unable to make the trip to Australia. This was the golden age of cricket, and the batting reflected the riches. A. C. MacLaren, J. T. Tyldesley, C. B. Fry, T. W. Hayward, F. S. Jackson, K. S.

Ranjitsinhji and G. L. Jessop were just some to consider. There were quality all-rounders in George Hirst, Len Braund and Bill Lockwood, and bowlers like Wilfred Rhodes and Sydney Barnes. The keeper, 'Dick' Lilley, was also a very capable batsman.

With two such strong sides, the series promised to be a good one, weather permitting. It was the weather that ruined the first two Tests. In the first Australia was saved from almost certain defeat after being bowled out for its lowest Test score, 36, in response to England's 376. At Lord's, England reached 3/102 when rain washed out the remainder of the match.

Australia broke the deadlock at Bramall Lane, Sheffield, winning the only Test ever played there by 143 runs, thanks to excellent bowling by Trumble, Saunders and Armstrong.

The Fourth Test, at Old Trafford, was one of the most exciting in history, with Australia winning by just three runs to take the series. Trumper made a hundred before lunch on the first day and Jackson scored a century for England. Joe Darling hit a brave 37 in difficult conditions in the second innings, giving Trumble (6/53) and Saunders (4/52) just enough runs to gather a famous victory. Much of the blame for England's defeat was laid at the door of Sussex bowler Fred Tate. An excellent slips fieldsman, Tate had dropped an outfield catch offered by Darling. Then, as last man—and with eight required to win—he hit a four and was bowled by Saunders on the next ball.

Tate was one of those replaced when the sides moved to The Oval for the final Test. With him went the Indian batting genius Ranjitsinhji and veteran opening batsman Bobby Abel. In their places came Abel's Surrey team-mate Tom Hayward, big hitting Gloucestershire batsman Gilbert Jessop and Yorkshire all-rounder George Hirst. This gave England a strong batting line-up of A. C. MacLaren, L. C. H. Palairet, J. T. Tyldesley, T. W. Hayward, F. S. Jackson, L. C. Braund, G. L. Jessop, G. H. Hirst, W. H. Lockwood, A. A. Lilley and W. Rhodes.

The Australians played the same eleven which won at Old Trafford. In batting order it read: V. T. Trumper, R. A. Duff, C. Hill, J. Darling, M. A. Noble, S. E. Gregory, W. W. Armstrong, A. J. Y Hopkins, H. Trumble, J. J. Kelly and J. V. Saunders.

Winning the toss and batting, the Australians recovered from 7/175 to make 324, thanks largely to 64 not out from Trumble. He then took 8/65 to dismiss England for just 183. With such a substantial lead, another Australian victory looked likely. However, the Australians did not make the most of their opportunity, slumping to 8/114 at stumps on the second day. It was still a substantial lead of 255, but not yet an impossible target.

As expected in this English summer, it rained during the night, but the day dawned fine. In a time of uncovered pitches, The Oval was wet. Good work from the groundstaff managed to get play underway before lunch.

Lockwood bowled Armstrong for 21 and had Kelly leg before for nought to end the innings for 121, collecting 5/45 in the process and leaving England the very difficult task of making 263 to win. The state of the pitch was guaranteed to assist the Australian bowlers, and they were quick to capitalise on it.

MacLaren played on to Saunders while attempting a defensive stroke, and then Tyldesley was bowled, also by Saunders, for nought, to leave England 2/5. Five runs later he gave Palairet a similar ball which hit Kelly in the face after breaking the wicket. After treatment to the wound the keeper was able to continue.

J.V. Saunders, whose left arm pace bowling wreaked havoc in the England top order. (Maurice Blunden)

Jackson and Hayward set about trying to repair the damage. The latter had a reprieve when he was put down by Gregory at short leg off Trumble with the total on 16. The pair had lifted the score to 28 when rain drove the players from the field for 35 minutes.

Three runs had been added after the resumption when Hayward was caught behind off a lifting delivery from Saunders for seven. The left-armer had all four wickets for just nine runs.

Braund now came in to partner Jackson, who was doing well in the difficult conditions. Runs were added slowly and there were few loose balls to punish. When the score reached 48, Braund played back to Trumble and Kelly took a good catch.

With half the side gone for such a low score few believed England would make 100, let alone score another 215 to win. However, if there was a batsman in the world capable of a miracle it was Gilbert Jessop, who now came in to bat. In all cricket's long history there has never been a player like him. Big hitters have come and gone. They have had their good days and their failures, but few have achieved any consistent run-scoring and none approached Jessop. On occasions Ian Botham might be comparable, but not even the mighty 'Beefy' scored his runs at 80 an hour for his entire career. Jessop made 26,698 first-class runs at 32.63 with 53 centuries, and achieved a highest score of 283 out of 355 in 175 minutes at Hove in 1903. On 18 occasions he reached 50 in no more than 25 minutes, and 15 of his centuries were made within the hour. A man of average height, with wrists of steel, his unusual stance at the crease had earned him the name of 'the Croucher'.

Wisden called him 'the most remarkable hitter cricket has ever produced'. Those wanting a more detailed look at this extraordinary cricketer could do no better than read Gerald Brodribb's biography *The Croucher*.

His batting had demolished attacks in county cricket, but he had done little of note in his few Test appearances, although he had made a good 55 at Bramall Lane in the Third Test. With 20 minutes to go to lunch and half the side gone, he certainly had nothing to lose.

The Australians had little time for Jessop. They considered him a fairly crude slogger, and one who would always struggle against good, consistent bowling.

He began with a single off Trumble's first ball, then struck the next three balls from Saunders for two, four and one. After another single he went down the pitch to Trumble and put the ball onto the pavilion awnings. It was counted as only four; the ball had to be hit out of the ground for a six. The next delivery went for another boundary.

After hitting Saunders for another four, he sprang down the pitch, missed, and Kelly fumbled the stumping chance. The crowd, now starting to throw off its depression, breathed a sigh of relief. Jessop responded by hitting the bowler high over cover for another boundary. Another slash just grazed the hand of a sprinting Trumper before lunch intervened. In those 20 minutes before the interval, 39 runs had been added: 29 of them to Jessop and eight to Jackson, who was a composed 39 not out.

Could Jessop keep it up? If he could, there was a chance the remaining 176 runs might be made. Odds, and logic, still favoured a comfortable Australian win.

After the break the pitch was still difficult, but not enough to worry Jessop, who late cut Trumble to the rope. Four byes brought up the 100 in only 80 minutes. Jessop continued to bat aggressively, although Jackson had a let off when Kelly missed another chance, then he played a cut through the slips which yielded five hectic runs. Off the next ball Jessop reached 50, made in 43 minutes out of 70, and the following delivery was cut off middle stump to the fence.

Jackson was missed by Armstrong off Trumble, but in the next over Jessop took Saunders apart. He went down on one knee to sweep the first ball for four, then charged out at the second and pulled it to the fence. A full toss was hammered over the infield and a half volley went to square leg again. Off the fifth ball he calmly placed a single to retain the strike. The over cost 17, and the crowd roared its appreciation.

Darling brought on the leg breaks of Armstrong to replace Saunders. Bowling outside the leg stump with five men on the on side, he managed to restrict Jessop for a time.

In the next over the hundred stand was reached in just 57 minutes, with Jessop on 75. He then found an answer for Armstrong, stepping back and

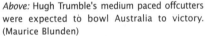

Above: Hugh Trumble's medium paced offcutters were expected to bowl Australia to victory. (Maurice Blunden)

Right: The Hon. F. S. Jackson's innings of 49 gave Jessop valuable support and steadied England's batting. (Maurice Blunden)

cutting him for four, then pulling him through the crowded leg side for another boundary.

At 6/157, the partnership had added 109 in 67 minutes when Jackson was caught and bowled by Trumble for 49. His steady play of the morning had deteriorated in the afternoon, and it was no surprise to see him go.

The new batsman, George Hirst, survived a confident appeal for leg before off Trumble, then celebrated by hitting Armstrong for two fours.

Jessop went on the attack to Trumble. He hit him onto the pavilion balcony for four, followed this with a pair of twos and drove him straight into the pavilion again, to take 12 from the over and bring his score to 96. To say the crowd was going crazy would be an understatement.

Off the next ball he faced he late cut Armstrong to reach his century. It came out of 139 in 75 minutes. It is still, and probably will remain, the fastest century in Ashes Tests. The applause was deafening, and hats, scarves, umbrellas and other items were hurled into the air.

Gilbert Jessop, whose hurricane batting turned certain defeat into eventual victory. (Maurice Blunden)

When the game resumed, Jessop swept Armstrong to the boundary, but in trying to repeat the shot, he gave Noble an easy catch at square leg. The hitter walked off to a tremendous ovation for the innings of a lifetime. Later, Jessop described the century as 'restrained', but as Lionel Brown points out in his book of the tour, it was performed on a bowler's pitch and at a very critical stage of the Test match. In his autobiography *Twenty-Four Years of Cricket*, England keeper 'Dick' Lilley said, 'the odds against him were unlimited', while of all innings ever played this was the one C. B. Fry believed should have been put on film.

Jessop's miracle had lifted England to 7/187, giving it the faint possibility of a win, but the odds still favoured Australia, as 76 runs were still needed in less than perfect conditions.

One paper published a ball by ball account of the innings:

12411... 441.4... 141. 111. 41... 1. 3. 1. 3514... 44441... 1... 12... 4... 41. 42. 244. 4. w.

Jessop later said that the greatest satisfaction came from restraining himself against Trumble's bowling. He resisted the temptation to play across the line, being content to settle for singles instead of trying to belt the cover off the ball—although he did admit to being tempted on a few occasions. After this innings the Australians had to admit that Jessop in form was a devastating proposition. They would not underestimate him again.

English playwright Ben Travers watched this game as a young boy, and nearly 80 years later he set down his impressions. 'It is obviously impossible to recall that Jessop innings in detail, but there are certain features of it and its effect upon the crowd that remain as clearly in my mind as though it all happened yesterday. To begin with, I was struck by Jessop's undaunted, almost heedless approach—no desperate situation about it. Jaunty. He was his own aggressive self right from the start... However despondent the crowd must have been during the morning, Jessop aroused them to a state of wild exhilaration.' The innings had a singular effect on the 15-year-old Travers, 'I know I was young and almost foolishly impressionable at the time but I have always treasured and still treasure that century of Jessop's above and apart from all the rest'.

Lockwood and Hirst set about the bowling, with the latter pulling and driving Saunders for two boundaries to bring up 200. Hirst did virtually all the scoring, but at 214 Trumble trapped Lockwood leg before for two.

With 49 still needed, keeper Lilley came in. He lived dangerously, nearly playing on to Saunders, then almost giving a return catch to Trumble. A boundary to each, some singles, another boundary, and the total was past 230.

As the score mounted so did the tension, but the batsmen seemed the two least concerned by it. Each run was frantically cheered, and the gap between the two sides became smaller.

When the total had reached 248—only 15 to go—Lilley lifted an off drive from Trumble, and Darling threw himself across to take the catch. Lilley had made 16 out of a partnership of 34, continuing to make victory a possibility.

The last man was left arm spinner Wilfred Rhodes, and he was no mere tailender. In the next series between the two countries he would add 130 for the last wicket with R. E. Foster. Within a decade he was one of England's opening batsmen, and at Sydney in the Fourth Test of the 1911–12 series he would make 179 in an opening partnership of 323 with Jack Hobbs. Both stands remain English records in Ashes Tests.

The meeting of the two Yorkshiremen on this day gave rise to the oft repeated, but untrue, story that they agreed to 'get them in singles'.

Rhodes survived the rest of Trumble's over, and Hirst took a single off Noble to reach his 50 in just 65 minutes. Good scoring, but it seemed slow after Jessop's onslaught.

Rhodes then put the crowd on edge again, by playing Noble through the slips for four. The batsman tried the shot again and Armstrong got a hand to it, but could not hold the catch.

A single off Trumble to Hirst. Rhodes was nearly caught and bowled off the next delivery, but they held on. There was another single to Hirst, before the game seemed to be decided in Trumble's next over. A run to each batsman was followed by two to Hirst, the second courtesy of an overthrow. When the incoming throw struck the batsman on the shoulder, it is difficult to imagine if he even felt it. His reply was to take a single off the last ball and keep the strike. Just to increase the tension, rain began to fall.

Cool in the crisis, Hirst played the over from Noble carefully, and took another single off the last ball. Just two to win, and Hirst made sure of the tie by placing a ball between the bowler and mid-off. With the knowledge that England could not lose, the crowd erupted.

It was obviously too much for one man of the cloth, who ran howling onto the field. Both batsmen smiled, and even some of the Australians laughed.

After playing three deliveries calmly, Rhodes pushed the next between Trumble and Duff, and ran. He did not stop until he reached the pavilion. Hirst was caught on the way off by the crowd and carried from the field. His 58 not out had continued the impetus created by Jessop. He had begun with half a dozen boundaries, but had adjusted his play to the situation to such an extent that 13 of his last 14 scoring strokes were singles. *Wisden* felt that in its own way, this innings was every bit as valuable as Jessop's. Criticism was also levelled at Darling for concentrating too much on the bowling of Saunders; it was felt that Noble could have been used more.

England had won, by a single wicket, a game that it had no right to win. In spite of the cool heads of Hirst and Rhodes, the situation was saved by one of Test cricket's most remarkable innings. *Wisden* commented, 'All things considered a more astonishing display has never been seen. What he did would have been scarcely possible under the same circumstances to any other living batsman'. Who could possibly argue with that?

Jessop would not repeat such heroics in Tests again. At first-class level he would make higher scores and he would make them more quickly than at The Oval in 1902, but he would never play a more important knock. The power to create a legend is given to very few. Gilbert Jessop was one.

ENGLAND v AUSTRALIA

Played at Kennington Oval, London on 11, 12, 13 August, 1902.
Toss: Australia.

AUSTRALIA

V. T. Trumper	b Hirst	42	run out	2
R. A. Duff	c Lilley b Hirst	23	b Lockwood	6
C. Hill	b Hirst	11	c MacLaren b Hirst	34
J. Darling *	c Lilley b Hirst	3	c MacLaren b Lockwood	15
M. A. Noble	c & b Jackson	52	b Braund	13
S. E. Gregory	b Hirst	23	b Braund	9
W. W. Armstrong	b Jackson	17	b Lockwood	21
A. J. Y. Hopkins	c MacLaren b Lockwood	40	c Lilley b Lockwood	3
H. Trumble	not out	64	(10) not out	7
J. J. Kelly +	c Rhodes b Braund	39	(11) lbw b Lockwood	0
J. V. Saunders	lbw b Braund	0	(9) c Tyldesley b Rhodes	2
Extras	(B 5, LB 3, NB 2)	10	(B 7, LB 2)	9
Total		**324**		**121**

Fall: 47, 63, 69, 82, 126, 174, 175, 256, 324, 324.   6, 9, 31, 71, 75, 91, 99, 114, 115, 121.

Bowling

First Innings: Lockwood 24–2–85–1, Rhodes 28–9–6–0, Hirst 29—5–77–5, Braund 16–5–29–2, Jackson 20–4–66–2, Jessop 6–2–11–0.

Second Innings: Lockwood 20–6–45–5, Rhodes 22–7–38–1, Hirst 5–1–7–1, Braund 9–1–15–2, Jackson 4–3–7–0.

ENGLAND

A. C. MacLaren *	c Armstrong b Trumble	10	b Saunders	2
L. C. H. Palairet	b Trumble	20	b Saunders	6
J. T. Tyldesley	b Trumble	33	b Saunders	0
T. W. Hayward	b Trumble	0	c Kelly b Saunders	7
Hon. F. S. Jackson	c Armstrong b Saunders	2	c & b Trumble	49
L. C. Braund	c Hill b Trumble	22	c Kelly b Trumble	2
G. L. Jessop	b Trumble	13	c Noble b Armstrong	104
G. H. Hirst	c & b Trumble	43	not out	58
W. H. Lockwood	c Noble b Saunders	25	lbw Trumble	2
A. F. A. Lilley +	c Trumper b Trumble	0	c Darling b Trumble	16
W. Rhodes	not out	0	not out	6
Extras	(B 13, LB 2)	15	(B 5, LB 6)	11
Total		**183**		**9/263**

Fall: 31, 36, 62, 67, 67, 83, 137, 179, 183, 183.   5, 5, 10, 31, 48, 157, 187, 214, 248.

Bowling

First Innings: Trumble 31–13–65–8, Saunders 23–7–79–2, Noble 7–3–24–0.

Second Innings: Trumble 33.5–4–108–4, Saunders 24–3–105–4, Noble 5–0–11–0, Armstrong 4-0–28–1.

England won by 1 wicket

4

Last Stand

SOUTH AFRICA V ENGLAND

The Wanderers, Johannesburg
4 January, 1906 – Day Three

SOUTH AFRICA had played eleven Tests before the first game of the 1905–06 series, losing ten and drawing one. It was hardly a record to be proud of, and indeed some cricket historians argue to this day that most of those early games have no right to be regarded as Tests.

English sides had made four previous visits to South Africa, playing eight Tests, and winning them all. Although the teams contained by no means the best players, being primarily a collection of those available and ready to travel, they were useful combinations, containing many fine players. The team of 1905–06 was no exception. It was the first trip to South Africa under the auspices of the MCC and it was led by Middlesex batsman Pelham Warner, who two seasons earlier captained England to victory in Australia. Although this side lacked the strength of that team, there were several good players, like the exciting all-rounder, 19-year-old J.N. Crawford, and left arm spinner Colin Blythe. Both were expected to make a big impact in the series.

The South Africans, on the other hand, were determined not to be easy-beats, and for this series they had produced something of a secret weapon. Warner's success in Australia owed much to the bowling of B.J.T. Bosanquet, the inventor of the googly. The off break delivered with a leg break action had bamboozled the Australians and added something new to the game of cricket. The South Africans had seized upon this style of bowling and in short order produced a number of googly bowlers. For this game, the home side had chosen six players to make their Test debuts, and four of them—Aubrey Faulkner, Ernie Vogler, Reggie Schwarz and Gordon White—all bowled googlies. The captain, keeper Percy Sherwell, was also playing in his first game.

No doubt the South Africans had improved. They had enjoyed a good tour of England in 1904, but they would still be at long odds to win a game, let alone the series. Although they were developing more experience, their batting seemed a little weak to deal with a spinner of Blythe's talent.

There seemed to be little to contradict this in the early part of the tour as the visitors demolished the various teams arrayed against them in the first five games. However, there was one hiccup when Transvaal beat them by 60 runs.

The First Test was to be played at the old Wanderers Ground in Johannesburg, an oval now buried beneath the city's railway station, early in the new year. This Test, like all others in the series and all Tests in South Africa until 1930–31, was played on matting, not turf.

Although Warner won the toss and decided to bat, his side could not take advantage of the situation, making 184. The googly bowlers captured eight of the wickets, and only Crawford, with 44, could get past the twenties.

That good start was frittered away as the Englishmen struck back to dismiss South Africa for just 91. Blythe took 3/33 and Crawford, who bowled right arm medium-pace off breaks, captured 2/14, but the best figures were achieved by Walter Lees, a right arm fast-medium bowler, who took 5/34.

With a useful lead of 93 the Englishmen set out to bat South Africa out of the game. Although Warner made 51, Crawford 43 and David Denton 34, the innings ended at 190. The googly bowlers again took eight wickets, with Faulkner, 4/26, the best of them.

This left South Africa 283 to win, by far the highest total in the game. By stumps they had made 68 of them, but had lost the wickets of Tancred and Hathorn for 22, before Shalders and White took them through to the close.

On the third day England had an ideal start when Shalders was run out for 38 before a run had been added. Snooke had made nine when he fell leg before to Lees, then big hitting Jimmy Sinclair was caught by F. L. Fane, also off Lees, for five. Further disaster was not long in coming when keeper Jack Board threw the stumps down to run out Faulkner for six.

At 6/105 the game looked well beyond the Springboks' capacity to win, when 'Dave' Nourse joined White in a vital partnership. The pair withstood everything the bowlers could send against them for over two hours to add 121 runs for the seventh wicket.

Nourse survived one chance. When he was 11 he gave the slips a very difficult catch, which was not accepted. In all fairness the fieldsman did well to get a hand to the ball, which went high and wide to his left.

'Dave' Nourse. (Brian Bassano)

White had taken his score to 81 when a fine delivery from Albert Relf bowled him. His four-hour innings had given his side a faint chance of an unlikely victory. That chance seemed to be rapidly snuffed out when Vogler was bowled by Hayes for two, with the total on 230.

Schwarz joined Nourse, and the pair played through to the tea interval without further loss, but shortly after the break Schwarz was caught and bowled for two by Relf.

The last pair now had the task of scoring 45 to win the game. South Africa had more chance than one would have thought under such circumstances. While Nourse was quite capable of getting the runs, not too many number elevens would have been able to stay with him. But Sherwell was not your average number eleven. He was, in fact, quite a good batsman, and he began by hitting the first ball he received to the boundary.

When Relf and Hayes were unable to secure the last wicket, Warner brought on Lees and Crawford. As the runs ticked away, Relf came back on in place of Crawford.

Finally, with the tension mounting, the required number of runs slipped below ten. With eight runs needed, Sherwell edged Crawford between Hayes and Relf to the boundary. A huge cheer, tinged with relief, split the air.

Nourse then hit Relf to leg for three to tie the score.

The tension had reached unbearable proportions as Warner brought the fieldsmen in around the bat to cut off the single. Sherwell played two balls carefully and let the third go through to the keeper. The pressure had to get to someone, and it got to Relf. He sent down a slow full toss outside the leg stump, which Sherwell gleefully smashed to the square leg boundary to win the game. According to *Wisden*, the Englishmen lost 'by one wicket after they had seemed to have the game in their hands'.

For a country to win its first Test is a special moment; to do it by adding 48 runs for the last wicket simply adds to the glory. Sherwell walked off with 22 not out against his name, and the knowledge that he led from the front at a critical time. Nourse remained 93 not out after over three hours at the crease, an innings of courage and determination, words that would symbolise his long career. 'In every way a splendid innings,' was the comment of *Wisden*.

Warner, in his book on the tour, was glowing in his praise of the pair. 'Nourse played a magnificent game... His back play was faultless. His back play was exceptionally strong, and he had a beautiful half-drive, half-cut behind point, while he was also very strong on the leg side. He scarcely ever drove a ball straight, but made most of his runs just in front or just behind point and on the leg side. His level-headedness and sterling cricket won the match for South Africa.

'Sherwell deserves just as much praise as Nourse, and no one could have played more calmly and coolly. Everything depended on him. If he failed the match

Percy Sherwell, the South African captain, partnered Nourse in a last wicket stand that produced his country's first Test win. (Brian Bassano)

was lost to his side, and the way he rose to the occasion and snatched a victory from the jaws of defeat stamps him as a big-hearted cricketer'.

Sherwell went on to play 13 Tests, ending his career by captaining South Africa on its first tour of Australia in 1910–11. In those games he scored 427 runs at 23.72 with one century and one fifty, caught 20 batsmen and stumped 16.

Nourse had a much longer career. He played for South Africa until 1924, representing his country in 45 Tests. He scored 2234 runs at 29.78, captured 41 wickets at 37.87 and took 43 catches. In first class cricket, he continued until 1936, when at the age of 57 he made good runs in his last match, against the might of the Australian tourists led by Vic Richardson, containing bowlers like Bill O'Reilly and Clarrie Grimmett. He was tough and uncompromising, and he—as much as anyone—gave South Africa a start on its road to cricket prominence. His son, Dudley, played 35 Tests—scoring 2960 runs at 53.81 and captaining South Africa in three series—and is rightly regarded as one of its finest batsmen.

Lees (3/74) and Relf (2/47) had led the bowling, but try as they might they could not finish the job. In fact the result was the start of a triumphant series, as the South Africans emerged 4–1 winners.

The scenes at the end of this wonderful day were memorable indeed. According to Warner, 'Men were shrieking hysterically, some were even crying, and hats and sticks were flying everywhere. When the winning hit had been made the crowd simply flung themselves at Nourse and Sherwell and carried them into the pavilion, while, for half an hour after it was all over, thousands lingered on, and the whole of the South African Eleven had to come forward on to the balcony of the committee-room'.

Abe Bailey, a strong supporter of South African cricket, asked Warner to address the crowd. The England captain did so, praising the effort in what he called a classic among cricket contests. 'And so we were beaten, but defeat in such a struggle was glorious, for the First Test match will be talked of in South Africa as long as cricket is played there.'

Indeed it has.

SOUTH AFRICA v ENGLAND

Played at Old Wanderers, Johannesburg on 2, 3, 4 January, 1906.
Toss: England.

ENGLAND

P. F. Warner *	c Snooke b Schwarz	6	b Vogler	51
F. L. Fane	c Schwarz b Faulkner	1	b Snooke	3
D. Denton	c Faulkner b Schwarz	0	b Faulkner	34
E. G. Wynyard	st Sherwell b Schwarz	29	b Vogler	0
E. G. Hayes	c & b Vogler	20	c Schwarz b Snooke	3
J. N. Crawford	c Nourse b Sinclair	44	b Nourse	43
A. E. Relf	b White	8	c Sherwell b Faulkner	17
S. Haigh	b Faulkner	23	lbw b Nourse	0
J. H. Board +	not out	9	lbw b Faulkner	7
W. S. Lees	st Sherwell b White	11	not out	1
C. Blythe	b Sinclair	17	b Faulkner	0
Extras	(B 6, LB 9, NB 1)	16	(B 23, LB8)	31
Total		184		190

Fall: 6, 6, 15, 53, 76, 97, 145, 147, 159, 184.

3, 55, 56, 73, 113, 166, 174,185, 190, 190.

Bowling

First Innings: Schwarz 21–5–72–3, Faulkner 22–7–35–2, Sinclair 11–1–36–2, Vogler 3–0–10–1, White 5–1–13–2, Nourse 1–0–2–0.

Second Innings: Schwarz 8–1–24–0, Faulkner 12.5–5–26–4, Sinclair 5–1–25–0, Vogler 11–3–24–2, White 4–0–15–0, Nourse 6–4–7–2, Snooke 12–4–38–2.

SOUTH AFRICA

L. J. Tancred	c Board b Lees	3	c Warner b Blythe	10
W. A. Shalders	c Haigh b Blythe	4	run out	38
C. M. H. Hathorn	b Lees	5	c Crawford b Lees	4
G. C. White	c Blythe b Lees	8	b Relf	81
S. J. Snooke	c Board b Blythe	19	lbw b Lees	9
J. H. Sinclair	c & b Lees	0	c Fane b Lees	5
G. A. Faulkner	b Blythe	4	run out	6
A. W. Nourse	not out	18	not out	93
A. E. E. Vogler	b Crawford	14	b Hayes	2
R. O. Schwarz	c Relf b Crawford	5	c & b Relf	2
P. W. Sherwell *+	lbw b Lees	1	not out	22
Extras	(B 9, LB 1)	10	(B 6, LB 2, NB 7)	15
Total		91		9/287

Fall: 5, 11, 13, 35, 39, 43, 44, 62, 82, 91.

11, 22, 68, 81, 89, 105, 226, 230, 239.

Bowling

First Innings: Lees 23.1–10–34–5, Blythe 16–5–33–3, Crawford 7–1–14–2.

Second Innings: Lees 33–10–74–3, Blythe 28–12–50–1, Crawford 17–4–49–0, Haigh 1–0–9–0, Relf 21.5–7–47–2, Wynyard 3–0–15–0, Hayes 9–1–28–1.

South Africa won by 1 wicket

Bradman v Bodyline

Melbourne Cricket Ground
2 January, 1933 – Day Three

T HERE HAS NEVER been a more controversial Test series than that of 1932–33. More than 60 years on, the acrimony of that summer remains, and the word 'Bodyline' overshadows everything else, including the actual cricket. So much happened during this series, that almost every day would have qualified for inclusion in this book.

When Douglas Jardine was named captain of the England side, he was faced with the prospect of curbing the run-scoring of Don Bradman. In the 1930 series, Bradman had made 974 runs, and any such repeat performance would make it impossible to regain the Ashes. If England was to win then Bradman had to be stopped, or at least restricted. To achieve this, Bodyline was born, not that it was called that in the beginning.

There are many stories and theories about how the tactic was created, and this is not the place to analyse them. Here, only the outcome is important. For whatever reason, Jardine believed that Bradman could be unsettled by fast, short-pitched bowling. In order to pursue this, his side was heavily loaded with fast men. The principal weapon was to be 'Notts Express' Harold Larwood, supported by his county partner, left armer Bill Voce, Middlesex amateur 'Gubby' Allen and Yorkshire quick Bill Bowes.

With so many fast bowlers, the Australians had an idea what to expect, but as the tour evolved, the pace, line and length of the bowlers was com-

Bill Woodfull is struck by a Larwood delivery. This picture clearly shows the packed leg-side field used for Bodyline.

plemented by an array of close catchers on the leg side, supported by fieldsmen protecting the boundary. The bowlers, except for the amateur Allen (who refused to bowl it, and whose letters show he had little liking for his captain) pitched short and at the batsmen. If a batsman defended he ran the risk of giving a catch to the close fielders, and if he attacked there was a good chance he would perish in the outfield. To duck and dodge produced a stalemate. The tactics were within the laws of cricket, but many considered them an affront to the game's spirit.

In his book, *The Larwood Story*, Larwood gave his version of what Bodyline meant. 'To bowl bodyline you had to be fast. Fast enough to make thunderbolts rear from the pitch in the direction of the batsman's ribs, shoulder or head. The faster the better. It left him with an even finer split-second to decide whether to attempt a stroke, dart out of the way or take a rib-roaster.

'They said I was the fastest bowler in the world. I hurled the ball at the batsman at close on a hundred miles an hour, giving him less than half a second from the precise moment of delivery to make a decision and act.'

For Jardine, the proof was in the result, and his side comfortably won the First Test, in spite of an incredible innings of 187 not out from Stan McCabe. He ferociously hooked Larwood and company, and on this day his luck was in. The young New South Welshman would not repeat his display in the remainder of the series.

While the victory was certainly a sweet one, it was not complete. Don Bradman was not a member of the Australian team. He had been involved in a dispute with the Board of Control over a contract to write about the series and was not in particularly good health. Although the issue of the contract was resolved when his employer released him from the agreement, Bradman's doctors decided a rest was needed.

The English knew that Bradman had to be mastered in Melbourne or the series could well be lost. The Australian batsman had put much thought into how he would deal with this form of attack. With his lightning footwork he could avoid being hit, but he had to make runs. There was no point dancing and dodging all day for no score, and the hook shot was out because he was too small to keep on top of it.

Bradman told journalist A.G. 'Johnnie' Moyes of his intentions. He would walk away from his wicket and try to hit the ball through the off-side field. If he succeeded, it would put the bowler off his balance and would force him to weaken the on-side field and strengthen the off-side field. Then he would revert to normal batsmanship. It was a daring tactic, which many (including Bradman himself) thought left the batsman more open to injury because of the unorthodox footwork required.

A number of people, in particular Jack Fingleton, were critical of Bradman's methods. For some perverse reason they felt that he should have stood and taken his punishment like a man, rather than dancing, dodging and playing shots. It's hard not to attach to their comments some malicious desire to see the great batsman injured. Jealousy of Bradman was not uncommon among certain sections of Australian cricket. The proof was surely in the outcome, and Bradman's methods were twice as successful as any others, in spite of the fact that Bodyline was delivered at him with more intensity than anyone else. He knew orthodox cricket would fail, and so determined to follow another course. Bradman believed that he achieved moderate success with these methods. It is hard to see what more effective methods could have been adopted.

For this particular game the Englishmen made a strange decision. They omitted their left arm spinner Hedley Verity and picked all four fast bowlers. This was the first time an England side played without a slow bowler. Vice-captain Bob Wyatt was critical of this decision, telling Jardine that if three bowlers could not do the job, then four wouldn't be any better. As usual, Jardine got his way, and the chosen team was Herbert Sutcliffe, Bob Wyatt, Wally Hammond, Nawab of Pataudi, Maurice Leyland, Douglas Jardine, Les Ames, 'Gubby' Allen, Harold Larwood, Bill Voce and Bill Bowes.

The Australians also made changes, the most important being the return of Bradman. Victorian left-hand batsman Leo O'Brien was chosen to bat at number three, the spot usually reserved for Bradman. It was felt that Bodyline might not be as effective against left-handers. Veteran left arm spinner Bert Ironmonger was included as well, and fast bowler Lisle Nagel and batsmen Alan Kippax and Bill Ponsford were dropped. This gave the Australians a line-up of Jack Fingleton, Bill Woodfull, Leo O'Brien, Don Bradman, Stan McCabe, Vic Richardson, Bert Oldfield, Clarrie Grimmett, 'Tim' Wall, Bill O'Reilly and Bert Ironmonger.

Australia won the toss and batted on a pitch looking more suited to slow—rather than fast—bowling, but could only manage 228. Fingleton made a brave 83, McCabe 32 and Richardson 34, but the sensation was Bradman, bowled off the edge, first ball aiming a pull at Bowes. He must seldom have played a worse stroke, or at least one with a worse outcome. The Englishmen could hardly believe their luck. However, they squandered the opportunity to build a match-winning lead, collapsing to 9/161 by stumps on the second day. Sutcliffe made 52 and Allen remained 26 not out. O'Reilly's mixture of leg breaks and googlies delivered at around medium pace and with plenty of aggression had accounted for four of the wickets, and fast-medium Wall also captured four.

The third day's play began with a record. The crowd of 68,238 was the largest ever to attend a single day's play at that time. It exceeded the previous record of 63,993 set on the first day. Public interest in this game and the series was intense. There had been queues outside the ground from eight o'clock in the morning, and the gates were closed at ten.

The last wicket added eight further runs before Allen fell to O'Reilly for 30, giving the bowler his fifth wicket for 63 runs. The batsman had just hit a four and was trying to repeat the shot when he found Richardson on the fence. England's total of 169 gave Australia a small, but important, lead of 59. With the problem of scoring on this pitch, it might be vital.

The advantage looked to be given away almost immediately as Fingleton fell for a single, caught by keeper Ames off Allen's third ball in the second over.

O'Brien was looking confident and Woodfull as solid as ever when Jardine relieved Allen after three overs, replacing him with Larwood, who would now have the use of the wind. A man of shorter than average height, the Notts professional had a beautiful rhythmic run to the wicket. Later followers would point out a similarity to Ray Lindwall, and he could produce frightening pace and sustained accuracy. His performance in this series was a spectacle more suited to an arena than a cricket field. The crowd would count the paces back to his mark. There would be silence as he delivered the ball, then tension was released in a roar.

O'Brien cut Larwood for two, then had his off stump cartwheel out of the ground to the next delivery. Extreme pace was the cause of his dismissal. He had made 11 and Australia was 2/27 as Bradman walked in to bat.

There can have been few times in his career when the great batsman was under more pressure. He had failed dismally in the first innings, and a great deal was expected of him to find the answers to the English attack. Bradman said that he did not feel under any extra pressure as he walked in to bat. After all that had happened, this sounds incredible, but when one remembers that everyone expected him to make a hundred every time he batted, nothing would have been altered by a first innings failure.

For Bradman facing Larwood, Jardine set three short and two long legs, a mid-on, straight and close in, and a gully. For Woodfull, he brought one of the long legs in close, and for both batsmen there was no one in front of the wicket on the off side. Leyland, square of the wicket at deep point, was the closest.

The pitch was not playing consistently and run scoring would be difficult, although the plan related to Moyes was not really necessary because of the placid nature of the surface. Interviewed on *The Bradman Tapes*, Sir Donald said, 'Despite it being a little slower than normal in Melbourne, the bowlers could still get the ball up'.

Bowes was brought on to confront Bradman. Perhaps Jardine was hoping that lightning would strike twice. It didn't. Bowes dropped one short and Bradman hooked it for four to open his account.

Jardine made repeated bowling changes in order to get a wicket. He could not afford to allow the batsmen, both of whom could make big scores, to settle in. However, the pair defied the bowling until lunch. The most memorable stroke came from Bradman, who stepped back and away from his wicket to force the ball back past Larwood to the fence. Could anyone else in the world have played that shot? 'A straight pull', one reporter called it. Twenty minutes after the break Jardine secured a wicket: the partnership had added an invaluable 51 runs before Woodfull fell to a catch at short leg by Allen off Larwood for 26. Woodfull had been batting well, but against this form of attack, a batsman could never believe he was set.

Three runs later, McCabe played on to a ball from Allen, to be out for no score. Australia's advantage was in danger of slipping away.

Richardson was a tough, aggressive, no-nonsense character—qualities which he passed on to his grandsons, the Chappells. In this series he played with more success than most, and was always prepared to take on the bowlers. This innings was no exception. He played the ball through the short legs and hooked it over them. When a rare delivery was pitched up he drove it, straight and beautifully, to the fence.

Interviewed late in his life, he gave his opinion of Bodyline. 'The worst thing was that it contravened the ethics, not the rules, of the game. The ball was delivered half-pitched and straight at you.'

Initially, the batsmen played carefully, hoping to tire Larwood and Allen, and then see if runs could be scored off the others. Bradman reached his half century in just on 90 minutes.

In their stand of 54, scored at better than a run a minute, Richardson made 32 before he was trapped in front to the fast-medium Hammond. Although used only as a part-time bowler, Hammond was frequently successful, as his figures in this innings show.

Voce came into the attack, bowling Oldfield for six and Grimmett for no score with a ball which kept low. At 7/156, just over 200 ahead, the lead did not seem enough. Bradman tried to take as much of the bowling as he could in order to gather a few more precious runs. Most considered that a lead of somewhere near 300 would be necessary.

Bradman took charge of the game after the tea interval, hitting nine off one over from Larwood. Wall made only three, but he stayed while 28 runs were added. When he fell leg before to Hammond, and O'Reilly was caught behind off the same bowler for no score two runs later, Australia was 9/186 and Bradman still two short of a century.

Last man in was left arm spinner Ironmonger, a true batting bunny. He is the man whose wife rang the dressing room and when told he was going in to bat said, 'I'll wait'. At least that's the story, and true or not it was inspired by his exceptionally ordinary performances with the bat. There was no guarantee he would last a ball, let alone long enough to help Bradman to a well deserved century. He greeted his batting partner with, 'Don't worry son, I won't let you down'. He then proceeded to

Veteran left arm spinner and number eleven batsman Bert Ironmonger, who told Bradman, 'Don't worry son, I won't let you down'. (Brian Bassano)

survive the remainder of Hammond's over, although Bradman said he had never seen two balls go closer to the stumps without hitting them.

Bradman was then pinned down by some excellent bowling from Voce. Off the last ball of the over he sent down a short one, which was dispatched over the leg side fieldsmen for three runs. The applause and cheering from the crowd held up the game for some minutes.

Shortly afterwards, in attempting a third run to keep Bradman in strike, the slow moving Ironmonger was run out by a huge distance to end the Australian innings at 191. Bradman remained a chanceless 103 not out, made in 185 minutes off 146 balls with seven fours. He had scored all but nine of the last 56 runs. He jogged off the field, cap in hand, to a tremendous reception.

All in all, it was a wonderful performance, fully atoning for the first innings and effectively countering his critics. Arthur Mailey said that it stood out like a diamond amidst glass. Many, including journalist Gilbert Mant, who was travelling with the English team, thought this was Bradman's greatest innings. A number also believed it was a more varied and resourceful innings than that played by McCabe in Sydney. Bill O'Reilly called it 'a beautiful century'.

Sir Donald Bradman himself ranks this innings as one of his very best.

Don Bradman, after a first innings failure, resisted the Bodyline attack and scored a matchwinning century. (Brian Bassano)

The Examiner was glowing in its praise and its words were typical of what was printed in newspapers all around the country, 'Although the Australian total was not large enough to make a victory more than a possibility, the most satisfactory feature from an Australian point of view was the convincing demonstration by Bradman that he is a match winner. He went in when two wickets had fallen cheaply and, batting with the restraint that indicated his determination to be revenged on the Englishmen for his first innings' failure, he made one of the best fighting centuries his admirers could hope for... There was no wild swishing, but there was the mixture of the stroke maker, the cool tactician, and the determined fighter'.

Perhaps the greatest praise came from his adversary Harold Larwood. In *The Larwood Story* the fast bowler said, 'That second innings of Don's must rank as one of the greatest of his life. He was under considerable strain but rose to the occasion. Although he was obviously put off his normal game he played well enough to make me think he might yet tame bodyline... I had to applaud some of the shots Don played. Bradman was a good one, all right'.

There was one question mark, however. The slowness of the pitch still left doubts in the minds of some, like that of former great England batsman Jack Hobbs, covering the tour as a journalist, that Bradman had not really countered the English leg theory tactics. *The Examiner* had reported that on this day there was practically no 'head attack', but that 'leg theory was exploited to the full'. Most would struggle to see the difference. Larwood did comment on the innocuous nature of the pitch, and wondered how Bradman would fare on one with a bit more life in it.

Contrary to expectations, Hammond with 3/21 had been the best of the bowlers, while Larwood, Voce and Allen each took two wickets. Bowes had only four overs, which cost 20 runs, and Jardine seemed a little reluctant to bowl him at Bradman.

Setting out in pursuit of 251 to win, the Englishmen must have believed they had a chance to get them. In an effort to counter O'Reilly, Jardine sent the left-handed Leyland in to open the innings with Sutcliffe. By stumps the pair had scored 43 of the runs, of which Sutcliffe made 33.

There was to be no successful run chase on the fourth day. O'Reilly bowled Sutcliffe straight away with a ball which pitched on middle and leg and hit off. From there England's batting collapsed and they were dismissed for just 139. O'Reilly, with 5/66 in the innings and ten wickets in a Test for the first time, and the veteran Ironmonger (4/26) had fatally exposed England's selection of so many fast bowlers.

Arthur Mailey, former Australian leg spinner, described this game as a victory for subtle bowling, of the 'rapier defeating the sandbag'.

Australia's victory by 111 runs squared the series as the teams moved on to Adelaide for the Third Test. This day in Melbourne had also left the English side with the nagging thought that Bradman just might have the answer to their tactics.

AUSTRALIA v ENGLAND

Played at Melbourne Cricket Ground, 30, 31 December, 1932, 2, 3 January, 1933
Toss: Australia.

AUSTRALIA

J.H.W. Fingleton	b Allen	83	c Ames b Allen	1
W.M. Woodfull *	b Allen	10	c Allen b Larwood	26
L.P.J. O'Brien	run out (Pataudi/Ames)	10	b Larwood	11
D.G. Bradman	b Bowes	0	not out	103
S.J. McCabe	c Jardine b Voce	32	b Allen	0
V.Y. Richardson	c Hammond b Voce	34	lbw b Hammond	32
W.A.S. Oldfield +	not out	27	b Voce	6
C.V. Grimmett	c Sutcliffe b Voce	2	b Voce	0
T.W. Wall	run out (Allen)	1	lbw b Hammond	3
W.J. O'Reilly	b Larwood	15	c Ames b Hammond	0
H. Ironmonger	b Larwood	4	run out (Larwood/Ames)	0
Extras	(B 5, LB 1, W 2, NB 2)	10	(B 3, LB 1, W 4, NB 1)	9
Total		**228**		**191**

Fall: 29, 67, 67, 131, 156, 188, 194, 200, 222, 228.　　1, 27, 78, 81, 135, 150, 156, 184, 186, 191.

Bowling

First Innings: Larwood 20.3–2–52–2, Voce 20–3–54–3, Allen 17–3–41–2, Hammond 10–3–21–0, Bowes 19–2–50–1.

Second Innings: Larwood 15–2–50–2, Allen 12–1–44–2, Bowes 4–0–20–0, Voce 15–2–47–2, Hammond 10.5–2–21–3.

ENGLAND

H. Sutcliffe	c Richardson b Wall	52	b O'Reilly	33
R.E.S. Wyatt	lbw b O'Reilly	13	(7) lbw b O'Reilly	25
W.R. Hammond	b Wall	8	(4) c O'Brien b O'Reilly	23
Nawab of Pataudi Sr	b O'Reilly	15	(3) c Fingleton b Ironmonger	5
M. Leyland	b O'Reilly	22	(2) b Wall	19
D.R. Jardine *	c Oldfield b Wall	1	(5) c McCabe b Ironmonger	0
L.E.G. Ames +	b Wall	4	(6) c Fingleton b O'Reilly	2
G.O.B. Allen	c Richardson b O'Reilly	30	st Oldfield b O'Reilly	23
H. Larwood	b O'Reilly	9	c Wall b Ironmonger	4
W. Voce	c McCabe b Grimmett	6	c O'Brien b O'Reilly	0
W.E. Bowes	not out	4	not out	0
Extras	(B 1, LB 2, NB 2)	5	(LB 4, NB 1)	5
Total		**169**		**139**

Fall: 30, 43, 83, 98, 104, 110, 122, 138, 161, 169.　　53, 53, 70, 70, 77, 85, 135, 137, 138, 139.

Bowling

First Innings: Wall 21–4–52–4, O'Reilly 34.3–17–63–5, Grimmett 16–4–21–1, Ironmonger 14–4–28–0.

Second Innings: Wall 8–2–23–1, O'Reilly 24–5–66–5, Ironmonger 19.1–8–26–4, Grimmett 4–0–19–0.

Australia won by 111 runs

6

Adelaide Assault

AUSTRALIA v ENGLAND

Adelaide Oval
16 January, 1933 – Day Three

THE BODYLINE SERIES reached its peak of animosity during the Third Test in Adelaide. With the rubber level at one-all, both sides were desperate for a victory. Sir Donald Bradman described this game as 'a regrettable affair', played in 'a deplorable atmosphere'. He felt that this was due to the injuries suffered by the Australian batsmen. The third day was certainly the most trying of the series.

Writing about this game in his history of the ground, Sydney Downer said, 'In the Adelaide Oval's 100 years of life, no single episode has possessed to such a degree the dramatic quality, fortified by elements of physical peril, a potential 'native' uprising and high-powered intervention, as the so-called Bodyline Test match in January 1933'.

For this crucial encounter the England side had a much more balanced attack. Bowes was dropped and replaced with the left arm spin of Verity, and batsman Eddie Paynter of Lancashire was brought in instead of the Nawab of Pataudi. As the Indian had made a century in the First Test, this was greeted with some surprise. The official reason was that Pataudi's batting was too slow, but many believed he was dropped because of his opposition to Jardine's tactics and his refusal to field in the leg trap. The batting order was also reshuffled and was as follows: Sutcliffe, Jardine, Hammond, Ames, Leyland, Wyatt, Paynter, Allen, Verity, Voce and Larwood.

43

The Australians made one change to their winning side, with Bill Ponsford returning in place of O'Brien. The batting order was: Fingleton, Woodfull, Bradman, McCabe, Ponsford, Richardson, Oldfield, Grimmett, Wall, O'Reilly and Ironmonger. This left the home side with rather a long tail, and the loss of some early wickets could be a problem. But it had avoided trouble in Melbourne and perhaps it would again.

Jardine won the toss and must have had little hesitation in batting. His cheer quickly turned to gloom as England collapsed to 4/30, three of the wickets to Tim Wall. However, thanks to Leyland (83), Wyatt (78), Paynter (77) and Verity (45) England fought back to a creditable 341. Wall, with 5/72, was by far the best of the bowlers.

Australia began badly, losing Fingleton for no score. Then came the first of the game's sensations. From the last ball of Larwood's second over, delivered to an orthodox field, Woodfull was struck a stunning blow over the heart. 'Well bowled, Harold,' was the comment of the England captain. The crowd, booed and jeered, then erupted when Jardine indicated he wanted the Bodyline field for the still groggy Woodfull.

The Australian captain 'toughed it out', but lost Bradman for eight and McCabe for the same score. Eventually, with his total on 22 and the score 51, he was bowled by Allen.

This left Ponsford and Richardson, the last two recognised batsmen to see out the day. This they did, with 45 and 21 respectively in the total of 4/109. This was not achieved without some luck, however, as Ponsford was dropped by Hammond in the slips, early in his innings. After that let-off he proceeded to play much more confidently than at any other time in the series.

According to O'Reilly, the Australian players were referring to the bowling as 'scone theory', because it was aimed at the head. He also remembered wishing players all the best as they went out to bat, with the feeling that he might never see them again.

Off the field things were warming up. When England's manager Pelham Warner entered the Australian rooms to offer some sympathy to Woodfull, the Australian captain quickly gave him his marching orders. 'I don't want to speak to you Mr Warner. There are two teams out there, but only one is playing cricket. It is too great a game for spoiling by the tactics your team are adopting'. When these events were leaked to the press Warner blamed Fingleton, a journalist by profession. He denied it and later named Bradman, who also denied it. Thus was created the reason for Fingleton's dislike of Bradman, which lasted, and even increased in intensity, throughout the rest of his life. It should be pointed out that at the time, according to journalist Gilbert Mant, most thought Fingleton to be the source of the leak.

An interesting sidelight is that Australian twelfth man, Leo O'Brien, was in the rooms at the time, and in an interview with *Wisden Cricket Monthly* said that neither Bradman nor Fingleton was present at the time, but former players Jack Ryder and Alan Kippax, who were both reporting the match, were.

Warner later issued a statement saying that Woodfull had apologised, but this was strenuously denied by the Australian captain, and reported as such by journalist Claude Corbett in *The Daily Telegraph*.

When Australians read of this incident in Monday's papers, members of the public now knew that their captain, and presumably his team, did not approve of what Jardine was

Australian captain, Bill Woodfull, was incensed by England's Bodyline tactics.

doing—that he was cheating in some way, or at the very least going against the spirit of the game. Armed with these thoughts a great many of them set off for the Adelaide Oval.

It was in the midst of such extraordinary goings on that the players assembled for the third day. Whatever feelings were around concerning England's bowling failed to bother Jardine, who began by setting a field with only two men on the off side.

In excellent weather the Australian batsmen began where they had left off the previous evening. The partnership was extended to 80 before Richardson tried to square cut Allen and chopped the ball onto his wicket to be out for 29. Some sources say it was an attempted pull. Like Bradman, but less extravagantly, Richardson had worked out his own method for dealing with Jardine's tactics. He used a short arm swing with a lot of forearm and wrist, and anything short was hooked and hooked hard. In this innings Richardson at one time took guard some half a metre outside his leg stump, leaving his wicket open, but the ball was still directed at him.

How tough it was is indicated by an incident recorded in Gerald Pawle's biography of Bob Wyatt. When a delivery from Larwood rose and struck Richardson on the hand, Jardine said, 'Well bowled! You made that rise nicely onto his thumb'. One of the team tried to pass this off as an example of English upper class humour.

At 5/131 keeper Oldfield came in to partner Ponsford, and he began

Bill Ponsford played one of his finest innings in the 'Battle of Adelaide', scoring 83. (Gordon Vidler)

well. When Jardine used Verity, he was struck for two boundaries, an off-drive and a late cut. An injury to Voce's ankle prevented him from bowling much before lunch, and this eased the pressure on the Australians, particularly when Larwood was not in the attack. In one of the few overs he did send down, Voce should have had Ponsford caught at short leg by Verity, but the chance was missed. The pair made it through to the break with the total 5/185. The problem was that there was very little to come once this stand was broken.

After lunch, Voce bowled around the wicket from the other end and was a more threatening proposition. The breakthrough should have come from a run out, but a wild throw from Larwood allowed Ponsford the chance to make his ground. The mistake was not costly, as two balls later he moved too far across to Voce and the ball hit leg stump. He and Oldfield had put on 63 for the sixth wicket.

Ponsford's innings of 85 in 221 minutes with eight fours was a very valuable one. In his only other Test, in Sydney, he attempted to evade the short balls by jumping aside. Here, he simply turned his back on them and took them on the body. Umpire George Hele was worried one would bounce a little more than expected and strike him on the head. During the course of his innings, he received some fearful blows, but never flinched. Lacking Bradman's quick footwork, he had to devise his own method and he did it well. In order to give himself some protection, he had rolled up some towels and placed them inside his shirt. It was not entirely successful, as his team-mates were able to count eleven huge bruises, ranging from red to purple to yellow, from Ponsford's shoulder to his hip. Larwood remembered hitting him more times than that. Looking at Ponsford's bruises and dividing them into his match payment, schoolmaster Woodfull calculated them at £2 10s each.

Ponsford was not the only one wearing some protection. Bradman wore a chest pad and Richardson used an extra batting glove to protect the inside of his knee after he was struck there by Larwood. Some players resembled the Michelin Man as they went in with as much padding as they could summon.

Keeper Bert Oldfield is struck on the head by a Larwood delivery.

Although the batsmen were bombarded with short-pitched bowling it was not quite as fierce as on the previous day. Perhaps this was because Bradman and Woodfull were already out.

Grimmett did not look at all happy against the quick bowling, particularly as the new ball was taken when the score reached 200. He repeatedly retreated towards the leg side and tried to cut anything short. One attempt finished up at fine leg. Such batting could not last, and his innings ended on ten when Voce took a good catch at third slip off Allen.

Discomfort almost turned to tragedy when Wall joined Oldfield. The Australian keeper had been batting well and had reached 41, with the total 7/218, when he attempted to hook a short ball from Larwood and was struck on the head. He was actually through the shot before the ball struck him via the edge of his bat. The bowler was quick to apologise, and the Australian keeper was just as quick to absolve Larwood from any blame. The fast bowler later said that he wouldn't have bowled the delivery except that Oldfield could bat and he had settled in.

Thankfully, Oldfield was able to leave the field under his own steam, escorted by his captain. Woodfull, dressed in his suit, jumped the fence and strode to the middle. 'This is war!' he said as he reached the centre. The news on Oldfield's injury was not completely satisfactory, as it was discovered that he had sustained a linear fracture of the frontal bone and would take no further part in the game. Nor would he be available for the next Test.

The noise of the crowd was incredible as Larwood walked back to his mark to bowl at O'Reilly. They booed, hooted and counted the bowler out. 'One. Two. Three. Four. Five. Six. Seven. Eight. Nine. Ten. Out, you bastard.' Cries of 'Go home, you pommy bastard' were also directed at the bowler, but mostly at Jardine. Larwood insisted that the barracking encouraged him to bowl faster, while Jardine probably revelled in the fact that he was annoying the Australians.

According to Arthur Mailey, the barracking was without parallel in Test cricket. In Gilbert Mant's words, 'the crowd went beserk'. The threat of a ground invasion was so real that mounted police were called in to restore order; they had been gathered outside the ground ready to go into action. Had one person run onto the ground there could have been a full scale riot, the consequences of which could have been catastrophic, particularly for Jardine and Larwood.

How close things came to a major disaster is best summed up by umpire Hele, who saw one man with his foot on the top of the fence ready to jump. What could have happened had he taken that next step does not bear thinking about. Bradman also thought that trouble was a distinct possibility. A number of those involved believed that had this occurred in front of the more volatile Melbourne crowd, an invasion would almost certainly have taken place.

Larwood remembered moving towards the stumps, so he could grab one if necessary, and he noticed that a number of his team-mates also wanted to field near the centre. Thankfully, only some rubbish was thrown onto the field and the spectators stayed put.

O'Reilly had to use his bat to force his way through the members, who were standing and jeering, in order to get onto the ground. The rather staid Adelaide members and their wives were standing booing and shaking their fists. One of them was former Australian captain, Clem Hill, incensed at what was happening. It was quite a few minutes before things settled down enough for the game to continue. Not too keen to get in line, and not delighted at being in the middle, the spinner played at six deliveries before being bowled by the seventh. He confessed later that he had never been so glad to get out.

Wall then played on to Allen and Australia was all out for 222, conceding a sizable lead of 119. Allen (4/71) and Larwood (3/55) had returned the best figures. Mailey thought Allen the best of the bowlers and considered that Jardine had overdone the leg theory on a pitch that really was not suited to quick bowling.

One could say many things (and a lot did) about Douglas Jardine, but one could never say he lacked courage. In the words of Australian fast bowler Harry 'Bull' Alexander, 'He had a ton of guts'. With the crowd screaming for blood—mostly his—he straightened the silk handkerchief around his neck, pulled his gaudiest Harlequin cap on and marched out with

Herbert Sutcliffe to open the innings. Jardine had been wearing his England cap in the field, but thought a change was required. The brightly coloured cap had been like a red rag to a bull all summer. To Australian crowds it represented English snobbery, and its wearer was the worst snob of all. In the words of Laurence Le Quesne in his book *The Bodyline Controversy*, he was 'the model of overbearing English arrogance'.

In his autobiography Harold Larwood said that after listening to the crowd noise, Jardine said, 'Listen to the bastards yelling. I think I'll go in myself and give the bastards something to yell at'. He certainly achieved his aim.

During this game the England captain had taken to reclining on the grass, making derisive comments about Australian cricketers and the public while he waited for the incoming batsmen. He loathed Australians, and they returned the compliment in equal measure.

Jack Hobbs commented that the crowd seemed to have gone mad when Jardine was involved in the play. The former England

The most hated man in Australia, Douglas Jardine, complete with Harlequin cap, walks out to bat.

batsman confessed to leaving the oval at the end of the day tired from the bellowing of the crowd.

No doubt they willed him to fail with every ounce of their collective being, but it was Sutcliffe who fell first. The Yorkshireman went to hook Wall and got the ball only on the bottom of his bat. O'Brien, who was fielding at fine leg as substitute for Oldfield, made plenty of ground to take a great catch. It was one of many occasions that the batsman fell to this stroke. Richardson acted as keeper during the second innings.

Joined by his vice-captain, Jardine was content to play quietly through to the end of the day, but Wyatt was in a much more aggressive frame of mind,

49

Australian vice-captain Vic Richardson.

reaching 47 at stumps to his captain's 24. Jardine took some 90 minutes over his first 15, much to the disgust of the still vocal crowd. England, at 1/85 and 204 ahead, was rapidly approaching an unbeatable position.

Throughout the last part of this day, Jardine was taunted with cries of 'You're out, you bastard', as he faced up to each ball, and Australian pace bowler Wall was encouraged with cries of 'Hit him on the bloody head, Tim!'

When drinks were taken during the last session, one spectator told the twelfth man, 'Don't give Jardine a drink. Let the bastard die of thirst'. *The Times* correspondent was, as expected, a little more subtle. 'An indignant crowd abused Larwood and Jardine and continued their wild shoutings when England opened their second innings.'

England's batsmen went on to score 412 in their second innings. Hammond (85), Ames (69), Wyatt (49), Leyland (42) and Verity (40) all played well. Jardine frustrated the bowlers and the crowd, who heckled him every step of the way, by staying in 254 minutes for 56. This was an important innings for Jardine, who had been under pressure for his poor batting form in the series. He had offered to stand down after the Melbourne Test, but the players would not hear of it. O'Reilly (4/79) and Ironmonger (3/87) did the best of the bowlers.

Faced with an impossible task, the Australians were dismissed for 193 to lose by 338 runs. Bradman made an electrifying 66 off 71 balls with ten fours and a six, Richardson made 21 and the Australian captain showed he was not short of courage also, by carrying his bat through the innings for 73.

By the conclusion of this game relations between the two sides were very strained. 'Absolutely hostile', was O'Reilly's description. There was no mixing and most just wanted the series to be over. This feeling was not just that of the Australians. England's top batsman Walter Hammond later wrote that only good luck prevented someone from being killed. He also said that if Bodyline had not been stopped he would have left the game. There may be some hypocrisy in this, as Vic Richardson believed that Hammond and senior professional Herbert Sutcliffe were both supporters of the tactics, but not, perhaps, when they were on the receiving end.

England went on to clinch the series in Brisbane, and then won the Fifth Test to complete a 4–1 win. Throughout the series Woodfull refused to contravene the ethics of the game by retaliating. It could have been done. According to Vic Richardson any quick bowler could have done it, and in Wall, Alexander and Laurie Nash, Australia had the players capable of doing it. Had he been in charge, Ian Chappell's grandfather would almost certainly have done so. He, like O'Reilly and a number of others, believed that Bodyline would have ended very rapidly had England received a taste of its own medicine.

The cables which started to be sent on the fifth day of this game threatened not just the continuation of the tour, but relationships between England and Australia. Like many others, Bradman believed that the time to complain about the English tactics was after Australia had won the Second Test. To complain from a position of one-all would carry more weight than after Australia lost in Adelaide. Such a tactic could be written off as moaning about a defeat.

In a later interview Sir Donald Bradman had this final comment to make about Bodyline. 'The man never lived who could consistently and successfully combat the 1932–33 bodyline attack as employed by England that summer.'

Bodyline succeeded to the extent that Bradman's average was reduced to human proportions of 56, and Larwood took 33 wickets. Those batsmen without Bradman's gifts—and that was all of them—suffered much more. 'The Don' returned to his run scoring eminence, but Larwood was destined to be the scapegoat for events well beyond his control. When he refused to apologise for bowling as his captain ordered, he was not chosen to play for England again. Later, he migrated to Australia where he remained a revered figure. When he died in 1995 aged 90, one of the most generous tributes came from Sir Donald Bradman.

Jardine did not play against Australia again, and when English crowds saw Bodyline delivered by West Indian fast bowlers in 1933, changes were made to the laws. Typically, Jardine made a century against them. He might have hated Australians and everything they stood for, and they certainly hated him, but he had the strength of character to see his plan through to the finish, regardless of the costs. He really did have 'a ton of guts'.

AUSTRALIA v ENGLAND

Played at Adelaide Oval on 13, 14, 16, 17, 18, 19 January, 1933.
Toss: England.

ENGLAND

H. Sutcliffe	c Wall b O'Reilly	9	c sub (O'Brien) b O'Reilly	7
D.R. Jardine *	b Wall	3	lbw b Ironmonger	56
W.R. Hammond	c Oldfield b Wall	2	(5) b Bradman	85
L.E.G. Ames +	b Ironmonger	3	(7) b O'Reilly	69
M. Leyland	b O'Reilly	83	(6) c Wall b Ironmonger	42
R.E.S. Wyatt	c Richardson b Grimmett	78	(3) c Wall b O'Reilly	49
E. Paynter	c Fingleton b Wall	77	(10) not out	1
G.O.B. Allen	lbw b Grimmett	15	(4) lbw b Grimmett	15
H. Verity	c Richardson b Wall	45	(8) lbw b O'Reilly	40
W. Voce	b Wall	8	(11) b O'Reilly	8
H. Larwood	not out	3	(9) c Bradman b Ironmonger	8
Extras	(B 1, LB 7, NB 7)	15	(B 17, LB 11, NB 4)	32
Total		**341**		**412**

Fall: 4, 16, 16, 30, 186, 196, 228, 324, 336, 341.

7, 91, 123, 154, 245, 296, 394, 395, 403, 412.

Bowling

First Innings: Wall 34.1–10–72–5, O'Reilly 50–19–82–2, Ironmonger 20–6–50–1, Grimmett 28–6–94–2, McCabe 14–3–28–0.

Second Innings: Wall 29–6–75–1, O'Reilly 50.3–21–79–4, Ironmonger 57–21–87–3, Grimmett 35–9–74–1, McCabe 16–0–42–0, Bradman 4–0–23–1.

AUSTRALIA

J.H.W. Fingleton	c Ames b Allen	0	b Larwood	0
W.M. Woodfull *	b Allen	22	not out	73
D.G. Bradman	c Allen b Larwood	8	(4) c & b Verity	66
S.J. McCabe	c Jardine b Larwood	8	(5) c Leyland b Allen	7
W.H. Ponsford	b Voce	85	(3) c Jardine b Larwood	3
V.Y. Richardson	b Allen	28	c Allen b LArwood	21
W.A.S. Oldfield +	retired hurt	41	absent hurt	-
C.V. Grimmett	c Voce b Allen	10	(7) b Allen	6
T.W. Wall	b Hammond	6	(8) b Allen	0
W.J. O'Reilly	b Larwood	0	(9) b Larwood	5
H. Ironmonger	not out	0	(10) b Allen	0
Extras	(B 2, LB 11, NB 1)	14	(B 4, LB 2, W 1, NB 5)	12
Total		**222**		**193**

Fall: 1, 18, 34, 51, 131, 194, 194, 212, 222, 222.

3, 12, 100, 116, 171, 183, 183, 192, 193.

Bowling

First Innings: Larwood 25–6–55–3, Allen 23–4–71–4, Hammond 17.4–4–30–1, Voce 14–5–21–1, Verity 16–7–31–0.

Second Innings: Larwood 19–3–71–4, Allen 17.2–5–50–4, Voce 4–1–7–0, Hammond 9–3–27–0, Verity 20–12–26–1.

England won by 338 runs

A Record Chase

ENGLAND v AUSTRALIA

Headingley, Leeds
27 July, 1948 – Day Five

WITH CONVINCING WINS in the first two Tests, and a draw in the third, Australia had dominated its first post-war tour of England. The team led by Don Bradman on his final tour had demolished all opposition to such an extent that it gave every indication of going through undefeated, although England had gained a significant lead in the first innings of the drawn game.

The Australians had a superbly balanced side, with strength in both batting and bowling, and they had been superior to England in all aspects so far. Perhaps Headingley would offer a change of fortune, but not if Bradman had anything to do with it. In 1930 and 1934 he had made triple hundreds in Tests on this ground, and in 1938 he had scored a mere hundred. Headingley could be called his turf. But then, he might be due to fail there after such an astonishing run.

England had to win this Test to keep their chance of squaring the series, and in order to do this they reinstated opener Len Hutton, who had been controversially left out of the previous Test because the selectors had been unconvinced of his capacity to deal with the Australian fast bowling. Lancashire all-rounder Ken Cranston and Surrey off-spinner Jim Laker were also included. Those left out of the previous side were Emmett, Dollery and Young.

In batting order the side was Hutton, Cyril Washbrook, Bill Edrich, Denis Compton, Jack Crapp, Norman Yardley, Cranston, Godfrey Evans, Alec Bedser, Laker and Dick Pollard.

The Australians were not without problems of their own. Opening batsman Sid Barnes was still suffering from the effects of the blow he received while fielding at short leg in the previous Test, and keeper Don Tallon was also unable to play. His understudy Ron Saggers came in to make his debut, while young left-hand batsman Neil Harvey was selected for his first Test against England. Vice-captain Lindsay Hassett had moved up to open with Arthur Morris. The Australian order was Morris, Hassett, Don Bradman, Keith Miller, Harvey, Sam Loxton, Ian Johnson, Ray Lindwall, Saggers, Bill Johnston and Ernie Toshack.

Things went well for England from the start when Norman Yardley won the toss and decided to bat. His players did not let him down, making an impressive 496. Hutton (81) and Cyril Washbrook (143) added 168 for the first wicket, then Bill Edrich (111) and night watchman Alec Bedser (79) drove home the advantage.

The Australians were in some trouble at 3/68, with Morris, Hassett and Bradman (33) all out. Keith Miller made a disciplined 58, then Harvey scored 112 in his Ashes debut. Sam Loxton hit five sixes in 93 and Ray Lindwall showed he was much more than just a bowler with 77. The final total of 458 gave England a minor lead.

They were quick to build on this, courtesy of another century opening stand between Hutton (57) and Washbrook (65). Their effort of 129 was followed by 54 from Edrich and 66 from Denis Compton. Keeper Godfrey Evans was 47 not out as England reached 8/362 at stumps.

Yardley was obviously prepared to give no hint of a chance to the Australians as he batted on for two overs and three runs on the final morning before declaring. This also allowed him to put the heavy roller on the pitch, perhaps helping it to break up a little more. When the Australians' turn came to bat, no roller was used at all.

The task given to Bradman and his team was to score 404 runs in 344 minutes on the fifth day of a Test, something which had never been done before. Would the Australians accept the challenge? In his autobiography *Farewell to Cricket*, Bradman said that he thought a total of 400 was beyond the Australians. Arthur Morris thought that it was generally accepted that England would win.

They were almost in trouble immediately. In Bedser's second over, Morris played the ball close to Cranston on the leg side. He had been dismissed off a similar stroke in the first innings, but this time he escaped.

There was a belief among many that the pitch was wearing and would suit the spinners. England's only specialist in this department was off-spinner

Jim Laker, and Yardley was quick to introduce him. The first over was a poor one. Hassett hit a four and a single then Morris struck a boundary. After being beaten by the following delivery, he put the next one into the rope.

In spite of this, the batsmen scored only 32 in the first 45 minutes. There seemed little urgency, but the bowling appeared to hold little concern, except for a missed stumping by Evans, Hassett being the lucky batsman.

Yardley then turned to the left arm wrist-spin of Compton. He had plenty of runs to play with, and the unorthodox nature of the bowling might just cause a mistake. It produced only easy runs, as Morris struck two boundaries to bring up 50 in 64 minutes. In Compton's next over, however, it might have paid off. Morris, on 32, moved down the pitch and missed, but Evans could not take the ball. Bradman described this as a very difficult chance, with the keeper obscured by the batsman playing over the ball. Laker was also now making some deliveries turn quite a long way.

Compton was compensated for the missed stumping when he turned one sharply to catch the leading edge of Hassett's bat, then ran up the pitch to take the catch. The vice-captain's dismissal for 17 left Australia 1/57 after 75 minutes.

The wicket brought in Bradman, playing his last Test innings at Leeds, and the one man likely to put Australia on the path to at least saving the game. His quick removal would give the bowlers great encouragement. The Australian captain admitted to being in a quandary as he walked to the wicket. He wanted to win, but he didn't want to lose. Just what approach should the batsmen take?

He was immediately off the mark with a single, then struck a pull and an off-drive to the boundary; this to a Laker field that contained three short legs. After six minutes he had made 12 runs.

Yardley, apparently searching in desperation, brought Hutton into the attack. A great batsman, but only a part-time leg spinner, he was hammered for three fours by Morris, who passed 50. It was strange that the England captain did not try Bedser or Pollard, his faster bowlers, before Bradman became settled. He didn't, and another over from Hutton brought further runs for Australia.

Bradman, in fact, regards the advent of Hutton as a crucial factor. He believes that this was a virtual admission that Yardley's established bowlers were not performing as he had hoped. The runs gained from the part-time bowler brought the Australians level with the clock, and gave them confidence to keep the runs ticking over.

Compton was the most likely wicket taker. In one over to Bradman he could have removed him a number of times. The first ball, an undetected wrong 'un, was edged past slip for four, and the second glanced to the boundary.

Jack Crapp misses Bradman at slip off Compton early in his innings.

Another undetected wrong 'un was edged into the slips, where Crapp dropped it, and the last ball hit the batsman on the pads.

Morris continued to enjoy himself at Hutton's expense; four overs cost 30 runs, until lunch, when the score was 1/121. The left-hander took a number of risks to do this, but thought that Hutton would get untidy under the pressure, and this proved to be the case. At lunch Morris was 63 and Bradman 35. Chances had been missed. Would they prove costly? Morris started to think in terms of a win during the break, although there was still a long way to go.

Compton was not the same force after lunch. Morris hit seven fours in two overs of what Jack Fingleton called 'indescribably bad bowling'. Less than 20 minutes after play resumed, Morris had reached his century, and had scored 37 runs while Bradman made three. There would have been few times when the Don had been outscored to such an extent.

The Australian captain was not at all bothered and kept going to reach his own 50 in an hour. Just after this he was dropped by Yardley off Cranston. Bradman mistimed a drive and the ball went in the air behind point. Yardley dived and got his hands to the ball, but failed to hang on.

Laker produced some full tosses which Morris despatched, and the 200 was on the board at ten past three.

In hooking Cranston to the fence, Bradman appeared to injure his side. Although he seemed in some pain, he was able to continue. During the previous season in Australia he had suffered a similar injury against India, and had been forced to retire hurt. What actually happened was a spasm of fibrositis, which gradually eased, so that, in spite of being uncomfortable for a short time, he was not greatly handicapped.

The milestones started to occur. At four o'clock the 250 was reached, with Morris 133 and Bradman 92. Then there was the 200 partnership, and at ten past the Australian captain reached his 29th Test century. Morris described the pitch as having uneven bounce, with quite a lot of turn, but slow. 'England was out for a win

Arthur Morris, in partnership with Bradman, dominated England's bowlers in the record run chase. (Brian Bassano)

and set an attacking field, which left lots of space in the outfield.' Morris also remembered the large number of boundaries struck by the batsmen.

At 108 Bradman was lured forward by Laker, and Evans, who was having a nightmare behind the stumps, once again fumbled the ball. In the next over, from Compton, Laker dropped Morris behind square leg. He got two hands to the ball, but the chance went begging.

Tea was taken with Australia needing 112 to win in 105 minutes with nine wickets in hand. A famous victory looked assured.

The batsmen continued in a similar vein after the break, until the score reached 358 and the partnership 301, when Morris was caught by Pollard off Yardley for 182. He had batted 291 minutes and hit 33 fours. Bradman believed this to be Morris's greatest innings.

With less than 50 runs required, Keith Miller decided to try to end the game in a flurry of big hitting. He made 12 before Cranston trapped him leg before.

Only eight runs were needed when young Neil Harvey walked in. His brave first innings century had done much to keep Australia in the game, and now he had the honour of striking the winning run, which came with 15 minutes of play still remaining.

Bradman was there to the end, 173 not out, made in 255 minutes with 29 fours. Although it was not one of his better centuries (there were a few

England keeper Godfrey Evans had the worst day of his long career, missing a number of chances. (Brian Bassano)

too many errors and false strokes for that) it was an immensely satisfying and valuable innings. It also meant that he had scored a hundred or better in every Test he played at Headingley. 'He perpetuated the legend that runs by right belonged to him on the Leeds ground', stated *The Times*.

It was a memorable innings because it produced a famous victory. Never before, and only once since (India against the West Indies in 1975–76), has a team scored in excess of 400 in the last innings to win a game.

The scorecard makes the pitch sound as if it was made for batting. Bradman disagreed. In his view it was not good, and Laker turned some deliveries prodigiously. At the time the ground was without sightscreens, and on the hot last day the ball was not easy to pick up.

For England, it was a case of missed opportunities and some poor bowling. One has only to look at the number of boundaries struck by Bradman and Morris to realise that there were plenty of loose deliveries, but the chances were there and they were not taken. Laker, the specialist spinner, had bowled too many bad balls, and part-timers like Compton and Hutton could not be expected to maintain the pressure. That having been said, there was some poor fielding, none worse than that of keeper Evans, who had the kind of day to haunt him for the rest of his life. In *Behind the Stumps*, the England keeper described his anguish. 'When we left the field at 6.20, I was so disgusted with my performance in that last innings, that I jumped straight into my car and drove the 236 miles non-stop to Maidstone—alone. I arrived home at 2 o'clock in the morning wishing I could forget what had happened.'

Bradman felt that the chances Evans missed were not easy, but in order to win at least some of the difficult ones needed to be taken. Most would have expected a player like Evans to accept at least one chance, and that would probably have been enough to ensure an England victory. In the words of *The Times* correspondent, Australia was 'generously encouraged by England's outcricket. England's bowling and fielding fell far short of what one would hope to see in a Test match'.

According to Bradman, the greatest problem for the England captain was the lack of a leg spinner. Had a player like Doug Wright or Eric Hollies been in the side, then Australia would have found the task much harder. Because he had only the off spinner Laker, Yardley had to turn to part-timers, and while Compton bowled quite well, it was asking too much for him to remove a strong batting line-up.

A critic might be tempted to say that the Australians were a little lucky to win, but then fortune favours the brave.

Bradman and Harvey leave Headingley in triumph.

At the crucial moment England could not, literally, grasp the chance, and the Australians played positively and rode their luck.

Cricket has a habit of producing the unexpected. This day at Leeds was just that. A victory against the odds, and another jewel in the crown of the the game's greatest batsman.

ENGLAND v AUSTRALIA

Played at Headingley, Leeds on 22, 23, 24, 26, 27 July, 1948.
Toss: England.

ENGLAND

L. Hutton	b Lindwall	81	c Bradman b Johnson	57
C. Washbrook	c Lindwall b Johnston	143	c Harvey b Johnston	65
W. J. Edrich	c Morris b Johnson	111	lbw Lindwall	54
A. V. Bedser	c & b Johnson	79	(9) c Hassett b Miller	17
D. C. S. Compton	c Saggers b Lindwall	23	(4) c Miller b Johnston	66
J. F. Crapp	b Toshack	5	(5) b Lindwall	18
N. W. D. Yardley *	b Miller	25	(6) c Harvey b Johnston	7
K. Cranston	b Loxton	10	(7) c Saggers b Johnston	0
T. G. Evans +	c Hassett b Loxton	3	(8) not out	47
J. C. Laker	c Saggers b Loxton	4	not out	15
R. Pollard	not out	0		
Extras	(B 2, LB 8, W 1, NB 1)	12	(B 4, LB 12, NB 3)	19
Total		**496**		**8/365**

Fall: 168, 268, 423, 426, 447, 473, 486, 490, 496, 496. 129, 129, 232, 260, 277, 278, 293, 330.

Bowling

First Innings: Lindwall 38–10–79–2, Miller 17.1–2–43–1, Johnston 38–12–86–1, Toshack 35–6–112–1, Loxton 26–4–55–3, Johnson 33–9–89–2, Morris 5–0–20–0.
Second Innings: Lindwall 26–6–84–2, Miller 21–5–53–1, Johnston 29–5–95–4, Loxton 10–2–29–0, Johnson 21–2–85–1.

AUSTRALIA

A. R. Morris	c Cranston b Bedser	6	c Pollard b Yardley	182
A. L. Hassett	c Crapp b Pollard	13	c & b Compton	17
D. G. Bradman *	b Pollard	33	not out	173
K. R. Miller	c Edrich b Yardley	58	lbw b Cranston	12
R. N. Harvey	b Laker	112	not out	4
S. J. E. Loxton	b Yardley	93		
I. W. Johnson	c Cranston b Laker	10		
R. R. Lindwall	c Crapp b Bedser	77		
R. A. Saggers +	st Evans b Laker	5		
W. A. Johnston	c Edrich b Bedser	13		
E. R. H. Toshack	not out	12		
Extras	(B 9, LB 14, NB 3)	26	(B 6, LB 9, NB 1)	16
Total		**458**		**3/404**

Fall: 13, 65, 68, 189, 294, 329, 344, 355, 403, 458. 57, 358, 396.

Bowling

First Innings: Bedser 31.2–4–92–3, Pollard 38–6–104–2, Cranston 14–1–51–0, Edrich 3–0–19–0, Laker 30–8–118–3, Yardley 17–6–38–2, Compton 3–0–15–0.
Second Innings: Bedser 21–2–56–0, Pollard 22–6–55–0, Cranston 7.1–0–28–1, Laker 32–11–93–0, Yardley 13–1–44–1, Compton 15–3–82–1, Hutton 4–1–30–0.

Australia won by 7 wickets

8

Exit The Don

ENGLAND v AUSTRALIA

The Oval
14 August, 1948 – Day One

WHEN ENGLAND confronted Australia for the fifth and final Test of the 1948 series the team had only pride to play for. The Australians, led by Don Bradman, were undefeated on tour and leading 3–0 in the Test series. Convincing wins in the first two Tests had been followed by a draw in the third, and at Leeds the Australians had scored an amazing 3/404 on the last day to snatch an unlikely victory.

English supporters could be forgiven for wondering if there was any possible way their team could win. The selectors had responded with some strange decisions, like that of leaving out Len Hutton, the country's best batsman, for the Third Test. A number of others had also been tried, most without any substantial return.

For the final game they had chosen, in batting order, Hutton, Dewes, Edrich, Compton, Crapp, Yardley, Watkins, Evans, Bedser, Young and Hollies. The biggest blow was the loss of opener Cyril Washbrook, who had made 143 in the previous Test, but whose injured thumb prevented him from playing. His replacement was to be young Cambridge batsman John Dewes. Fast bowler Dick Pollard was dropped, as was off spinner Jim Laker, who had bowled particularly poorly at Headingley. The new players were leg spinner Eric Hollies and all-rounder Allan Watkins, the first Welshman to play against Australia in a Test. This meant that the selectors had used 22 different players in the five games.

The Australians, on the other hand, made few changes in the series. They had used 15 players and three of the changes had been made because of injury. For this game opening batsman Sid Barnes and keeper Don Tallon returned from injury. Leg spinner Doug Ring came into the side, with off spinner Ian Johnson being relegated to twelfth man, and that probably would not have happened had left armer Ernie Toshack not been injured. This gave the Australians a batting order of Barnes, Morris, Bradman, Hassett, Miller, Harvey, Loxton, Lindwall, Tallon, Ring and Johnston. It was a formidable combination indeed, one which was already being called the finest Australian team ever.

While the locals were playing only to salvage some pride, the Australians had a couple of spurs to keep them going. Bradman wanted to lead the first team through a tour of England undefeated. As the end loomed closer, the skipper was even more keen not to let the unbeaten record slip. There was to be no relaxation of effort.

The other spur was that this would be Bradman's last Test. He had already announced his retirement for the end of the tour. Cricket's most successful batsman had tortured Test bowlers for 20 years, and this would be the last opportunity. He would be as keen to do well as his side would be to win this last game for him.

The weather leading up to the match had been poor, and there was the possibility that the Kennington Oval pitch, usually very much in favour of batting, might have something in it for the bowlers.

The former Australian cricketer, Jack Fingleton, who was covering the tour as a journalist, thought that whoever won the toss would have an advantage. Fingleton's book of the tour, *Brightly Fades the Don*, is regarded as a classic of the game's literature.

Yardley won the toss and decided to bat, a decision which puzzled most at the ground. If there was anything in the pitch, giving first use of it to Lindwall, Miller and Johnston did not seem a good idea. Australians usually struggled on rain-affected pitches, and the temptation for many spectators would have been to see how they went on it. Sir Donald Bradman said later that had he won the toss he would probably have sent England in, although he maintains that what happened had as much to do with good bowling and some weak batting.

The pitch actually played quite well—it was the England batting which had the problems. According to Arthur Morris, Lindwall and Miller bowled very fast, and extracted some lift and pace out of the pitch.

Dewes took strike and scored a single off the first over from Lindwall. Miller began from the other end. He sent down one ball, sprinkled some

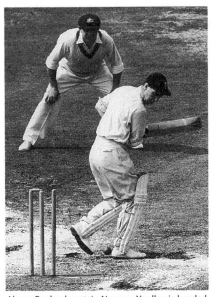

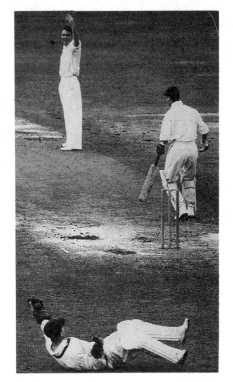

Above: England captain Norman Yardley is bowled by Ray Lindwall for seven. (Brian Bassano)

Right: Don Tallon takes a fantastic catch to dismiss Hutton for 30 off the bowling of Lindwall, ending England's innings for just 52. (Brian Bassano)

saw-dust on the run-up, then clean bowled Dewes, who played across the ball.

Hutton and Edrich batted slowly. Bradman changed his bowlers around, looking for some assistance from the pitch, and the switch to Bill Johnston worked. A left armer capable of bowling anything from pace to spin, he was one of the most underrated players in Test cricket history. On this tour he had been consistently successful, and would end up taking over a hundred first-class wickets.

Johnston bowled a bouncer, Edrich did not hit it well enough, and Hassett dived away from backward square leg to take an excellent catch.

Denis Compton was the next batsman. He had been England's player of the series, the one capable of attacking the fast bowlers, but he looked far from comfortable. One delivery from Lindwall was edged to Hassett at third man, and in watching the ball Compton dropped his bat. The fieldsman sportingly held off returning the ball until the batsman regained his ground.

Another bouncer from Lindwall produced a well-struck hook, but Morris at square leg took a spectacular catch to leave England at 3/17. Fingleton said that Bradman told Compton he remembered such a shot from The Oval Test ten years before and had put the man there for it.

Jack Crapp fought for 20 minutes without scoring before he edged Miller

Norman Yardley leads his team in giving Don Bradman three cheers. (Brian Bassano)

to Tallon to have England in dire trouble at 4/23. Miller had figures of 2/3 off six overs. Lunch was reached without further loss, with Hutton on 17 and captain Yardley on four.

There was to be no revival. Shortly after the resumption Lindwall yorked Yardley for seven, and Watkins came in to play his first Test innings with the score 5/35. He played and missed one bouncer, then took another on the shoulder, before playing across the line to Johnston to be leg before for nought.

Keeper Godfrey Evans could be a difficult customer in a crisis, but he had no chance on this day, as an express delivery from Lindwall uprooted his stumps for one. Although better known as a bowler, Alec Bedser had played a couple of useful innings in the series, but he, too, lost his stumps to Lindwall. The new bat he carried in with him was still spotless as he trudged off.

Lindwall put another rapid delivery through Young's defence, and at 9/47 only last man Hollies was left to partner Hutton. With support running out, the Yorkshireman hit Lindwall back over his head for the only boundary of the innings. Indeed, he had looked in little trouble throughout and seemed certain to bat through the innings, when he was out to one of the great catches.

Hutton leg glanced Lindwall fine and a diving Tallon scooped the ball up in his outstretched left hand. Fingleton thought it the best catch by a keeper he had ever seen.

England was all out for a paltry 52, the lowest total ever made against Australia at home, of which Hutton had made 30. Lindwall had 6/20, and in eight overs since lunch had taken 5/8. The last time England had batted at The Oval in a Test against Australia they had made 7/903. Certainly, the Australians had gained some measure of revenge. The game ended as a contest about halfway through the first day, and while all considered Australia the better team, not too many had thought there was this great a difference.

This superiority was underlined as Morris and Barnes went past the England score in quick time, and with no apparent difficulty. The 100 part-

Bradman is bowled by Eric Hollies, second ball for a duck. (Brian Bassano)

nership was reached and the stand was extended to 117 before Hollies, who had been the best of the bowlers, turned a leg break away from Barnes. He could only edge it to the keeper, and trudged off with 61 to his name.

Then, as Bradman walked in to bat for what would almost certainly be his last time in Test cricket, there was one final piece of drama. Needing to score just four runs to secure an unbelievable Test average of 100 he walked in to a huge ovation.

As he reached the crease Norman Yardley called his team in to give the Australian three cheers. He then shook hands and the game continued. In his autobiography, Bradman admitted that the ovation had stirred his emotions, and that he dearly wanted to do well.

Bradman played the first ball defensively, although he said he was not quite sure that he saw it very well. The next delivery was slightly fuller, and the batsman moved forward and was bowled. Arthur Morris, watching at the non–striker's end, said, 'The wrong 'un was perfectly pitched, just outside off stump, and he got a slight inside edge'.

After the initial cheer of seeing an important wicket fall, the crowd was left to ponder on this most unusual of events. It seemed not to know what to make of it all. John Arlott, who was commentating at the time, said to his listeners, 'What do you say under those circumstances?'

Bradman looked back at the stumps and then walked slowly away. Seeking a reason for what happened, many have said that the Don was emotionally affected by the reception he had received, and that he did not spot Hollies' wrong 'un because of tears in his eyes. Sir Donald denies this, stating that it was not the end of the match and there was still the possibility that he would have to bat again. 'I did not feel the drama the scribes made of it', he said in a letter to the author. When interviewed on the *Bradman Tapes* he again strenuously denied that his emotions affected his performance, saying that to suggest this denigrated a fine ball from a fine bowler. While the author is not prepared to argue with such an eminent figure and his generous praise, it is hard to imagine the memories of 20 years of Test cricket not crowding in on the Australian captain as he walked out to bat.

It is difficult to see humour here, but Sid Barnes managed to inject some. No greater larrikin has pulled on the baggy green cap, and stories about him are many. This is one of the best.

A keen photographer, Barnes had walked into the dressing room, grabbed his camera and walked straight onto the balcony, where he filmed his captain's exit. He then entered the dressing room and unbuckled his pads beside his skipper, while telling him that he had captured his entire innings on film. Not many people would have risked the great man's ire. When he returned to Australia Barnes travelled around the countryside showing his movies, talking about the tour and 'making a quid'.

There was no further excitement as Morris (77) and Hassett (10) played out the remainder of the day, leaving Australia comfortably placed at 2/153. *The Times* commented on the day's play, 'It is quite easy to say that England's batting was deplorable. It certainly was; but it is more to the point that Australia's bowling, catching, and ground fielding were superb'. And the batsmen had reinforced the advantage.

The match continued on its predictable course with Morris making 196 in Australia's innings of 389. Hollies took 5/131 and troubled not just Bradman in the process.

Left with a deficit of 337, England could manage only 188 in the second innings to lose by an innings and 149 runs. Hutton again top scored, this time with 64. At one stage the score stood at 2/125, but the later batting fell away to the bowling of Johnston (4/40), Lindwall (3/50) and Miller (2/22).

Australia won the series 4–0, and Bradman achieved his ambition of completing the tour undefeated by leading his side successfully through the remaining games.

As a contest, Jack Fingleton was correct when he said that this Oval Test was one of the poorest between the two countries, but the drama of England's collapse to Lindwall and company on the first day and the exit of Bradman the batsman from the Test arena make it a day to remember.

ENGLAND v AUSTRALIA

Played at Kennington Oval, London, on 14, 16, 17, 18 August, 1948.
Toss: England.

ENGLAND

L. Hutton	c Tallon b Lindwall	30	c Tallon b Miller	64
J. G. Dewes	b Miller	1	b Lindwall	10
W. J. Edrich	c Hassett b Johnston	3	b Lindwall	28
D. C. S. Compton	c Morris b Lindwall	4	c Lindwall b Johnston	39
J. F. Crapp	c Tallon b Miller	0	b Miller	9
N. W. D. Yardley *	b Lindwall	7	c Miller b Johnston	9
A. J. Watkins	lbw b Johnston	0	c Hassett b Ring	2
T. G. Evans +	b Lindwall	1	b Lindwall	8
A. V. Bedser	b Lindwall	0	b Johnston	0
J. A. Young	b Lindwall	0	not out	3
W. E. Hollies	not out	0	c Morris b Johnston	0
Extras	(B 6)	6	(B9, LB 4, NB 3)	16
Total		**52**		**188**

Fall: 2, 10, 17, 23, 35, 42, 45, 45, 47, 52.   20, 64, 125, 153, 164, 167, 178, 181, 188, 188.

Bowling
First Innings: Lindwall 16.1–5–20–6, Miller 8–5–5–2, Johnston 16–4–20–2, Loxton 2–1–1–0.
Second Innings: Lindwall 25–3–50–3, Miller 15–6–22–2, Johnston 27.3–12–40–4,
    Loxton 10–2–16–0, Ring 28–13–44–1.

AUSTRALIA

S. G. Barnes	c Evans b Hollies	61
A. R. Morris	run out	196
D. G. Bradman *	b Hollies	0
A. L. Hassett	lbw b Young	37
K. R. Miller	st Evans b Hollies	5
R. N. Harvey	c Young b Hollies	17
S. J. E. Loxton	c Evans b Edrich	15
R. R. Lindwall	c Edrich b Young	9
D. Tallon +	c Crapp b Hollies	31
D. T. Ring	c Crapp b Bedser	9
W. A. Johnston	not out	0
Extras	(B 4, LB 2, NB 3)	9
Total		**389**

Fall: 117, 117, 226, 243, 265, 304, 332, 359, 389, 389.
Bowling:
Bedser 31.2–9–61–1, Watkins 4–1–19–0, Young 51–16–118–2, Hollies 56–14–131–5,
Compton 2–0–6–0, Edrich 9–1–38–1, Yardley 5–1–7–0.

Australia won by an innings and 149 runs

9

'Coometh the Hour'

SOUTH AFRICA V ENGLAND

Kingsmead, Durban
20 December, 1948 – Day Four

WHEN ENGLAND toured South Africa in the 1948–49 season, they were doing so after a home summer in which they were comprehensively defeated by an Australian team led by Don Bradman. Although England had emerged comfortable winners the last time the two sides met, in England in 1947, there was ample evidence to believe that the result could be different this time.

Victory for England in the previous series was due in no small part to the batting of the Middlesex twins, Bill Edrich and Denis Compton, at the peak of their form. Edrich was not selected for the tour, and it might be asking too much for Compton to achieve the same standards again, although he had been successful against the Australians. England's bowlers had also suffered at the hands of a strong Australian batting line-up, and only fast-medium Alec Bedser had emerged with his reputation reasonably intact.

However, the Springboks, in spite of any improvement they may have made, were not in the same class as Bradman's Australians, and England was expected to emerge victorious, principally through the batting of openers Len Hutton and Cyril Washbrook, and Compton. Bedser looked the best bowler on either side. England also had a new captain in George Mann, whose father had led the 1922–23 team to South Africa. Mann's selection was something of a surprise, as he had not played in a Test before, but he proved a capable and popular choice.

The team began in encouraging fashion, winning six and drawing three of the nine lead-up games to the First Test. Hutton, Compton and Washbrook had all played substantial innings, and Nottinghamshire's Reg Simpson, on his first tour, also made plenty of runs. Leg spinner Roly Jenkins had proved devastating, running through a succession of batting line-ups. So by the time the teams reached Durban for the beginning of the series, the visitors were firm favourites.

But, as is often said, cricket is a funny game, and the South Africans proved to be much more of a handful than was expected. So much so that the game provided one of the most exciting finishes in Test history.

This was the first Test played in South Africa since the so-called 'Timeless Test' at Durban in 1938–39. Springbok keeper 'Billy' Wade remembers everyone being delighted with the prospect of sitting and watching some Test cricket after so long. It did not seem to matter who won as long as there was some cricket to see. This desire is best illustrated in story told by Wade, who met a friend at the end of the War after both had been released from P.O.W. camps. 'I said, "Well Bill, it's all over, thank goodness, we'll soon be home now." To which he replied, "Maybe, but until I am sitting at Castle Corner at Kingsmead watching cricket, eating peanuts and drnking beer with a roaring headache, only then will I know I am really back home".'

Dudley Nourse captained South Africa in the absence of Alan Melville, who had led the Springboks on their 1947 tour of England but was unavailable due to injury. Nourse won the toss and decided to bat on what looked like a good pitch. His batsmen, however, made no real use of it and were dismissed for only 161. Veteran Bruce Mitchell and Denis Begbie, in his maiden Test, each made 37, while Bedser (4/39) and Derbyshire seamer Cliff Gladwin (3/21) both bowled well.

In the field the South Africans performed a little better, dismissing a strong line-up for 253. Almost as expected, Hutton (83) and Compton (72), were the stars of the show, but the rest could make no headway against the left arm spin of 'Tufty' Mann (6/59) and the off-breaks of Athol Rowan (4/108).

In spite of their sterling efforts, the Springboks faced a sizeable deficit of 92 as they went into their second innings, and it would require a substantial effort to set England a target to chase. By stumps on the third day they had made 90, but lost the wickets of Eric Rowan, Owen Wynne, Mitchell and Nourse — the cream of their batting.

When the fourth and last day began, an England win looked a mere formality. But the not out batsmen 'Billy' Wade and Begbie had other ideas.

Fast bowler Cuan McCarthy took 6/43 on his Test debut and almost won the game for his side. (Brian Bassano)

With some excellent batting they added 85 in only 82 minutes in a partnership which looked like saving the game. Wade said that quite a bit of rain had fallen during the game, making the pitch increasingly more difficult to bat on.

Jenkins then turned the match by bowling Wade for an excellent 63, and five runs later 'Osie' Dawson was caught by Compton off the leg spin of Doug Wright. With South Africa 6/179, the possibility of an England win began to emerge.

Athol Rowan held out with Begbie while 29 valuable runs were added. Time was almost as important as runs, and every minute the batsmen occupied the crease brought South Africa closer to the safety of a draw. Then both batsmen fell with the score on 208. Begbie went to a catch by Mann off Bedser for 48, completing an excellent debut, and Wright bowled Rowan for 15 made in 70 minutes.

A few more precious runs were added before Compton, with his left arm wrist spin, had 'Tufty' Mann caught by George Mann for 10. This event prompted famous broadcaster John Arlott to speak of 'Mann's inhumanity to Mann'.

Jenkins bowled Cuan McCarthy for a duck and the South Africans were all out for 219. Lindsay Tuckett had occupied the crease for 55 minutes for three not out. This left England the task of making 128 runs in 135 minutes to win the game. (The South African papers say 131 minutes.) The England captain accepted the challenge and encouraged his side to go for the runs. Rain was also a threat to be considered.

That this was to be an afternoon of high tension was quickly apparent as Washbrook hooked Tuckett's first ball to Wynne at fine leg; Wynne dropped it. Shortly afterwards a square cut hit Nourse on the knee, and five minutes were lost while he received treatment. Then a shower of rain caused a 12 minute delay, making the run chase a little more difficult.

After the break, Tuckett had Hutton caught by Dawson at short leg for five. England was now 1/25. Captain Mann was missed twice, scored 13 and took the total to 49, then both he and Washbrook fell within the space of three runs. The latter was leg before to the spin of 'Tufty' Mann for 25, and the former brilliantly caught in the slips by Mitchell off fast man McCarthy,

Above: Cyril Washbrook leaving the crease after being leg before to Mann for 25. (Brian Bassano)

Right: Godfrey Evans has his stumps shattered by McCarthy for four. (Brian Bassano)

another playing in his first Test. The light was not good by this time. McCarthy was becoming difficult to see, and to make matters worse it began to drizzle.

Allan Watkins made only four before McCarthy shattered his stumps as well. Then, without addition to the score, Simpson registered a duck in his first Test, caught by Eric Rowan off McCarthy from the first ball he received. He simply pushed the delivery straight into the hands of the fieldsman, who hurled it into the air with delight. The fast bowler's three wickets had put his team back in the game, and six runs later he had a fourth when keeper Godfrey Evans was beaten and bowled for four.

At 6/70 England was really struggling, and the Springboks could seriously think about forcing an unlikely victory. An hour remained in which England had to score 58 runs or South Africa take four wickets. They reckoned without the skills of Compton, who, assisted by Jenkins, pushed the total calmly along. Nothing the bowlers could produce seemed to trouble them, and victory began to be a possibility again, although the players on both sides had to be conscious of the minutes ticking away.

The pair had added 45, taking England to within 13 runs of victory, when McCarthy bowled Compton for 28. One run later he had Jenkins caught by keeper Wade for 22. Throughout their partnership the light was so bad that any appeal would certainly have been granted, but there was no desire to complete the game in any way other than by playing it out. 'Billy' Wade said it became so dark that the players in the middle could barely see the crowd. About half an hour before the end a light drizzle set in, causing problems for both batsmen and fielders.

Derbyshire's Cliff Gladwin, whose meaty thigh carried England to victory to fulfil his prediction. (Brian Bassano)

The new batsman, Gladwin, entered to join Bedser with a soon to be immortal comment, 'Coometh the hour, coometh the man', when Nourse asked him what he was looking so cheerful about. He admitted in a later interview that he wasn't nearly as confident as he tried to sound. They were almost his last words as he lofted McCarthy to Tuckett at mid-on. The fieldsman so badly misjudged the ball that not only did he miss the catch, but the batsmen scored two runs as well. Bedser then managed to avoid being run out, but not by much, and there remained time for only one more over. England needed eight runs, or South Africa two wickets off the eight deliveries.

By now, the drizzle had become heavier and it was so dark the streetlights outside the ground appeared to be blazing.

McCarthy ended his spell with 6/43, a brilliant, almost matchwinning display from a young man in his maiden Test, and Nourse had to look for someone to bowl the last over. He initially went to left arm spinner 'Tufty' Mann, a move which pleased 'Billy' Wade, as he could stand up to the stumps. Mann told Nourse he was unable to see through his glasses because of the rain and couldn't see without them. With his first choice out of action the captain turned to the steadiness of Tuckett, no doubt also hoping that he might want to atone for his missed catch a few minutes earlier. This was not something the bowler was looking forward to. He hadn't bowled for quite a while, and was stiff and wet as it had been drizzling for some time. The ball was soft and the grass slippery to run in on. It was not going to be easy for the batsmen either, as the ball was nearly impossible to see in the murk. Wade decided not to stand as far back as he would normally, so that he could get to the wicket quickly and prevent the batsmen stealing any byes.

Nourse set the field with Eric Rowan covering 'cow-shot corner' at deep mid wicket. Bedser missed the first ball, but he got some pad on it. As second slip fumbled the ball a leg bye was scrambled. Gladwin heaved the next ball, a slower one, towards deep mid-on. Rowan had moved in only to see the ball carry over his head. He ran for it, but could not get there before the ball bounced into the crowd. Had he stayed put a wicket might have resulted, or three vital runs might have been saved. Wade excused the fieldsman, saying that Rowan failed to pick it up in the gloom. Under normal circumstances he thought the catch would have been taken.

Gladwin scored a leg bye to fine leg off the third ball, so just two were needed to win. Bedser could make nothing of the next two deliveries. One of them struck the batsman in the stomach, drawing a rebuke from Nourse. 'What are you doing? Bowl at the wicket', he ordered Tuckett. As he was doing this the crowd appealed for leg before.

Fast–medium Lindsay Tuckett, who was entrusted with bowling the last over. (Brian Bassano)

The sixth ball of the over was pushed into the covers and the single taken, although Bedser would have been run out had the throw hit the stumps. The scores were level with two deliveries remaining. Tuckett was contemplating running out the non-striker. In his opinion the batsmen were pinching yards, but Nourse vetoed the plan: 'We don't do that in a Test'. He would not even contemplate issuing a warning.

At the resulting mid-pitch conference the batsmen decided that they would run for the next delivery, no matter what. Gladwin took a swing, missed, and Bedser set off for the winning run. He went into rapid reverse when he realised that his partner had not moved and Wade had taken the ball. Amid shrieks and near hysteria from the crowd, he made it safely back.

With one delivery to go Tuckett asked if Nourse had any instructions. 'Just bowl at the wicket', was the reply. It wasn't a bad delivery either, just short of a length on leg stump. Gladwin moved down the pitch, aimed a stroke towards the leg side, missed, and the ball hit his thigh. This time both batsmen were off at such speed that 'Tufty' Mann, fielding close on the leg side, was unable to get the ball in time to beat Bedser home. Two other fieldsmen also tried to get there. Viewing film of this delivery, it certainly seems that Bedser was off before Tuckett released the ball.

England had recorded an incredible two wicket victory off the last ball of the game. The umpire was so excited that he forgot to signal a leg bye. A run was recorded, but this was later changed. The bruise on Gladwin's thigh was photographed and displayed almost as a badge of honour. 'I hope that bruise stays there for 50 years', he said.

Gladwin and McCarthy were chaired from the field, and while celebrations went on in the England dressing room, the South Africans sat in silence, thinking about what might have been. They certainly had much to consider. A number of catches had been dropped, any one of which might have changed the result, but considering their first innings had ended at four o'clock on the first day, it was a remarkable achievement to hold out until the very last ball of the match.

In a game most thought would be dominated by batsmen, the bowlers had controlled proceedings, although the pitch was a sporting one and not conducive to brilliant batting.

At the start of the tour George Mann had promised that his side would play bright cricket. He couldn't have planned it better, and described the game as one of the most exciting anyone could wish to see. 'What a finish for any man captaining his first Test team and playing in his first Test! If I took part in many more matches like this I should think of retiring early. The strain is too much.'

Opposing captain Dudley Nourse said also that it was an unforgettable game. He praised the fightback made by his team, but sounded a note of realism: 'The only trouble is that we are now one down in the series'. Eric Rowan felt that Nourse's field placings towards the end could have prevented the loss. He wanted to crowd the batsmen and force them into playing big shots, rather than scrambling singles. Nourse would not do this.

'Billy' Wade said there was some discussion after the game about field placings and whether or not Tuckett should have warned the batsmen for backing up too far, but he was also full of praise for the South African team. 'I think our team did wonderfully well, especially as we were all amateurs, some of whom were past their best cricketing years, which they had spent serving in the armed forces during World War II.'

The journalists also waxed lyrical. Charles Bray of the *Daily Herald* said the last hour was the most exciting he had ever spent. Apparently the tension was such that he found himself lighting a pipe which had no tobacco in it. E. W. Swanton, covering the tour, described it as 'a game none should lose', while Alex Bannister in the *Daily Mail* said, 'it was a fitting finish to a truly great match'.

The next three Tests were drawn and England won the last game to take the series 2–0, but the lasting memory was of the ball rebounding off Cliff Gladwin's thigh and the batsmen scampering through for the winning run. The man and the hour had indeed come together.

SOUTH AFRICA v ENGLAND

Played at Kingsmead, Durban on 16, 17, 18, 20 December, 1948.
Toss: South Africa.

SOUTH AFRICA

E. A. B. Rowan	c Evans b Jenkins	7	c Compton b Jenkins	16
O. E. Wynne	c Compton b Bedser	5	c Watkins b Wright	4
B. Mitchell	c Evans b Bedser	27	b Wright	19
A. D. Nourse *	c Watkins b Wright	37	c & b Bedser	32
W. W. Wade +	run out	8	b Jenkins	63
D. W. Begbie	c Compton b Bedser	37	c Mann b Bedser	48
O. C. Dawson	b Gladwin	24	c Compton b Wright	3
A. M. B. Rowan	not out	5	b Wright	15
L. Tuckett	lbw b Gladwin	1	not out	3
N. B. F. Mann	c Evans b Gladwin	4	c Mann b Compton	10
C. N. McCarthy	b Bedser	0	b Jenkins	0
Extras	(B 3, LB 2, NB 1)	6	(B 1, LB 5)	6
Total		**161**		**219**

Fall: 9, 18, 69, 80, 99, 148, 150, 152, 160, 161.
22, 22, 67, 89, 174, 179, 208, 208, 219, 219.

Bowling

First Innings: Bedser 13.5–2–39–4, Gladwin 12–3–21–3, Jenkins 14–3–50–1, Wright 9–3–29–1, Compton 2–0–5–0, Watkins 3–0–11–0.

Second Innings: Bedser 18–5–51–2, Gladwin 7–3–15–0, Jenkins 22.3–6–64–3, Wright 26–3–72–4, Compton 16–11–11–1.

ENGLAND

L. Hutton	c McCarthy b A. Rowan	83	c Dawson b Tuckett	5
C. Washbrook	c Wade b Mann	35	lbw b Mann	25
R. T. Simpson	c Begbie b Mann	5	(6) c E. Rowan b McCarthy	0
D. C. S. Compton	c Wade b Mann	72	b McCarthy	28
A. J. Watkins	c Nourse b A. Rowan	9	b McCarthy	4
F. G. Mann *	c E. Rowan b A. Rowan	19	(3) c Mitchell b McCarthy	13
T. G. Evans +	c Wynne b A. Rowan	0	b McCarthy	4
R. O. Jenkins	c Mitchell b Mann	5	c Wade b McCarthy	22
A. V. Bedser	c Tuckett b Mann	11	not out	1
C. Gladwin	not out	0	not out	7
D. V. P. Wright	c Tuckett b Mann	0		
Extras	(B 2, LB 12)	14	(B 9, LB 10)	19
Total		**253**		**8/128**

Fall: 84, 104, 146, 172, 212, 212, 221, 247, 253, 253.
25, 49, 52, 64, 64, 70, 115, 116.

Bowling

First Innings: McCarthy 9–2–20–0, Dawson 3–0–16–0, Tuckett 6–0–36–0, A. Rowan 44–8–108–4, Mann 37.4–14–59–6.

Second Innings: McCarthy 12–2–43–6, Tuckett 10–0–38–1, A. Rowan 4–0–15–0, Mann 2–0–13–1.

England won by 2 wickets

10

Ramadhin and Valentine

ENGLAND v WEST INDIES

Lord's Cricket Ground, London
26 June, 1950 – Day Two

For those people who have watched cricket only over the past 20 years, it seems that the one unchangeable force has been the dominance of the West Indies. A frightening array of fast bowlers has consistently destroyed batsmen, breaking reputations, and sometimes a few bones in the process. To gain a victory against the West Indies was rare enough; to win a series was unheard of. Only recently have some chinks begun to show in the previously impenetrable armour, but even now it would take a brave man to predict the demise of the West Indies.

But this was not always the case. There were times in the past when the cricketers from the Caribbean were a disorganised and poorly performed group. They would produce outstanding individual cricketers like batsman George Headley and all-rounder Learie Constantine, but the support players lacked depth and the results were generally poor, particularly when teams were playing way from home.

If there was a time when the cricket world began to sit up and take notice of the West Indies as a cricket power, it might just have been the 1950 tour of England. Up to this time the West Indies had never won a Test in England.

They had enjoyed some success at home, but this was against sides which were not the strongest England could have provided.

There was some cause to think that 1950 might be a little different. In the period following the end of the Second World War, the West Indies had built up a formidable array of batting talent led by Frank Worrell, Everton Weekes and Clyde Walcott—the famous three Ws. Each was different in style and technique, but all were capable of destroying any attack. To support them was an excellent opening combination in Jeff Stollmeyer and Allan Rae, along with players like Gerry Gomez, Bob Christiani and skipper John Goddard, all of whom could make useful runs.

If there was a concern it was with the bowling, and here the selectors made two inspired choices. From cricketing obscurity they plucked young spinners Alf Valentine and Sonny Ramadhin. Valentine was a left arm spinner, whose large hands and long fingers gave the ball a vicious tweak. His first class record consisted of two wickets captured in a couple of games. Ramadhin's methods, on the other hand, were far from orthodox. Wearing a cap, and with his sleeves buttoned to the wrist, he delivered a mixture of off and leg breaks which could prove difficult for the Englishmen to pick. His only first-class experience before the tour was two trial games. Before the tour he had never left Trinidad, and he had never bowled on any other surface than matting. Both players owed their selection to some lobbying by captain Goddard and vice-captain Stollmeyer, who believed them to be worth the risk.

Although the visitors' batting might prove hard to shift, England found it difficult to believe that two young, untried spinners would worry the likes of Len Hutton and Denis Compton.

This seemed to be the case when England won the First Test by 202 runs. Although Valentine had taken 8/104 and 3/100 in his Test debut, and Ramadhin had been economical in capturing four wickets, England's batting had performed well. The West Indians, on the other hand, had succumbed to the spin of Eric Hollies and Bob Berry, who captured eight and nine wickets respectively. Their efforts ensured that England moved on to the Lord's Test with some confidence. The West Indians, on the other hand, were extremely unhappy with the pitch, and hoped for a better surface in the Second Test.

Goddard won the toss and the West Indies batted, reaching 7/320 at stumps on the first day. Opener Rae held the innings together with a composed 106, while Worrell (52) and Weekes (63) added some punch.

As the players moved onto the field for the second day, the West Indies were determined to push the score along, while England wanted a quick finish to the innings.

It was the locals who had their wish granted. Christiani was bowled by the third ball of the day, from Alec Bedser, for 33, then Roly Jenkins removed Prior Jones and Valentine to end the innings at 326 and give himself

Alf Valentine, whose left arm spinners destroyed the leaden–footed England batting.
(Brian Bassano)

5/116. The West Indies had produced a good, but not brilliant, total, and England could look forward with some confidence to taking a first innings lead.

Jones, right arm, and Worrell, left arm, opened the bowling against Hutton and Washbrook. Although one or two deliveries caused some discomfort, particularly when Worrell was bowling to Hutton, there seemed to be little cause for concern. The innings had been in progress for an hour before Goddard brought Valentine and Ramadhin into the attack together.

Initially the batsmen increased the scoring. Two overs from Valentine went for ten, three from Ramadhin for 13, and the total reached 55. The spinners then tightened their accuracy and delivered five maidens in a row before Hutton took a single off Valentine. When he struck Ramadhin through the covers to the boundary, most thought the batsmen had weathered any threat.

Within 15 minutes of lunch Hutton seemed intent on attacking Valentine. Three times he moved down the wicket, but did not get to the pitch of the ball. For all his limited experience Valentine was a hard man to get to, and when Hutton tried again, he was beaten by the flight and Walcott completed the stumping. England was 1/62 and its finest batsman out for 35.

In the 15 minutes before lunch, the spinners bowled 46 balls from which no runs were scored.

Bill Edrich took a single off the second ball after the break, and Washbrook drove a boundary, but this was followed by four more maidens. Fieldsmen crowded around the bat, as run scoring began to look a difficult task.

Although Ramadhin bowled mostly off-breaks, the batsmen could never be certain. Attacking strokes were a rarity, but Washbrook played one, striking the little Trinidadian to the boundary. It was his last act of defiance. Later in the over he moved down the pitch to drive but was beaten by an off-break; Walcott did the rest. He had made 36 and the score was 2/74.

Hubert Doggart, playing in only his second Test, came in to join Edrich. He played a maiden, then fell to a classic piece of deception. Ramadhin bowled an off-break from the edge of the crease which spun away outside leg stump. Doggart swung and missed. The next ball landed in the same spot, and again the batsman swung and missed. But this one was the leg break. It spun and trapped the batsman in front. Doggart was out for nought, and England 3/74.

Gilbert Parkhouse, the next batsman, had been in top form in county cricket, and was chosen to make his Test debut in this game. The problem was that he had been most successful as an opening batsman for Glamorgan. Batting number five against spinners was not something he was particularly used to.

The West Indians tightened the screws, with each bowler delivering four maidens. After 13 scoreless overs Edrich broke the drought, getting a single off Valentine. Perhaps facing the other spinner was too much for Parkhouse. He swung across the line and was bowled for nought. With a duck on debut he trudged off.

Captain Norman Yardley came in to join the fray. Edrich, who had spent an hour over two runs, hit Ramadhin to the boundary, but this proved a false hope as it was followed by six maidens.

The sequence was broken by a single and a three to Yardley and two to Edrich, which took the total to 86. Then Ramadhin struck the next blow. Edrich stretched forward to what was a leg break and edged it to Walcott. His 90 minute sojourn ended with his total on eight, and England now in desperate straits at 5/86. Edrich received a deal of criticism for this innings. Many thought he should have played with more aggression, in particular *The Times* correspondent, who said he utterly refused to play any shot but 'a smothering dab, allowing Valentine to bowl to two silly mid-offs, two slips with no third man and no one in the region of extra cover'. But bowlers have always looked easy from the stands, and having watched Hutton and Washbrook dismissed, and with Compton not playing, the weight of responsibility was heavy upon him. He knew he could not afford to get out and played accordingly.

Keeper Godfrey Evans was in good form, having made a century in the First Test, and although he began by playing a maiden, he soon hit two boundaries off Ramadhin, just after Yardley had struck two fours off Valentine. Those blows added 16 runs in five minutes, after just 14 had been made in the previous 80.

Any ideas of a recovery were quickly removed as Ramadhin bowled Evans, who was attempting to hit the ball a vast distance. Then eight runs later Yardley was bowled by Valentine for 16 to leave England tottering at 7/110. When Jenkins was caught behind off Valentine for four ten minutes later, it was 8/113.

Tea was reached without further loss, but after the break, Johnny Wardle, with only Bedser and Berry left, decided to attack. Bedser chose to play in the same vein and struck the second ball to the boundary, but was bowled by the next. Another wicket to Ramadhin, his fifth, and England was 9/122.

Wardle found support in last man Berry, so much so that the pair added 29 for the last wicket, of which Berry made only two. Wardle hit six fours, and was so successful that Goddard had to remove the spinners and bring back Jones and Worrell. This proved the correct tactic, as Jones had Berry caught by Goddard to end the innings at 151. Wardle's 33 not out was the

Sonny Ramadhin, bowling with cap on and sleeves down. His mystery spin was a problem England's batsmen could not solve. (Brian Bassano)

one attacking innings of note, and the thought was that perhaps some others needed to be more positive, although five of them—Hutton, Washbrook, Doggart, Parkhouse and Evans—were all out playing aggressive strokes. *The Times* correspondent called it 'preposterously bad batting'.

If the batting was disappointing, then the bowling was inspired. Ramadhin captured 5/66 off 43 overs, and Valentine had 4/48 off 45. At one stage they bowled 44 maidens out of 76 overs, while in conceding 16 scoring shots each, Valentine delivered 234 balls and Ramadhin 222. Between 12.50 and 4 pm, Ramadhin sent down 204 deliveries, of which just nine were scored from. It was an amazing display of control, especially from two such inexperienced players, against some very capable batsmen. It was hard to believe that the spinners had not been playing Test cricket for many years.

With such a substantial lead, Rae (16 not out) and Stollmeyer (29 not out) played carefully through the last 75 minutes of the day, adding 45 runs, although the fieldsmen did give Rae two lives, courtesy of dropped catches.

The West Indies went on to declare at 6/425, with Walcott making 168 not out, Weekes 63 and Gomez 70. Faced with an awesome task England did better second time around, but were dismissed for 274 to lose by 326 runs, giving the West Indians their first Test victory in England. Washbrook made 114, but no one else reached 50. Parkhouse was next best, going some way towards atoning for his first innings duck with 48. Ramadhin and Valentine again emphasised their dominance, with 6/86 off 72 overs and 3/79 off 71 overs respectively.

With their dominance established the West Indies won the remaining two Tests by ten wickets and an innings and 56 runs to take the series 3–1. The spinners were the key. Valentine took 33 wickets at 20.42 and Ramadhin 26 wickets at 23.23 in the series. No one else got close to ten. Such was their effort that they inspired the famous calypso about 'two little pals of mine, Ramadhin and Valentine'. Both also captured over a hundred wickets on the tour.

So in England in 1950, the West Indies took the first steps along the road to cricket dominance. Given recent history, it is ironic to think that it was all through the performance of two young and inexperienced spinners.

ENGLAND v WEST INDIES

Played at Lord's, London on 24, 26, 27, 28, 29 June, 1950.
Toss: West Indies

WEST INDIES

A. F. Rae	c & b Jenkins	106	b Jenkins	24
J. B. Stollmeyer	lbw b Wardle	20	b Jenkins	30
F. M. M. Worrell	b Bedser	52	c Doggart b Jenkins	45
E. de C. Weekes	b Bedser	63	run out	63
C. L. Walcott +	st Evans b Jenkins	14	(6) not out	168
G. E. Gomez	st Evans b Jenkins	1	(7) c Edrich b Bedser	70
R. J. Christiani	b Bedser	33	(8) not out	5
J. D. C. Goddard *	b Wardle	14	(5) c Evans b Jenkins	11
P. E. Jones	c Evans b Jenkins	0		
S. Ramadhin	not out	1		
A. L. Valentine	c Hutton b Jenkins	5		
Extras	(B 10, LB 5, W 1, NB 1)	17	(LB 8, NB 1)	9
Total		**326**		**6/425**

Fall: 37, 128, 233, 262, 273, 274, 320, 320, 320, 326.   48, 75, 108, 146, 199, 410.

Bowling:

First Innings: Bedser 40–14–60–3, Edrich 16–4–30–0, Jenkins 35.2–6–115–5, Wardle 17–6–46–2, Berry 19–7–45–0, Yardley 4–1–12–0.

Second Innings: Bedser 44–16–80–1, Edrich 13–2–37–0, Jenkins 59–13–174–4, Wardle 30–10–58–0, Berry 32–15–67–0.

ENGLAND

L. Hutton	st Walcott b Valentine	35	b Valentine	10
C. Washbrook	st Walcott b Ramadhin	36	b Ramadhin	114
W. J. Edrich	c Walcott b Ramadhin	8	c Jones b Ramadhin	8
G. H. G. Doggart	lbw Ramadhin	0	b Ramadhin	25
W. G. A. Parkhouse	b Valentine	0	c Goddard b Valentine	48
N. W. D. Yardley *	b Valentine	16	c Weekes b Valentine	19
T. G. Evans +	b Ramadhin	8	c Rae b Ramadhin	2
R. O. Jenkins	c Walcott b Valentine	4	b Ramadhin	4
J. H. Wardle	not out	33	lbw b Worrell	21
A. V. Bedser	b Ramadhin	5	b Ramadhin	0
R. Berry	c Goddard b Jones	2	not out	0
Extras	(B 2, LB 1, W 1)	4	(B 16, LB 7)	23
Total		**151**		**274**

Fall: 62, 74, 74, 75, 86, 102, 110, 113, 122, 151.   28, 57, 140, 218, 228, 238, 245, 248, 258, 274.

Bowling:

First Innings: Jones 8.4–2–13–1, Worrell 10–4–20–0, Valentine 45–28–48–4, Ramadhin 43–27–66–5.

Second Innings: Jones 7–1–22–0, Worrell 22.3–9–39–1, Valentine 71–47–79–3, Ramadhin 72–43–86–6, Gomez 13–1–25–0, Goddard 6–6–0–0.

West Indies won by 326 runs

11

A Different Kind of Courage

SOUTH AFRICA V NEW ZEALAND

Ellis Park, Johannesburg
26 December, 1953 – Day Two

T EST CRICKET had never seen the kind of drama played out at Ellis Park, Johannesburg on Boxing Day, 1953. A writer would not have dared to produce an account of this day's events, lest his fiction be termed too unbelievable. It was a day of tragedy and triumph, of brutal and spectacular cricket, but above all, of breathtaking courage that lifted the match out of the realms of mere sport to show some of the finest human qualities.

New Zealand had found the going tough on its first tour of South Africa. In spite of some good individual performances the First Test was lost by an innings. Moving on to Ellis Park, Johannesburg, the Second Test was a more even competition, South Africa having struggled to 8/259 at the end of the first day. The visitors would have been in an even better position had they not dropped seven catches. However, the pitch was moist and full of life, and the Kiwis knew runs would be hard to come by.

The drama began early on Boxing Day when news came through of the Tangiwai rail disaster in New Zealand's North Island, where a train of holidaymakers had lost their lives when a mudslide had destroyed a bridge just before the express arrived. Tragic enough anyway, the disaster became more personal when one of the 150 dead was identified as the fiancee of Kiwi fast bowler Bob Blair.

Manager Jack Kerr remembered, 'I was awoken by the phone ringing on Saturday morning. It was an urgent cable message from New Zealand to break the news to Bob Blair that his fiancee had been killed. I immediately contacted Geoff Rabone, our skipper, and with Eric Dempster, a pal of Bob's, we then told him the sad news'.

Obviously too distressed for anything as mundane as a cricket match, Blair stayed in the hotel. As he prepared to leave, John Reid saw his distraught team-mate sitting in his room with his head in his hands. It was a quiet group which arrived at the ground to find the flags flying at half-mast.

Rabone held a team meeting and asked that the players try to concentrate on the cricket. This was difficult, as the players were upset for Blair, and as they had not received a full casualty list they were left to ponder whether any of their friends or relatives were involved. Bert Sutcliffe remembered a feeling of lethargy, 'a sort of what are we doing here anyway feeling'.

Trying to concentrate on the game, the Kiwis wrapped up the Springbok innings for 271, then found themselves facing the swing of Dave Ironside and the ferocious pace of Neil Adcock. The latter was only 22, but at this stage, arguably the fastest bowler in the world. Adcock had just been run out without facing a ball in his first innings in Tests. He was furious, and announced that someone was going to pay. Former Springbok Jackie McGlew remembered that Ellis Park was so suited to the tall fast bowler that it was known as 'Adcock's Alley'.

Both openers, Rabone and Murray Chapple, were struck on the body in the first over on a pitch which Bert Sutcliffe later described as 'almost lethal'. The innings started badly when skipper Rabone, a century maker in the First Test, was caught in the slips off Ironside for 1. Adcock struck, removing Chapple for eight with a ball that went from gloves to chest to stumps to have the Kiwis 2/9.

Neil Adcock was positively lethal on the Ellis Park pitch, which was known locally as 'Adcock's Alley'. (Brian Bassano)

Left: Kiwi skipper Geoff Rabone on his knees after being hit. (Brian Bassano) *Right:* Bert Sutcliffe is hit by an Adcock flier. (Brian Bassano)

Sutcliffe is assisted from the field. (Brian Bassano)

According to Rabone, Adcock was lifting the ball head-high from a length, and 'it was extremely difficult to handle. The pitch was the greenest, longest grass growth that I had to perform on'.

Enter New Zealand's best batsman, left-hander Sutcliffe. He hardly had time to look around when Adcock struck again. His third ball was a vicious lifter, striking the batsman a dreadful blow behind the ear. Sutcliffe said later that it was his own fault as he turned his head instead of swaying away from the ball. Sutcliffe confessed to 'going out like a light', and although bleeding badly and very shaky, he managed to get from the field under his own steam. Taken to hospital for treatment, he fainted twice, and at the ground it was announced that he wouldn't bat again.

The aftermath of Sutcliffe's injury had incensed Geoff Rabone. Photographers had run onto the ground to get a picture of the stricken batsman. The New Zealand captain went out and did his best to remove them.

Back at Ellis Park the carnage continued. Reid, the ironman of Kiwi cricket, was hit five times in 25 minutes at the crease by Adcock while making three runs. On his dismissal, the score stood at 3/23 with one retired hurt. Tough as he undoubtedly is Reid still cannot think of that day without getting a lump in his throat.

Lawrie Miller took Adcock's first delivery on the chest, and left the field coughing blood. It took some persuasion to make the brave Miller leave, and he too, looked unlikely to bat again—'The next one butchered to make an Ellis Park holiday', said New Zealand writer Dick Brittenden.

Frank Mooney's bat flies from his hands after he received a blow to the body. (Brian Bassano)

Shortly before lunch Adcock thundered a delivery into Matt Poore's ribs; it deflected onto the stumps.

So it was 4/41 and two retired hurt. Even saving the follow-on looked a long way away. Sutcliffe remembered that every one of the first six batsmen was bruised in their efforts to counter Adcock. He felt that this tended to be forgotten in the emotion later in the day, but not by him or any of those concerned.

After the break some of the fire seemed to leave the wicket, although batting was still far from easy. Nineteen-year-old John Beck, in one of Test cricket's most daunting debuts, hung on for an hour and 16 runs, and on his dismissal Miller returned to join wicketkeeper Frank Mooney. After discussion between captain and manager, the decision of whether to go out again was left to the batsman. There was no question what he would do. Miller's brave innings ended at 14 when Ironside bowled him.

At 6/82 in walked a pale-faced Bert Sutcliffe, his head swathed in bandages and looking more like a Sikh hockey player than a cricketer. The decision of whether to bat had been left up to him, just as it had with Miller. He confessed to being strongly fortified by a product of Scotland which he refused to name, except to say that it was not porridge. Manager Kerr has a vivid memory of the event. 'Not the normal therapy in such situations', he said. The left-hander's courage caught the crowd and he received a tremendous ovation. With such a small total and little to follow he decided that attack was the only way to go. His third ball, from Ironside, disappeared over the fence. After another boundary Adcock was brought back, only to be cut for four. South African skipper Jack Cheetham turned to his other trump card,

Bert Sutcliffe, head swathed in bandages, hammers Tayfield for six during his heroic innings. (Brian Bassano)

off spinner Hugh Tayfield. Sutcliffe responded to the challenge by driving his first ball for six. When Tayfield tried to fire the ball in, it was just short of a length and hammered through square leg for four. At the tea interval Sutcliffe and Mooney had added 50 in half an hour.

Mooney went shortly after the break for a brave 35, and at 7/138 Sutcliffe was joined by tall medium pacer Tony MacGibbon. They added eight before MacGibbon fell to Ironside for nought. Now joined by Guy Overton, Sutcliffe realised the end was near, but he wasn't going down without a fight, dispatching Tayfield out of the ground for yet another six. But when Ironside dismissed Overton at 154 the players headed toward the pavilion.

Suddenly the crowd fell utterly silent. Sutcliffe looked up to see what had happened. Bob Blair was walking out to bat. He had been listening to the game and decided to help his mates, if he could. Now he moved slowly to the wicket, fumbling to put on his gloves, a task which seemed beyond him. In the unearthly silence Sutcliffe walked to meet Blair, putting an arm about his shoulders and escorting him to the centre.

Sutcliffe remembered what he called 'a bloody marvellous moment', the most vivid of his memories of the day.

'I said, "What the hell are you doing here?" He half-smiled through teary eyes, "I'd like to feel I can help." I told him we had just avoided the follow on and to throw the bat and let's get out of here.'

As Blair waited for Ironside to bowl he frequently brushed his hand across his eyes in an endeavour to see through his tears. A spectator later wrote that Blair reminded him 'of a small boy, beaten, but still defiant'. To come back from injury as Sutcliffe had was one thing, but to come back when your whole world has crashed around you requires courage of an altogether different kind. This, at least, was the thought of Dick Brittenden watching from the stands. In a day requiring plenty of bravery, he felt Blair's courage was unexcelled. The New Zealand players looking on were moved to tears by their colleague's display. Sutcliffe said he, too, was trying hard not to cry.

The situation was just as poignant for the South Africans. Jackie McGlew was the fieldsman closest to Blair as he walked out. 'It was hard to decide what one should do. A pat on the back might have helped him just a little; or the right word, whatever that might be at a moment such as this. But as I approached him I saw that Blair was walking out with his face a taut and anguished mask. His shoulders heaved, for he was a man who had been deeply stricken. I saw this and turned away, for this was not the time for whatever sympathetic gesture one might have in mind.'

Still the eerie silence continued as Blair somehow survived the remainder of the over. It is doubtful if he even saw the ball. He played down a line and the ball missed bat, stumps, everything. Sutcliffe believes Blair would have been unable even to see the bowler, let alone the ball.

Tayfield came on to deliver the next over, and Sutcliffe broke the

Bob Blair, whose courage gave a dramatic day its most poignant moment. (Brian Bassano)

silence by hitting him for three sixes. Taking a single with one delivery to go, the left-hander watched Blair take a huge swing and deposit Tayfield into the crowd for the fourth time in an over which cost 25 runs. The crowd, so still and silent before, were yelling and screaming as if it was a Rugby international.

There was time for another six by Sutcliffe before Blair was stumped to end the innings at 187. The pair had added 33 in just ten minutes. Sutcliffe had scored his unbeaten 80 out of 106 in 112 minutes. He had hit seven sixes and four fours. South Africa's finest cricket writer, Louis Duffus, had this to say about Sutcliffe's batting. 'It is difficult to imagine that a more electrifying or more moving innings than that of the injured left-hander was ever played in a South African Test match. When he walked back to the stand, bandaged, bruised, but unbeaten, the crowd rose to acclaim him.'

Sutcliffe felt that it was not his best innings, as he should have been caught by Tayfield early on, but luck stayed with him. 'Luck's an incredible thing. If Tayfield hadn't missed that easy catch none of the rest would have taken place.' But statistics, no matter how impressive, lose their relevance at a time like this. Brittenden best summed up the feelings at the end of the innings. 'They went off together arm in arm, into the pavilion and immortality. How could the loss of a thousand Test matches be set against an occasion such as this—a day when skill and courage and love fused so fiercely?'

In the long run that sums it up. Although they had the Springboks 3/35 at stumps, the first innings lead was too great, and New Zealand lost the Test by 132 runs—and later the series—but most of the details have been forgotten. What has been remembered is the courage displayed by Bert Sutcliffe and Bob Blair on that day. They gave New Zealand cricket perhaps its finest moment. 'Someone decided to give it legend status', says the ever–modest Sutcliffe. The legend the pair created lives on and will continue to do so.

And what of the principal players in this extraordinary drama? Bert Sutcliffe continued to charm the cricket world with his skills for many years, although his injury may have cost him a little in confidence when dealing with the fastest bowlers. In 42 Tests he scored 2727 runs at 40.10. An innings of 230 not out was the highest of his five centuries. Sutcliffe had the misfortune never to play in a winning Test side, but in spite of that he left some enviable achievements. His 2627 runs on the 1949 tour of England is a total exceeded only by Bradman for a visiting batsman, and until the advent of Brian Lara he held the world record score for a left-hander, 385 for Otago against Canterbury. (His ten partners contributed 86.) From 1947 to 1965 the talents of Bert Sutcliffe were frequently on display, but he never had a finer moment than Boxing Day 1953 at Ellis Park in Johannesburg.

This was the second of Springbok fast bowler Neil Adcock's 26 Tests, in which he captured 104 wickets at the excellent average of 21.10. When he was joined in the Test team by Peter Heine the Springboks possessed a pair of quicks as lethal as any in the world.

Adcock was South Africa's spearhead for a decade, retiring in 1962. Perhaps his finest moment came on the 1960 England Tour, when he took 26 wickets at 22.57 in the Tests and 108 at 14.02 altogether. Adcock's 8/87 in this game secured his place in the side, and he never sent down a more hostile spell.

Bob Blair never reached the heights of Sutcliffe and Adcock, but his rhythmic action was capable of producing genuine speed, and he was the first New Zealander to take 500 first class wickets. Between 1953 and 1964 he played 19 Tests and his 43 wickets cost 35.23 apiece. His best performance came in his last Test, when he took 4/85 and 3/57 against South Africa at Eden Park, Auckland. On that day, Blair and Kiwi skipper John Reid were the only survivors from Ellis Park's day of drama. But then you would expect Bob Blair to keep trying, to keep going, and to be there to help, regardless of the situation. After all, it was something he'd proved a long time ago.

SOUTH AFRICA v NEW ZEALAND

Played at Ellis Park, Johannesburg on 24, 26, 28, 29 December, 1953.
Toss: South Africa.

SOUTH AFRICA

D.J. McGlew	c Reid b MacGibbon	13	b MacGibbon	8
A.R.A. Murray	c Chapple b Blair	7	(9) c Blair b Overton	13
W.R. Endean	c Sutcliffe b Reid	93	c sub (Leggat) b Reid	1
K.J. Funston	lbw b Overton	0	c Overton b MacGibbon	11
R.A. McLean	c Blair b Overton	27	(7) lbw b Reid	36
C.B. van Ryneveld	b Blair	65	(8) c Reid b MacGibbon	17
J.E. Cheetham *	c Mooney b MacGibbon	20	(6) c Sutcliffe b Reid	1
H.J. Tayfield	not out	20	(5) b Reid	34
J.H.B. Waite +	c Mooney b MacGibbon	0	(2) c Reid b MacGibbon	5
D.E.J. Ironside	b Reid	13	not out	11
N.A.T. Adcock	run out	0	c Poore b Overton	6
Extras	(B 3, LB 2, NB 8)	13	(LB 3, NB 2)	5
Total		**271**		**148**

Fall: 13, 37, 43, 100, 168, 226, 244, 244, 271, 271.   11, 13, 24, 37, 44, 67, 112, 122, 138, 148.

Bowling
First Innings: Blair 17–4–50–2, Reid 18–3–63–2, Overton 20–4–68–2, MacGibbon 22–5–61–3, Rabone 3–0–16–0.
Second Innings: Blair 5–0–14–0, Reid 16–5–34–4, Overton 12.1–1–33–2, MacGibbon 20–2–62–4.

NEW ZEALAND

G.O. Rabone *	c Endean b Ironside	1	c Van Ryneveld b Adcock	22
M.E. Chapple	b Adcock	8	c Waite b Ironside	22
M.B. Poore	b Adcock	15	b Adcock	1
B. Sutcliffe	not out	80	c Endean b Murray	10
J.R. Reid	c Endean b Adcock	3	(6) c Funston b Ironside	1
L.S.M. Miller	b Ironside	14	(7) c Waite b Adcock	0
J.E.F. Beck	c Waite b Murray	16	(8) c Endean b Ironside	7
F.L.H. Mooney +	b Ironside	35	(5) c Funston b Adcock	10
A.R. MacGibbon	c Endean b Ironside	0	not out	11
G.W.F. Overton	c Murray b Ironside	0	(11) run out	2
R.W. Blair	st Waite b Tayfield	6	(10) b Adcock	4
Extras	(B 3, LB 4, W 2)	9	(B 3, LB 5, NB 2)	10
Total		**187**		**100**

Fall: 5, 9, 23, 35, 57, 81, 138, 146, 154, 187.   35, 38, 58, 75, 75, 76, 76, 84, 89, 100.

Bowling
First Innings: Adcock 14–2–44–3, Ironside 19–4–51–5, Murray 12–3–30–1, Tayfield 8.2–2–53–1.
Second Innings: Adcock 19–4–43–5, Ironside 20.5–10–37–3, Murray 8–3–10–1.

South Africa won by 132 runs

12

'It's a Tie!'

Brisbane Cricket Ground
14 December, 1960 – Day Five

THE 1960–61 series between Australia and the West Indies was a vital one for both sides for a number of reasons. The last Australian home series, in 1958–59 against England, had been successful, but the cricket played had been tedious. There was a need to play positively in order to bring the crowds back to the game, and to sustain interest in Australia's number one sport. Sir Donald Bradman, in his capacities as selector and Board member, had addressed the Australian players before the Brisbane Test, and impressed upon them the need for positive cricket.

For the West Indians, this was also a vital series. It was their third tour of Australia, and the others in 1930–31 and 1951–52 had both been relatively unsuccessful. They were keen to improve on a disappointing record. The other factor was that after many years of lobbying, the West Indians would be led by a black man, Frank Worrell. The pressure would be on Worrell to show that he could weld the different talents and backgrounds of his side into a cohesive force. It would prove to be an inspiring choice.

The first Test of this series would be important in establishing a tone for the series. No one, even in their wildest dreams, could have predicted what would happen in Brisbane during those five days.

The West Indies chose, in batting order: Conrad Hunte, Cammie Smith, Rohan Kanhai, Gary Sobers, Frank Worrell, Joe Solomon, Peter Lashley,

Gerry Alexander, Sonny Ramadhin, Wes Hall and Alf Valentine. The side was full of dazzling batting, but slightly weaker in bowling, in spite of the presence of the very fast Hall.

The Australians chose Colin McDonald, Bobby Simpson, Neil Harvey, Norm O'Neill, Les Favell, Ken Mackay, Alan Davidson, Richie Benaud, Wally Grout, Ian Meckiff and Lindsay Kline. This, too, was a capable side, again perhaps slightly stronger in batting than bowling. Worrell won the toss and the West Indies got the game away to a flying start by making 453 (7/359 on the first day). Sobers led the way with a brilliant 132, ably supported by Worrell and Solomon (65 each), keeper Alexander (60), and fast bowler Hall with an entertaining 50. Davidson, with 5/135, was a long way ahead of the rest of the bowlers. Australia replied with 505. O'Neill made his highest Test score of 181, Simpson 92, McDonald 57, Favell 45 and Davidson 44. Hall took 4/140, and unsettled everyone with his express pace.

At stumps on the fourth day, the West Indies had reached 9/259. Worrell made his second 65, Rohan Kanhai 54 and Solomon 47. Davidson again led the attack with 5/70, including the prize wicket of Sobers, whom he yorked for 14.

The Australians' task on this final day was to take the last West Indian wicket as quickly as possible in order to give themselves the reasonable total of just over 200 to win.

The West Indians Hall and spinner Alf Valentine frustrated Benaud's plans for 40 minutes, during which they extended their last wicket partnership to 31. Davidson took the last wicket, bowling Hall, attempting a huge swing, for 18, to give him 6/87 for the innings, and 11/222 for the match.

The West Indies' dismissal for 284 left Australia 233 to win, a rate of 45 per hour on a pitch which had stood up well and was offering little help to the bowlers. Bob Simpson and Alan Davidson were among those who thought that Australia would certainly win.

McDonald, who had taken a battering from Hall in the first innings, had his ribs padded as he walked in to open with Simpson. In the third over Hall got one to lift at Simpson, who could only fend it off one-handed to substitute fieldsman Lance Gibbs at short leg. He had tried to duck instead of swaying away from the ball as was his usual method. Australia 1/1, Simpson out for nought, had made the worst of starts.

Neil Harvey was the veteran of the Australian order. Having made his debut in 1947–48, the small left-hander was his country's most capped player. He began with a boundary through square leg off Hall, then in the fast bowler's next over he edged a ball into the slips only to see Sobers dive forward and to the right to take a great catch. In getting his hand under the ball the all-rounder dislocated a finger, which Alexander—a vet—put back into place. As the finger was also cut Sobers left the field for attention.

At 2/7 O'Neill appeared, and was greeted by a screaming bumper which sat him on the pitch. In spite of everything Hall could throw at them (and that was plenty) the batsmen held on. O'Neill took 24 minutes to get off the mark, and at lunch he had eight and McDonald 14. Australia's 2/28 had taken 70 minutes.

After the break O'Neill went on the attack. Acting on his captain's advice of 'Have a look and then thrash them', he played Hall to leg for three, leg glanced him for four, and in his next over twice cut him to the fence. Worrell did not use a third man, leaving the shot open for O'Neill, who tried it again and was caught behind by Alexander for 26. Australia was 3/49. Favell, an aggressive South Australian right-hander, was almost bowled first ball.

Worrell, who had been bowling economically while Hall attacked, made the next break by bowling McDonald for 16, scored in 91 minutes. This was a vital wicket, as the Victorian had taken on the role of sheet anchor and was quite capable of batting out the rest of the day. At 4/49 the game was swinging towards the visitors. Australian success looked more unlikely when Hall fired three deliveries straight through the new batsman Ken Mackay.

Hall dropped in a short one to Favell, who smashed it past point to the boundary, but when he pitched one up, the South Australian whipped it off his toes, straight into Solomon's hands. Favell walked off, no doubt regretting his impetuous shot.

The last three wickets had fallen for eight runs, and at 5/57 defeat seemed only a matter of time. To achieve victory Australia required 176 runs in 200 minutes. A draw looked the best option, if they could survive. In 'Slasher' Mackay, the Australians had the perfect brick wall, and Davidson, Benaud and company could all bat to some effect.

After his heroics with the ball Davidson found himself in the centre again. 'What the hell am I doing here? I shouldn't be batting at all', were his thoughts at the time.

Hall went off, after sending down 12 overs in succession, during which he captured 4/38. This brought Sobers into the attack. Surely the most versatile of all bowlers, he could deliver fast, medium, orthodox left arm spin, and wrist spin. In this spell he came on to bowl his spinners into the footmarks at the other end.

Things were quiet for a while as the batsmen struggled to rebuild the innings. Sobers gave way to the spin of Sonny Ramadhin, who should have had Mackay caught in the slips, but Gibbs dropped the catch. The little spinner had his revenge 12 runs later when he put one through Mackay's defence. The pair had added 35 in an hour.

At 6/92 and with the major defensive power of Mackay gone, a West Indies victory looked more likely than ever. The situation could have been even worse when Ramadhin's second ball shaved the stumps of the

Australian captain, going for byes. Shortly afterwards he was off the mark with an off-drive to the boundary from Valentine. 'Never had a half volley looked so good', he said later.

When the tea interval was reached Davidson had 16 and Benaud six, and in 120 minutes of play Australia needed 123 runs with four wickets in hand. Alan Davidson remembers the Australian dressing room was like a morgue during the adjournment. No one spoke, although Bob Simpson said he remained confident, believing that Australia would still win.

During the break Sir Donald Bradman asked the Australian captain what his plans were. When told he was going for a win, he replied, 'I'm very pleased to hear it'. Benaud felt that the West Indians would crack if the batsmen could keep the pressure on, but he reckoned without the calm assurance of Worrell.

The Herald which went to press at this time had a different view, proclaiming the West Indies to be on the brink of victory.

When the players returned to the field, Benaud turned to his partner and said, 'Let's give it a go'. Under the circumstances not many captains would have been so brave. The Australian skipper had great confidence in his partner. 'Davidson was a wonderful attacking player and that was what was needed on that final afternoon in Brisbane, so that the initiative could be taken away from the West Indies.'

Davidson scored his first boundary after 84 minutes at the crease, and runs flowed steadily after the break. The equation was reduced to 105 in 100 minutes, with both batsmen playing well. Hall had three overs and was then rested. Worrell needed him to have something in reserve if the new ball had to be taken at 200.

In between the boundary hits there were plenty of short singles as the Australians tried to unsettle the fielders. The West Indian temperament had a reputation for collapsing under pressure, and this could be its sternest test. Worrell was constantly calming and reassuring his players.

The captain brought himself into the attack and Benaud immediately hit him past mid-on for four to bring up the 150. The pair had been maintaining a steady rate, and in the 75 minutes remaining 80 runs were needed.

The Australians went after Ramadhin. Benaud lofted him down the ground, hitting the fence on the first bounce. Davidson square cut him for four, and at the drinks break the target had been reduced to 60. A run a ball from here, and the possibility of an Australian win—thought by many to have been buried long ago—resurfaced.

Lindsay Kline remembers the tension in the rooms. 'Slasher Mackay was very superstitious. We were not allowed to move, and if we went to the toilet we could only go between overs and we had to back before play restarted.'

Davidson is run out via a direct hit from Joe Solomon for a brilliant 80. (*The Age*)

The small crowd of 4100 was certainly getting its money's worth. In view of the day's play, there should have been many more there to witness it. Perhaps there were, as Richie Benaud says he has met at least 50,000 people who swear they were there on that last day.

Ramadhin continued after the break and Davidson hit him forward of square leg for six to bring up his 50 in 141 minutes. When Sobers came on to replace Worrell, Benaud swung him to the square leg fence. The spinner kept bowling and Davidson, with a straight hit and a pull shot, produced two more boundaries. The second of these brought up the 100 partnership in just 95 minutes.

Although the running between the wickets was superb, the fieldsmen did not panic. When Sobers bowled a full toss Benaud hit it with enormous power, only to see Worrell field it one-handed and save a boundary. The captains of both sides were setting the example.

With the total on 198 and the new ball imminent, the batsmen decided to have one last assault on Ramadhin. They hit two singles, followed by a two to Davidson from a square cut and a boundary to an off-drive.

The last roll of the dice for Worrell was the new ball. Hall took it at 5.30 with the score on 206. The batsmen needed 27 in 30 minutes, and it was hard to see how Australia could now lose. What happened next would defy the imagination of the best scriptwriter.

The Australians began with three singles, one of them a near catch to Hunte from Benaud. Davidson then moved inside a bouncer and hooked it superbly to the fence. The next ball was pushed away for a single, leaving 19 to get.

In this over there should have been a run out, but Valentine threw the ball to the wrong end, and Davidson managed to make it home.

With 21 minutes to go and 19 to get Sobers bowled from the other end, three singles came off the first three balls, a leg bye and one to each batsman. Benaud then played a magnificent off-drive to the fence. Sobers bowled a no ball, then Benaud took a single to reach his 50 in 124 minutes with six fours. Australia was set to win, as only ten were needed in 15 minutes. During these last minutes Worrell was continually urging his players to 'relax and concentrate'.

Alan Davidson became the first man to score over a hundred runs and take ten wickets in the same Test. (Arthur James Collection)

Hall put the first delivery of the next over through Benaud. He followed it with a scorching bouncer which nearly removed the Australian captain's nose. The next ball was a yorker, which he somehow kept out and pushed away for a single. There were no more runs, and with ten minutes to go, nine were needed.

Two more singles were taken off Sobers, one of them to Solomon, who, the batsmen thought, moved a little slowly to the ball. Then Benaud pushed the third ball wide of square leg and the batsmen set off. Solomon picked up the ball, hit the base of the stumps from side on, and Davidson was run out. He had made 80, his highest Test score, in 194 minutes with eight fours and a six. Given his long spell of bowling, it was an incredible effort. In the course of this innings Davidson became the first man to score 100 runs and take ten wickets in a Test. Benaud blamed himself for a bad call that might cost the game.

The new batsman, keeper Wally Grout, was capable of some aggressive strokeplay, but would he be up to the tension of these next few minutes? In the dressing room he had been nervously chain-smoking, and when the moment came to go in he could not find his batting gloves because he was sitting on them. Grout was keen not to waste time, meeting Davidson half way in. There was no minimum number of overs in the day, or the last hour, so every second counted. Seven runs were required in six minutes. That meant one more over from Hall after this one from Sobers, which still had four balls remaining.

Grout survived the first two balls, then took a quick single off the next. This would leave him on strike unless Benaud could get a run from Sobers's last ball. He couldn't, as fieldsmen converged from everywhere.

Six runs to get, eight balls to be bowled and three wickets in hand. Five days of excellent cricket had come down to one over.

The first delivery from Hall hit Grout in the groin. He would have fallen, but he saw Benaud charging down the pitch and scrambled to the other end, clutching bits of his anatomy. One leg bye stolen.

Worrell had ordered Hall not to bowl a bouncer at Benaud. The fast bowler ignored, or forgot, the instruction and let one go. The Australian captain went for it, but succeeded only in gloving it to the keeper. Alexander screamed his appeal and Benaud was on his way for 52 made in 136 minutes with six fours. In his book *A Tale of Two Tests*, the Australian captain wrote of his feelings as he trudged off: 'Have you ever tried so hard to do something... concentrated so desperately that everything else was pushed from your mind... and then seen it disappear in a fraction of a second?' As he passed Grout, he said, 'All yours, Wal'.

'Thanks very much', was the less than pleased reply.

In the celebrations onfield, Hall had trouble looking Worrell in the eye. The captain ambled over to remind his fast bowler that he had disobeyed orders. Hall was made aware that a top edge could have cost the match. There would be no more bouncers.

Meckiff, the new batsman, played the first ball defensively and there was no run. The next one went down the leg side to the keeper and Grout charged through for a bye. Four to win, four balls to go.

Grout had decided to end it all in one big hit. His mistimed stroke spooned up in the air towards mid wicket. A number of fieldsmen could have taken it, but Kanhai camped under it and waited. He never touched it as Hall charged across, got the ball in both hands, and dropped it. The West Indians could not believe it, and to add insult to injury the batsmen took a run.

In the dressing room the tension was so great many believed they couldn't take any more. But there was plenty more to come.

Meckiff now decided to follow Grout's lead. He took a huge swing, and connected. 'A five iron shot', Benaud called it. The ball flew towards the square leg boundary and victory. As the Australians sprinted up and down the pitch, Conrad Hunte chased the ball as if his life depended on it. He overhauled it just inside the fence and threw it low and straight to Alexander.

The batsmen had completed two, so the scores were now tied. They set off for what would be the winning run. Alexander got the ball in his gloves

Wally Grout dives for the crease and victory, but is run out by a superb throw from Conrad Hunte. (*The Age*)

and broke the wicket as Grout dived for the line and victory. The appeal roared out and the umpire's finger went up. Grout trudged slowly away. He had fallen literally centimetres from glory.

To Benaud, this throw of Hunte's was the best of the day's miracles. He had to throw the ball on the turn directly into the keeper's gloves over a distance of some 80 metres. It was low, flat, straight, perfect.

Two balls left, one run to win. Enter Lindsay Kline, a definite number eleven. Hit the ball and run was the obvious tactic. But could he hit the ball? Kline said, 'I had been sitting in the dressing room terrified at the prospect of going in'. In near panic the batsman was unable to find his gloves, only to discover that like Grout he was sitting on them. The nervousness must have shown because as he walked past Worrell, the West Indian captain said, 'You look a little pale, Lindsay'. The Australian number eleven was forced to agree that he did indeed feel a little pale.

Meckiff actually thought there was only one ball to go, and so was determined to run whatever happened. They would not leave it to the last ball. He said to Kline, 'If you hit it, we'll go. It doesn't matter where it goes'.

Before the delivery was bowled Worrell walked over to Hall and said, 'Do you realise that if you bowl a no ball you will never be able to go home?' Hall agreed, making sure his foot was well behind the line as he bowled.

Kline, who cannot even remember taking guard (although he does remember wishing Hall would hurry up and get there as he was charging in), played the ball pitched on middle and leg, with the full face of the bat

Joe Solomon (far left) hits the stumps and Ian Meckiff is run out to record Test cricket's first tie.
(Ron Lovitt/*The Age*)

towards square leg, and the batsmen ran. 'I thought I played it pretty well', he remembered. Some ten or eleven metres away Joe Solomon moved in, picked up the ball and threw the stumps down from side-on for the second time in two overs. Meckiff was well out. Meckiff said he got such a shock that Kline hit it that he hesitated and lost the race for the crease.

Joe Solomon, who twice hit the stumps from side–on in the last few hectic minutes.
(Brian Bassano)

'He's out! He's run out! The stumps are thrown down!' screamed commentators Clive Harberg and Johnnie Moyes in the climax to an amazing over.

A tie—the first in Test history—had been achieved, although not all were aware of it. Some thought the West Indies had won. The umpires themselves were not aware of the result until they reached the dressing rooms. Meckiff said he found out 45 minutes later that the game had been tied.

Solomon, at the centre of it all, was well aware of the situation. 'I gathered the ball soon after the batsmen crossed, with full knowledge of the result if the run was made. I strained every sinew and aimed. I could see little more than one stump. There wasn't much time. I let go. It hit.' Typically modest, Solomon, whose two miraculous throws had made it possible, said he was just happy to have contributed.

Three Australian batsmen had been dismissed in seven balls, two of them run out while going for the winning run.

As the players left the field, many in disbelief at what had happened, Benaud came onto the field, put an arm round Worrell's shoulder and walked off with him. In an extraordinary day both captains had achieved their aims. Benaud had led from the front in his quest for attacking, positive cricket, while Worrell had proved—if anyone had ever doubted it—that a black man could captain the West Indies, and that he could weld their different personalities together and mould them together in the most desperate of circumstances. 'I'm very proud of my boys', he said afterwards. 'Every man played his part.' The joint contributions of the captains had set the scene for what many think was the finest Test series of all.

Later, journalist Jack Fingleton wrote a book on this game. He called it *The Greatest Test of All*, and who could possibly argue with that?

AUSTRALIA v WEST INDIES

Played at Woolloongabba Oval, Brisbane on 9, 10, 12, 13, 14 December, 1960.
Toss: West Indies.

WEST INDIES

C.C. Hunte	c Benaud b Davidson	24	c Simpson b Mackay	39
C.W. Smith	c Grout b Davidson	7	c O'Neill b Davidson	6
R.B. Kanhai	c Grout b Davidson	15	c Grout b Davidson	54
G. St A. Sobers	c Kline b Meckiff	132	b Davidson	14
F.M.M. Worrell *	c Grout b Davidson	65	c Grout b Davidson	65
J.S. Solomon	hit wkt b Simpson	65	lbw b Simpson	47
P.D. Lashley	c Grout b Kline	19	b Davidson	0
F.C.M. Alexander +	c Davidson b Kline	60	b Benaud	5
S. Ramadhin	c Harvey b Davidson	12	c Harvey b Simpson	6
W.W. Hall	st Grout b Kline	50	b Davidson	18
A.L. Valentine	not out	0	not out	7
Extras	(LB 3, W 1)	4	(B 14, LB 7, W 2)	23
Total		**453**		**284**

Fall: 23, 42, 65, 239, 243, 283, 347, 366, 452, 453.

13, 88, 114, 127, 210, 210, 241, 250, 253, 284.

Bowling

First Innings: Davidson 30–2–135–5, Meckiff 18–0–129–1, Mackay 3–0–15–0, Benaud 24–3–93–0, Simpson 8–0–25–1, Kline 17.6–6–52–3.

Second Innings: Davidson 24.6–4–87–6, Meckiff 4–1–19–0, Mackay 21–7–52–1, Benaud 31–6–69–1, Simpson 7–2–18–2, Kline 4–0–14–0, O'Neill 1–0–2–0.

AUSTRALIA

C.C. McDonald	c Hunte b Sobers	57	b Worrell	16
R.B. Simpson	b Ramadhin	92	c sub (L.Gibbs) b Hall	0
R.N. Harvey	b Valentine	15	c Sobers b Hall	5
N.C. O'Neill	c Valentine b Hall	181	c Alexander b Hall	26
L.E. Favell	run out	45	c Solomon b Hall	7
K.D. Mackay	b Sobers	35	b Ramadhin	28
A.K. Davidson	c Alexander b Hall	44	run out (Solomon)	80
R. Benaud *	lbw b Hall	10	c Alexander b Hall	52
A.T.W. Grout +	lbw b Hall	4	run out (Hunte/Alexander)	2
I. Meckiff	run out	4	run out (Solomon)	2
L.F. Kline	not out	3	not out	0
Extras	(B 2, LB 8, W 1, NB 4)	15	(B 2, LB 9, NB 3)	14
Total		**505**		**232**

Fall: 84, 138, 194, 278, 381, 469, 484, 489, 496, 505.

1, 7, 49, 49, 57, 92, 226, 228, 232, 232.

Bowling

First Innings: Hall 29.3–1–140–4, Worrell 30–0–93–0, Sobers 32–0–115–2, Valentine 24–6–82–1, Ramadhin 15–1–60–1.

Second Innings: Hall 17.7–3–65–5, Worrell 16–3–41–1, Sobers 8–0–30–0, Valentine 10–4–27–0, Ramadhin 17–3–57–1.

Match tied

13

Mackay and Kline

Adelaide Oval
1 February, 1961 – Day Five

AFTER THE DRAMA of the tie in the First Test at Brisbane, the Australians emerged winners by seven wickets in the next game, at Melbourne. This was principally due to some poor West Indian batting which produced totals of only 181 and 233. Alan Davidson took eight wickets to be the leading force in the victory.

Many believed that the West Indies had made their run. The Brisbane effort would not be repeated and the Australians would walk away with the series. How wrong they were, as the visitors came roaring back to win the Third Test by 222 runs. Sobers made 168 in the first innings and Gerry Alexander 108 and Worrell 82 in the second, while Davidson took another eight wickets. In the face of excellent spin bowling from off spinner Lance Gibbs and left armer Valentine, who took eight wickets each, the Australians could muster only 202 and 241.

So the teams came to Adelaide for the Fourth Test and with the series locked at one all. If anything, the situation favoured the West Indies, as Davidson, who had 27 wickets in three Tests, was injured and unable to play. Without him the Australian attack looked decidedly thin, particularly as Western Australian paceman Des Hoare was making his debut, and (apart from Benaud) the remainder had precious little experience. The batting also looked a little suspect without both Davidson in the lower order and Neil

Harvey, the most experienced player, whose injured leg had not yet healed.

The Australian side, in batting order, was Colin McDonald, Les Favell, Norm O'Neill, Bobby Simpson, Peter Burge, Richie Benaud, Ken Mackay, Wally Grout, Frank Misson, Hoare and Lindsay Kline.

The West Indian line-up was Conrad Hunte, Cammie Smith, Rohan Kanhai, Gary Sobers, Frank Worrell, Seymour Nurse, Gerry Alexander, Joe Solomon, Lance Gibbs, Wes Hall and Alf Valentine. With the dependable Solomon at number eight, the batting looked impressively strong, and the addition of the thin Guyanese off spinner Gibbs had given another dimension to the attack. On paper, the visitors looked ahead in every department.

Worrell won the toss and batted. He scored 71 himself, but it was Kanhai, with 117, who really dominated. Alexander, 63 not out, continued his good series, and Nurse made 49 in a very respectable total of 393. Benaud, with 5/96, was the only real threat.

Thanks to McDonald (71), Simpson (85), Benaud (77), Burge (45) and Hoare (35), the Australians reached 366. It looked at one stage as if it would be much better. With the score a healthy 5/281, Gibbs removed Mackay, Grout and Misson with successive deliveries, completing a superb hat-trick.

Setting out to build on the slender lead, Kanhai completed his second century of the game, this time 115. This was accomplished after Hunte (79) and Smith (46) had got the side away to an excellent start. Worrell made 53 and Alexander remained 87 not out when the declaration was made at 6/432.

A target of 460 in about 395 minutes was near to impossible for the Australian batsmen, but a draw could certainly be achieved. This calculation was shot to pieces when Favell, McDonald and Simpson were dismissed for just 31 runs before stumps on the fourth day. In fact there were some who attacked Worrell for delaying the declaration too long. There was a strong feeling that a target of about 400 would be far too many for the home side.

So Australia entered the fifth day with very little hope of survival, and the West Indies expected to take a 2–1 lead in the series.

Peter Burge, the burly Queensland right-hander, and Norm O'Neill resumed an Australian innings which was not expected to last until the tea break. Although they looked safe in defence the batsmen were prepared to play strokes when the need arose, and they took 13 from one Hall over. The fast bowler found the lifeless turf not to his liking and had real trouble getting the ball above stump high.

In the first hour 17 overs were bowled and 45 runs scored as Worrell tried his main attacking bowlers, Hall, Sobers and Gibbs. It appeared strange that, with so many runs to play with, the West Indian captain did not set more attacking fields.

The pair brought up the hundred, although runs did not really matter, and the batsmen looked well in control.

Worrell decided to introduce the left arm spin of Valentine. He made one bounce and turn away, and Burge's attempted cut only found its way into Alexander's gloves. The Queenslander's 49 was his second useful contribution in the game, and he had added 82 with O'Neill.

Benaud was the new batsman, and Australia reached the luncheon interval without further loss. The fall of just one wicket in the morning session strengthened the chances of the locals batting it out for a draw.

Resuming after the break, the pair played carefully until just past two o'clock, when O'Neill hit a ball back to Sobers to be caught and bowled for a valuable 65. At 5/129 only Mackay and Benaud were left of the established batsmen. There remained the small matter of 210 minutes' play to be negotiated until stumps.

With his gum chewing and slouching walk, Mackay looked more a figure of comedy than a Test

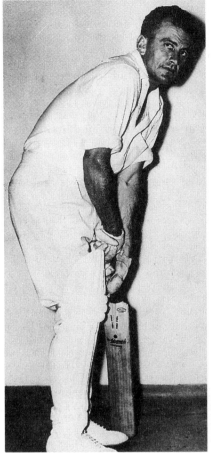

Ken 'Slasher' Mackay's endless patience was ideal for the situation. (Brian Bassano)

cricketer, but the 'Slasher', so called for his defensive powers, was a force to be reckoned with. No one placed a higher price on his wicket, and no one was a better man for a crisis. This was a situation tailor-made for him.

His innings was almost immediately terminated when he was nearly caught at slip off the first ball he received. Worrell brought Gibbs back into the attack, no doubt hoping to trouble the left-hander with the ball turning away from the bat. On his first tour, to England in 1956, Mackay had been a consistent victim of off spinner Jim Laker. The West Indians were hoping his technique was still a little suspect.

Benaud stepped in and struck a couple of boundaries, but then he also went caught and bowled trying to drive Sobers. With the Australian captain out for 17, and the score 6/144, only four wickets stood between the West Indies and victory. For the Australians, an uncomfortably long time still remained.

Keeper Wally Grout was more at home hitting the bowling than playing for draws. He arrived at the crease to be surrounded by fieldsmen, but refused to be dismayed by the situation and began playing his natural game. After running through his main bowlers without securing the wicket, Worrell introduced Solomon into the attack, and when that failed to work, brought himself on from the river end.

Grout hit him to the boundary, then was struck on the pads. That appeal was turned down, but two balls later another leg before shout was answered in the affirmative by umpire Colin Egar. The Australian keeper was on his way for a good 42, and (more importantly) he and Mackay had used about 75 minutes.

Unfortunately for Australia, there was still plenty of time remaining and only Hoare, Misson and Kline to stay with Mackay, who seemed to have taken root at the crease.

Misson came in and managed to hang on until tea, but soon after the interval he was caught by Solomon at leg slip off Worrell for one. Hoare, who had batted quite well in the first innings, was bowled for no score, attempting to sweep Worrell.

Australia was 9/207, an irrelevant statistic as Lindsay Kline walked out to bat. What was more important was that 110 minutes still remained and that would be ample time for the West Indians to take the last wicket and the lead in the series.

The Australians were under no illusions about what would happen. Some of the players had taken the Victorian out into the nets to bowl a few at him, in order to give him some confidence in case he was needed. After he had been bowled some nine or ten times in a few minutes they all returned to the dressing room, reluctant to destroy what little confidence he might have had left. As for surviving 110 minutes in the middle — well, it just would not happen. Bob Simpson was so certain of defeat that he had packed his gear and was ready to go.

Worrell kept shuffling through his bowlers, and the batsmen survived. Occasionally, there was a faulty stroke, but nothing went to hand. The minutes ticked by.

With just over an hour remaining, Mackay on 17 played forward to Worrell. Sobers took the ball at his position close to the pitch, and he and some others started walking off. They didn't get very far as umpire Egar quickly rejected the appeal. Mackay stood, chewing his gum. He wasn't going anywhere. A number of the West Indians, including Worrell, believed it was a catch, but would say nothing more about it after the game.

The new ball was then taken, but Hall was unable to gain any life from the pitch. Both batsmen held on and Worrell turned back to his spinners.

Runs were unimportant, as they had been all day, and the fieldsmen crowded around the bat waiting for an error, a wavering in concentration. It never came, and still the clock moved on. As time passed a change came

Surrounded by the entire West Indies team, Lindsay Kline defends grimly. (*The News*, Adelaide)

over both the West Indians and the Australians. The fielding side, assured of victory for most of the day, started to doubt. They hurried through their overs in an endeavour to get as many balls in as possible. Surely, one would do the job. This was an ill-considered tactic because they moved through far too quickly, and in their haste failed to think about what they were doing. Towards the end they were bowling an eight ball over every two minutes, with nine fieldsmen clustered around the bat. 'Johnnie' Moyes said later that he marvelled at how the bowlers could get the ball through to the batsmen without hitting anyone.

Bob Simpson does not think the West Indians panicked to any great extent. 'Apart from Wes Hall their bowlers didn't take very long to bowl an over, and as few runs were being scored the over rate was obviously going to be very high.' Richie Benaud, on the other hand, thought they did rush things a little towards the end.

In the Australian dressing room the advancing clock produced a different sensation. Slowly, the possibility began to dawn that the pair might just do it. There was absolutely no margin for error, but every minute increased the realisation. With about 30 minutes to go, Bob Simpson started to think that the pair just might hold on. As in Brisbane earlier in the season, the Australian players were not allowed to move lest they court disaster. With about ten minutes remaining, Benaud started to believe that a draw was a possibility.

Mackay and Kline stuck to their task magnificently. There was no relaxation, and at one minute to six Worrell, who had been unable to remove Kline in his last over, threw the ball to Hall for the final over of the game.

Running in to deliver the first ball, he lost his step and threw the ball down on the ground. Children had jumped the fence and had to be removed

Mackay and Kline celebrate their unlikely stand. (Brian Bassano)

from the ground. Hall, who had bowled that last pulsating over in Brisbane not that long ago, must have wondered if his nerve could stand the pressure. It did, and life in the pitch or not, he gave it everything he had.

Finally, with the tension reaching almost unbearbale proportions in the Australian dressing room, Hall moved in for the final delivery, and bowled a no ball. Once again, thousands of spectators, most of them children, had to be removed from the ground.

Mackay continued chewing his gum as Hall returned to his mark, and then came thundering in for the last roll of the dice. The 'Slasher' would make no mistake. As the ball reared fast and short of a length he removed his bat from the line and took it on the body, and the game was saved. Mackay remained 62 not out and Kline 17. Together, they had added 66 for the last wicket and occupied the final 110 minutes of the game. In the process they had saved the match and the series for their side. The exuberance among the Australians was fantastic. They had 'got out of gaol'.

Mackay might well have been the only player in the world capable of performing this rescue act. He was a cricketer born to play under pressure, and one who would never let his side down. Bob Simpson summed up the 'Slasher'. 'He possessed a calm, cool, controlled temperament and technique and he had plenty of courage. If he decided he wasn't going to get out he could be very difficult.'

Richie Benaud had this to say about him: 'Mackay in Adelaide was the ideal player to have facing the last over from Wes Hall. Not many would have worked out that the final ball was almost certain to be a bumper and, therefore, he could take out some possibilities of dismissal by determining to take it on the body. However, he was also alive to the possibility of it being a yorker, therefore he determined to play it with his body, providing it was short'.

Mackay said, 'We were lucky to see it through. I don't know how many overs we played, or what the score was. I was interested in only one thing — the clock'.

In spite of all his poor form in the nets, Lindsay Kline had exercised a straight bat and great determination. 'I just tried to play every ball as it came along', he said afterwards.

In the Fifth Test in Melbourne Australia scraped home by just two wickets to win the series. It was yet another classic contest.

Was this the finest Test series ever played? Richie Benaud had this to say. 'It was just a great series of matches right to the end, not merely a series where one of the games was tied. The two teams played excellent cricket throughout.' Certainly, the thousands who gave the West Indians a ticker tape farewell parade thought so too, and they may well have been right. Surely, in all Test history there is nothing to match Australia versus West Indies 1960–61.

AUSTRALIA v WEST INDIES

Played at Adelaide Oval, on 27, 28, 30, 31 January, 1 February, 1961.
Toss: West Indies.

WEST INDIES

C. C. Hunte	lbw b Hoare	6	run out	79
C. W. Smith	c & b Benaud	28	c Hoare b Mackay	46
R. B. Kanhai	c Simpson b Benaud	117	lbw b Benaud	115
G. St A. Sobers	b Benaud	1	run out	20
F. M. M. Worrell *	c Misson b Hoare	71	c Burge b Mackay	53
S. M. Nurse	c & b Misson	49	c Simpson b Benaud	5
J. S. Solomon	c & b Benaud	22	(8) not out	16
F. C. M. Alexander +	not out	63	(7) not out	87
L. R. Gibbs	b Misson	18		
W. W. Hall	c Hoare b Benaud	5		
A. L. Valentine	lbw b Misson	0		
Extras	(B 3, LB 3, W 5, NB 2)	13	(B 2, LB 6, W 2, NB 1)	11
Total		**393**		**6/432**

Fall: 12, 83, 91, 198, 271, 288, 316, 375, 392, 393.   66, 229, 263, 270, 275, 388.

Bowling:
First Innings: Hoare 16–0–68–2, Misson 17.5–2–79–3, Mackay 2–0–11–0, Benaud 27–5–96–5, Kline 21–3–109–0, Simpson 5–0–17–0.
Second Innings: Hoare 13–0–88–0, Misson 28–3–106–0, Mackay 12–0–72–2, Benaud 27–3–107–2, Kline 12–2–48–0.

AUSTRALIA

C. C. McDonald	c Hunte b Gibbs	71	run out	2
L. E. Favell	c Alexander b Worrell	1	c Alexander b Hall	4
N. C. O'Neill	c Alexander b Sobers	11	c & b Sobers	65
R. B. Simpson	c Aleaxnder b Hall	85	c Alexander b Hall	3
P. J. P. Burge	b Sobers	45	c Alexander b Valentine	49
R. Benaud *	c Solomon b Gibbs	77	c & b Sobers	17
K. D. Mackay	lbw b Gibbs	29	not out	62
A. T. W. Grout +	c Sobers b Gibbs	0	lbw b Worrell	42
F. M. Misson	b Gibbs	0	c Solomon b Worrell	1
D. E. Hoare	b Sobers	35	b Worrell	0
L. F. Kline	not out	0	not out	15
Extras	(B 2, LB 3, NB 7)	12	(B 9, LB 1, NB 3)	13
Total		**366**		**9/273**

Fall: 9, 45, 119, 213, 221, 281, 281, 281, 366, 366.   6, 7, 31, 113, 129, 144, 203, 207, 207.

Bowling:
First Innings: Hall 22–3–85–1, Worrell 7–0–34–1, Sobers 24–3–64–3, Gibbs 35.6–4–97–5, Valentine 21–4–74–0.
Second Innings: Hall 13–4–61–2, Worrell 17–9–27–3, Sobers 39–11–87–2, Gibbs 28–13–44–0, Valentine 20–7–40–1, Solomon 3–2–1–0.

Match drawn

14

Benaud's Match

ENGLAND v AUSTRALIA

Old Trafford, Manchester
1 August, 1961 – Day Five

THE AUSTRALIAN team which toured England in 1961 was very much an unknown quantity. There were few players (only six in fact) who had previously visited England, and the way in which the newcomers would perform under conditions vastly different from those at home would be a key factor in the series. Mind you, it would not do to underestimate them, as Benaud's team had emerged victorious against the West Indies a few months earlier in perhaps the finest series of all time.

In addition to the captain, Neil Harvey and Alan Davidson had plenty of English experience, and Colin McDonald, Peter Burge and Ken Mackay had been on the previous tour in 1956. Much would be expected of batsmen Bob Simpson, Bill Lawry, Norm O'Neill and Brian Booth, and it was hoped that the young Western Australian fast bowler, Graham McKenzie, would develop into an effective partner for Davidson.

The last series between the Ashes rivals, in 1958–59, had resulted in a comprehensive win for Australia. The Englishmen, led by Peter May, would be keen to overturn what had been an embarrassing defeat for a side regarded as one of the strongest ever sent to Australia. The previous series provoked much controversy over the bowling actions of certain Australians, in particular Ian Meckiff and Gordon Rorke, but neither was chosen for this tour.

Coming to the Fourth Test at Old Trafford, the series was level at one all. England had been forced to fight a rearguard action to save the First Test. This it did, thanks to 180 from Ted Dexter and 112 from Raman Subba Row, after Australia had compiled 516 in response to England's first innings 195.

A shoulder injury forced Benaud out of the Second Test, where vice-captain Harvey led Australia to victory by five wickets. Lawry, in his second Test, made 130 on a difficult pitch. Davidson took 5/42 in the first innings and McKenzie, who was making his debut, captured 5/37 in the second.

England struck back in the Third Test thanks to an 11 wicket haul by fast bowler Freddie Trueman to square the series.

With the Ashes very much in the balance Australia won the toss at Old Trafford and batted. Apart from a 74 from Lawry and 46 from Booth, the batting was disappointing, and the total of 190 looked decidedly insufficient.

England set about building a substantial lead, which they did by making 367. Geoff Pullar (63), Peter May (95), and Ken Barrington (78) did best in a consistent effort.

Faced with a deficit of 177 the Australians fought back. Initially, this was through a century opening stand from Simpson (51) and Lawry (102), Lawry's second hundred of the series. O'Neill played well for 67 and Harvey made 35. At stumps on the fourth day, Australia was 6/331—a lead of 154. The English bowlers were hoping to restrict the lead to something under 200, while the Australians needed another 100 runs at the very least. On a pitch still in reasonable condition, England must have been favourite in a fourth innings run chase.

In his book on the tour, *The Challenging Tests*, Ray Lindwall described this last day as being 'memorable for the quality of play it produced and for the nerve-tearing fluctuations in fortune that shaped the game'.

The day could not have begun worse for the visitors. Before most spectators had found their seats, off spinner David Allen had taken three wickets, and victory for England looked a formality.

The left-handed Mackay was caught by Close at slip off one that turned, Benaud played back and was leg before, and Grout tried to hit Allen out of the attack and merely lofted an easy catch to Statham in the covers. Three wickets had fallen for three runs, and only the last wicket pair of Davidson and McKenzie was left to add some runs and occupy some time. The latter had been receiving some treatment for a sore leg from physio Arthur James, and had to make a mad scramble to get on the field.

As Davidson had shown in the Tied Test a few months earlier, he was capable of batting well under pressure. Had he not been such a vital bowler, his run scoring would have been much more consistent. He had a good defence, and his selection of which ball to hit and his power when on the attack made him a player to be feared. He walked over to McKenzie and said, 'Just play straight, Garth, and we'll see what we can do'. The youngster remembered his partner looking like 'an old, old man'.

The young Western Australian had batted well at Lord's, and here he played no rash strokes. He employed a straight bat and put his body behind the ball, following Davidson's advice to the letter.

As England off spinner David Allen remembers the situation, 'Davidson took all the strike from me; the others were unable to bowl McKenzie out at the other end and there was a stalemate. Peter May decided I should try and bait Davidson and get him to come after me'.

Davidson realised that Allen was the danger man, particularly for McKenzie, and decided to do something about him. When he came on for his tenth over of the morning, the left-hander jumped down the pitch and hit the first ball over cover for six. The third ball went back over the bowler's head and into the crowd on the first bounce, then the fifth ball beat the man at deep cover for another boundary. The over ended in perfect fashion for the Australians as Davidson clouted the ball way over long off for six more. It may have been the biggest hit ever made on the ground.

After watching the over disappear for 20 runs, May decided there would be no more Allen and removed him from the attack. Davidson had won the battle. Many believed this to have been a huge blunder on the part of the England captain. Allen was regarded by the batsmen as the greatest threat. Davidson was sure he would have got McKenzie if he had kept bowling, and the left-hander himself ran the risk of mis-hitting a ball which was spinning away from him. Hindsight is a wonderful thing, and in defence of May, not too many captains would have kept Allen on after what Davidson had done to him. Allen, himself, felt he would have liked to continue—but that was the captain's decision. England opening batsman Raman Subba Row felt that keeping Allen on would not have helped. In his autobiography, *A Game Enjoyed*, May said that Davidson's shots had been played with confidence off the middle of the bat. He also stated that he believed England would have had trouble chasing any score over 200 and that keeping the runs down also figured in his thinking.

Close was brought into the attack, but he could not get the length right, sending down a series of poor deliveries, three of which McKenzie hit for four. This was another of the strange tactical moves made by May during the partnership. Close would not have been most people's choice to throw in at a number eleven.

Trueman and Statham took over the bowling, and the batsmen looked at ease against them. McKenzie emerged to cut the former and drive the latter for runs. The lead continued to build past 200 and well beyond.

Davidson saw no need to protect McKenzie from the strike, especially as May had banished Allen from the attack.

The partnership was worth 98 runs in 102 minutes when Jack Flavell finally got one through McKenzie's defence to bowl him for 32. Davidson remained 77 not out, and England now required 256 to win at 67 an hour. The reactions of the batsmen on entering the rooms provided an interesting contrast. The youngster apologised for getting out, while the veteran Davidson threw his bat into a corner and announced that Australia would win.

Richie Benaud feels this partnership was the turning point for the Australians, giving them the runs to make victory a possibility. In the England camp, victory was also considered a possibility.

In the 20 minutes before lunch Pullar and Subba Row scored 20 runs. After the break they extended that to 40 when Davidson dropped one short to Pullar. An instinctively aggressive player, the batsman went for the hook, but succeeded only in lobbing a catch to O'Neill at square leg.

The match appeared to swing back towards England with the advent of Ted Dexter. He tore into the attack from the moment he arrived at the crease, and went on to play what Benaud later described as 'the finest short innings I have seen in a Test match'. Watching at the other end, Subba Row considered it a tremendous innings. 'He hit the ball all over the place.'

'Lord Ted' struck Davidson with tremendous power and Benaud was forced to remove his star bowler from the firing line. Davidson had batted all morning and then sent down 13 overs, and was looking very much in need of a rest.

McKenzie came on and Dexter hit him for eleven in the over. With just over two hours remaining England needed 130 with nine wickets in hand. Any attempt to bottle up the game and play defensively on Australia's part would result in a defeat. There was, Benaud considered, just one thing to do: go all out for a win. He walked over to vice-captain Harvey and said, 'We've had it as far as saving this. The only way we'll get out of it is to win'.

'Get into it then', Harvey replied with a grin.

Benaud's first move was to bring the leg spin of Simpson into the attack in the hope that he might induce Dexter to make a mistake. That didn't happen, as four overs went for 21 runs. Attacking fields were maintained as there was no going back now. When told what the tactics were, keeper Grout laughed, and said, 'Good luck'.

Using the steady medium pace of Mackay in place of Simpson, Benaud, at the other end, persisted in his tactic of bowling around the wicket in the bowler's footmarks. Benaud described the area. 'There were four marks, and those nearer the stumps were in excellent position for bowling to the left-handed batsmen. They were deep holes, not just surface scratches as they had been in the first innings, and even the area between them and around them was scarred and dusty. The holes had been made partly by Fred Trueman, but also by Ted Dexter and Jack Flavell.' England had five left-

The turning point. Ted Dexter is caught by keeper Grout off Benaud for 76, and Australia is on the way to a famous victory. (Brian Bassano)

handers to work on, and the Australian captain was now bowling around the wicket to the right-handers as well. This was no spur of the moment decision. Benaud had been keeping a close eye on the footmarks, and on the previous evening he spoke to Ray Lindwall about the possibility of attacking the batsmen around the wicket, believing it would make life difficult for a player chasing runs.

Bowling around the wicket to the right-handed Dexter, Benaud was determined to keep him tied down. If he could tie him down he might do something foolish. After failing to score off the first five balls, he tried to thrash the sixth, a top spinner, through the covers off the back foot. All he succeeded in doing was getting an outside edge, and Grout did the rest.

Dexter walked off with 76 runs beside his name, and to a huge ovation from the crowd. It was the second great innings of the day, and he had batted for only 84 minutes. At 2/150 he had made victory appear a formality.

England's captain, Peter May, was the next man in. For the previous half-dozen years he had been regarded by most experts as the best batsman in the world. He possessed a classic technique, with his driving the feature of his game. May was not as vicious a strokemaker as Dexter, but he, too, could win the game. There was no point in keeping him quiet. He had to be dismissed.

May defended the first ball, but the second landed in the rough, bowling him around his legs as he attempted a sweep shot. England's captain was out for a duck, with just the faintest hope of an Australian win.

Yorkshireman Brian Close was the new batsman, and one that Benaud feared. Close was, like Dexter, a player capable of destroying an attack in a very short time.

He attempted to do just that, and in a situation where a quick 20 could be vital he had to be dismissed quickly. He played the first ball over fine leg for two. Close swung twice more and missed. Then he went down the pitch and hit Benaud over long on for six. After one more failed sweep shot, he top edged one and O'Neill took a good catch at square leg. Close out for eight and England 4/158.

Immediately after the game, and in the years to follow, Close was castigated for his dismissal as if he alone was to blame for what happened. Journalist E. W. Swanton was particularly severe on him. 'To describe Close's innings taxes charity beyond endurance, as indeed it taxed credibility to behold.' West Indian captain Frank Worrell, who was reporting the series for *The Observer,* called Close's tactics 'incomprehensible'.

Benaud felt the tactics were justified, and with a little luck Close's hitting could have won the game. To lay the blame entirely at his door is an unduly harsh punishment. The innings did, however, cost Close his Test place for some two years. According to Benaud the criticism of Close was unjust.

Subba Row also feels the criticism was harsh. 'The way Benaud was turning the ball you had to play him onto the on side. Close decided to belt him, and was hitting in the right direction. I thought of having a chat with him, but I didn't want him to change. If he had been successful we would have won.'

While all this had been happening Subba Row had defied the bowling and fought his way to 49. He had been an almost silent partner in the partnership of 110 with Dexter, and now it seemed all he needed was someone to stay with him and finish the job. However, the game turned again, as he tried to drive the last ball before tea from Benaud and was yorked. The Australian captain had taken four wickets in 19 balls.

At the break England needed 93 in 85 minutes, but now had only five wickets in hand. Australia was back in business. The captain's 'attack at all costs' policy had paid some handsome dividends. For those watching in the dressing room the tension was becoming unbearable. No one was allowed to move from his seat and Ron Gaunt was stopped from taking photos. Apparently each time he had reached for his camera earlier in the tour, disaster had followed.

After tea Benaud decided to bowl himself and Mackay. The latter was to be used to tie up an end, but he had a badly torn hamstring and was in some pain. There was never any doubt that he wouldn't bowl. 'Any time you say so', was the reply to his captain's request. Benaud remains glowing in his praise of Mackay's courage.

In Barrington and keeper Murray England still had batsmen who could win the game. Mackay justified his captain's faith by trapping Barrington leg before for five. At 6/171 the balance had shifted toward Australia.

This became even more obvious when Simpson took an excellent catch at slip from Murray off Benaud without addition to the score. The Australian captain had to come back over the wicket, as the batsmen were now playing defensively.

Simpson did even better shortly afterwards when he took what Benaud described as 'one of the best catches I have seen anywhere' to remove Allen for ten, once again off the bowling of Benaud. The bats-

Richie Benaud, who took 6/70, bowling around the wicket, and won the Ashes in the process. (Brian Bassano)

man had tried to drive the ball and got an edge which flew just wide of Grout. Simpson dived to the left and caught the ball one-handed. Benaud believes Simpson to be the best slips fieldsman he has ever seen, and cites these as perfect examples. Simpson's comment was, 'Yes, they were okay, but I had a good look at them'.

The pair captured the next wicket—that of Trueman—but this time it was Simpson the bowler and Benaud the catcher. The batsman slashed at a leg break and the captain took it brilliantly. At 9/193, England's only hope was for Statham and Flavell to bat through to stumps and secure a draw. The pair held out well enough to begin frustrating Benaud. 'I wanted to get at Flavell, but I couldn't', he recalled.

When the 200 was reached the new ball was due, so Davidson was recalled to the attack. With the fourth ball of his first over he knocked Statham's off stump out of the ground. 'One of the loveliest sights I've ever seen', recalled Benaud. Australia had won by 54 runs with 20 minutes to spare.

A match that had looked lost on at least two separate occasions during the day, had been won. By refusing to try to force a draw and playing aggressively, Benaud, with 6/70, had led his team to an unlikely but famous victory, and in doing so retained the Ashes. This was the first time Benaud had bowled around the wicket for a specific reason, and between this game and his retirement in 1964, he used the tactic with what he describes as 'reasonable frequency, though only when there was a reason for doing so'. He feels that it can be overdone.

On the subject of leg spinners bowling around the wicket, Bob Simpson used the memory of this day to persuade Shane Warne to adopt the tactic. 'I had to get him to bowl to me for some time before he was convinced. Richie was not as good a spinner as Shane, but he worked very hard at his game.'

While sitting on the balcony, enjoying a celebratory drink, the Australian captain remembered the last Test he had played at Old Trafford, in 1956, when Jim Laker had taken 19 wickets to destroy Australia. Here, at least, was a comforting revenge. The situation of five years before was reversed. The Australians were jubilant, while there was substantial gloom in the England team.

The last Test was drawn, so Australia took the series 2–1.

Benaud had never enjoyed great success as a bowler in England. But on this day, he produced a display which confounded the critics, who believed his style was not suited to English conditions. In doing so, he won a game that appeared lost. But the efforts of Davidson and McKenzie should not be forgotten. It was, after all, their partnership of 98 for the last wicket which gave Benaud the runs to work his magic.

Subba Row believes that Benaud also out-captained May. The Australian was shrewd and a good tactician, while the Englishman was a little too straightforward. Benaud's flair had turned the game.

Simpson felt that Benaud possessed a great team of men who were unselfish in their play and who were rewarded by his loyalty and confidence. 'He was a great man for flair and drama and situations like this suited him down to the ground.'

The Times correspondent also thought it was the captain's day. 'It was one of their most famous and thrilling victories, made possible at the last by the daring and skill of their captain.'

Subba Row also cited an incident earlier in the game which, he felt, had repercussions for England. 'We were going well on the third day. We were in the lead with wickets left. Gubby Allen, then chairman of selectors, told Peter May to get on with it. I didn't agree. I thought we should get as big a lead as possible and play them out of the game. As a result of following his advice we lost wickets and didn't get the lead we should have.'

For Richie Benaud, Old Trafford provides the best and worst of his cricket memories. 'The best day in which I was involved was the final day at Old Trafford in 1961. My favourite day as a commentator was when David Boon hit the winning run at Old Trafford in 1989 to regain the Ashes in England for the first time in 55 years. My least favourite day was when Jim Laker took his 19th wicket for the match at Old Trafford in 1956. Remarkably, Old Trafford features in all three.'

ENGLAND v AUSTRALIA

Played at Old Trafford, Manchester, on 27, 28, 29, 31 July, 1 August, 1961.
Toss: Australia.

AUSTRALIA

W. M. Lawry	lbw b Statham	74	c Trueman b Allen	102
R. B. Simpson	c Murray b Statham	4	c Murray b Flavell	51
R. N. Harvey	c Subba Row b Statham	19	c Murray b Dexter	35
N. C. O'Neill	hit wkt b Trueman	11	c Murray b Statham	67
P. J. P. Burge	b Flavell	15	c Murray b Dexter	23
B. C. Booth	c Close b Statham	46	lbw b Dexter	9
K. D. Mackay	c Murray b Statham	11	c Close b Allen	18
A. K. Davidson	c Barrington b Dexter	0	not out	77
R. Benaud *	b Dexter	2	lbw b Allen	1
A. T. W. Grout +	c Murray b Dexter	2	c Statham b Allen	0
G. D. McKenzie	not out	1	b Flavell	32
Extras	(B4, LB1)	5	(B 6, LB 9, W 2)	17
Total		**190**		**432**

Fall: 8, 51, 89, 106, 150, 174, 185, 185, 189, 190.

113, 175, 210, 274, 290, 296, 332, 334, 334, 432.

Bowling

First Innings: Trueman 14–1–55–1, Statham 21–3–53–5, Flavell 22–8–61–1, Dexter 6.4–2–16–3.

Second Innings: Trueman 32–6–92–0, Statham 44–9–106–1, Flavell 29–4–4–65–2, Dexter 20–4–61–3, Allen 38–25–58–4, Close 8–1–33–0.

ENGLAND

G. Pullar	b Davidson	63	c O'Neill b Davidson	26
R. Subba Row	c Simpson b Davidson	2	b Benaud	49
E. R. Dexter	c Davidson b McKenzie	16	c Grout b Benaud	76
P. B. H. May *	c Simpson b Davidson	95	b Benaud	0
D. B. Close	lbw b McKenzie	33	c O'Neill b Benaud	8
K. F. Barrington	c O'Neill b Simpson	78	lbw b Mackay	5
J. T. Murray +	c Grout b Mackay	24	c Simpson b Benaud	4
D. A. Allen	c Booth b Simpson	42	c Simpson b Benaud	10
F. S. Trueman	c Harvey b Simpson	3	c Benaud b Simpson	8
J. B. Statham	c Mackay b Simpson	4	b Davidson	8
J. A. Flavell	not out	0	not out	0
Extras	(B 2, LB 4, W 1)	7	(B 5, W 2)	7
Total		**367**		**201**

Fall: 3, 43, 154, 212, 212, 272, 358, 362, 367, 367.

40, 150, 150, 158, 163, 171, 171, 189, 193, 201.

Bowling

First Innings: Davidson 39–11–70–3, McKenzie 38–11–106–2, Mackay 40–9–81–1, Benaud 35–15–80–0, Simpson 11.4–4–23–4.

Second Innings: Davidson 14.4–1–50–2, McKenzie 4–1–20–0, Mackay 13–7–33–1, Benaud 32–11–70–6, Simpson 8–4–21–1.

Australia won by 54 runs

15

Lord's Classic

ENGLAND v WEST INDIES

Lord's Cricket Ground, London
25 June, 1963 – Day Five

THE 1963 West Indies tour of England had been eagerly awaited by all cricket followers. Frank Worrell's team had played one of the great series in Australia in 1960–61, and there was considerable anticipation to see whether another classic encounter would occur.

England had returned from a rather lifeless tour of Australia which had ended in a 1–1 draw. Despite the expressed desires of the captains to play bright cricket, it was something of an anticlimax after the West Indians. No one was really sure how Dexter's team would fare against a side which was now close to the best in the world.

Since the Australian tour, Worrell's side had become even stronger, with the addition of the fearsome fast bowler Charlie Griffith. Although some expressed doubts about his action, particularly when delivering the yorker and the bouncer, there was no denying his pace. Griffith had teamed with Wesley Hall to route India 5–0 in the Caribbean, and he had ended the Test career of captain Nari Contractor, who received a fractured skull from a rising delivery. Off spinner Lance Gibbs had become the number one slow bowler, and teamed with the all-round skills of Gary Sobers he gave the West Indians a strong attack. The batting had increased in depth, too, with the advancement of Seymour Nurse and the addition of the small aggressive

Guyanese, Basil Butcher. The only weak point was the lack of an adequate opening partner for Conrad Hunte.

The West Indians began the series with a comfortable win in the First Test by ten wickets. The batsmen ran up a total of 6/501 declared, then Gibbs took 5/59 and 6/98 to bowl England out for 205 and 296. It was a comprehensive victory and it was difficult to see how England could turn the tables in the Second Test at Lord's. Against considerable odds it managed to do this, and in doing so played in one of the most exciting Tests of all time, and arguably the best ever seen at Lord's.

Out of the team from the First Test went keeper Keith Andrew, replaced by Sussex's Jim Parks, perhaps not quite as good behind the stumps, but a far better batsman. Hampshire medium pacer Derek Shackelton also came into the side, at the expense of Brian Statham. The West Indies made one change, bringing Easton McMorris into the troublesome opening batting position to partner Hunte.

Worrell won the toss and elected to bat. The game started in electrifying fashion when Hunte hit the first three balls from Trueman to the boundary. The bowler fought back to claim 6/100 as the West Indies were dismissed for 301. Rohan Kanhai (73) and Joe Solomon (56) were the only two to pass 50.

England replied with 297 thanks to 80 from Ken Barrington, 70 from Ted Dexter and 52 not out from off spinner Fred Titmus. Griffith, who had taken only one wicket in the First Test, captured 5/91.

The West Indies owed their second innings almost entirely to Butcher, who made a brilliant 133 out of a team total of 229. Worrell (33) and Kanhai (21) were the only others to reach double figures. Trueman continued his excellent form with 5/52 and Shackleton justified his selection with 4/72.

In spite of the brilliance of Butcher England was left to make a not impossible 234 to win and square the series. The home team was soon in trouble at 3/31, with Mickey Stewart, John Edrich and Dexter all back in the pavilion. Barrington and Cowdrey were righting the situation before a delivery from Hall broke Cowdrey's arm, forcing him off the field, and presumably out of the game. Brian Close survived with Barrington, who had reached 55 not out, to stumps, when the total was 3/116, effectively four with Cowdrey's injury. The game was balanced on a knife edge for the final day. It was not to be a place for the faint-hearted.

For a long time it seemed that the game might end there. Drizzle through the morning prevented play from beginning on time. It was hoped to start at twelve, but the rain returned again. By 1.50 the rain had stopped and the pitch was fit for play, but the light was not. It was another 30 minutes before the match recommenced, and this meant that the factor of time was added into the balance of runs and wickets. The pitch was reasonably good, although offering a bit of bounce, as England set off after a further 118 runs,

Frank Worrell led his team with great calm as the game drew to its tense climax. (Brian Bassano)

while the West Indies looked at six, perhaps seven, wickets. The pitch, under covers, was not affected by the rain, and the outfield was surprisingly dry.

In front of a small crowd (due to the poor weather) Gibbs began the attack, knowing that given England's suspect lower order, Barrington and Close would have to get most of the runs. Gibbs bowled just one over before Griffith came on to partner Hall. Worrell's tactic throughout the day would be to use his fast bowlers and keep to a minimum the number of deliveries available to the batsman.

Close had a reputation in English cricket as a 'hard man', and it was this day which went a long way towards creating it. Rather than play deliveries from Hall, he chose to take them on the body, and the sound of ball hitting flesh echoed around the ground.

Barrington was struggling to find his touch of the previous day, taking 40 minutes before he flicked a ball to the leg boundary, just after scoring a single off his glove. It was his last act of defiance, as aiming a cut at a Griffith delivery which was too close to his body and not really short enough for the stroke, he succeeded only in edging it to keeper Murray. Barrington's 60 had been his second good innings of the match, but his dismissal opened the way for the West Indies to push towards victory.

After 13 overs the score had reached 4/130 as Parks arrived at the crease. He was almost leg before to Griffith's first ball, then began to play in the aggressive fashion which had earned him a place in the side. Twice he got Griffith away to mid-wicket, then twice cover drove him to the boundary.

Close, who had been struggling to score runs other than with jabs and pushes, now started to play more fluently, but disaster struck when Parks went back to turn Griffith through the leg side, missed, and was lbw for 17. It was an awful stroke, attempting to play across the line of a straight half volley. With the total 5/158 the West Indies were now back on top.

Titmus, who had also batted well in the first innings, opted for a different approach, taking short singles whenever the opportunity arose, and by tea the total had reached 171. This left 63 runs to get in 20 overs.

Close decided that these runs would not be made unless he took some positive steps. This he did by attempting to hit anything from Hall that was in reach. In one over he swung the fast bowler to the fine leg fence, missed twice, then swung him away again, only to see Butcher make a brilliant save.

While all this was happening, the crowd was building up as spectators hurried into the ground in order to catch the last act of this enthralling game.

Worrell gave Gibbs four overs after Griffith had bowled two following tea. Titmus held on, and with one hour remaining, 48 runs were needed. Close kept going. He missed a hook shot at a Hall bouncer, then connected with another to reach his 50. Gibbs was pulled for four and the target was 31 in 50 minutes.

The West Indies now desperately needed a wicket, and Hall, who had been bowling all day, obliged. Titmus failed to get over a leg stump delivery, which jumped a little at him, and turned it to McMorris,

Wes Hall bowled unchanged in what he later called his 'finest hour'. (*The Examiner*)

who took a good catch at short leg. The partnership had added 42 priceless runs in just 45 minutes. Having got one wicket, Hall grabbed another with his next ball when Trueman followed a very fast, lifting delivery outside off stump and edged it to Murray. Thoughts of victory for England now faded as the possibility of defeat raised its head.

England was now 7/203. Close decided that he had to keep attacking, and he swung two more deliveries away to the leg side boundary. His partner, off spinner David Allen, sensibly adopted a defensive role. Allen felt that England was still in with a good chance of winning at this point.

Close produced consternation by moving down the pitch before Hall had delivered the ball. The bowler, not knowing what was going on, pulled up sharply and held on to the ball. He looked as if he might have been injured as he stood clutching his back, but Worrell walked over and had a quiet word, and Hall returned to his mark.

The batsman continued with the tactic, not always successfully, although he did manage to hit a couple, including a hook off Griffith and a four to fine leg off Hall. In his autobiography, *MCC*, Cowdrey praised Close for a

Charlie Griffith, whose fearsome bowling gave Worrell another attacking weapon. (Doug Crampton)

carefully planned assault, which (while it might have looked reckless) stood a good chance of putting the bowlers off their game.

Griffith then returned to the attack after just four overs from Gibbs. With 20 minutes to go, 15 runs were needed when Close chanced his arm once too often. Moving down the pitch and swinging across a good length ball from Griffith, he got a faint edge and Murray did the rest. Close's 70 had occupied 230 minutes and he had hit eight fours. He walked off to a tremendous ovation, having taken England to the brink of victory.

The following day, the papers were loud in their praise of Close's effort, and printed pictures of him displaying a number of bruises collected from the fast bowlers. No doubt the batsman appreciated the irony. In his previous Test series, he had been condemned for his tactics in trying to hit Benaud off his length at Old Trafford in 1961. That day his tactics failed and England lost. On this day, he scored runs and was cheered to the echo. *The Times* headline read 'Close, cricket's enigma, now a hero'. While most praised his performance, a few still attacked the recklessness of the latter half of his innings. The vagaries of cricket certainly had their fun with Close.

Allen felt that the balance of the game had now shifted away from an England win. Close's dismissal had taken England to 8/219, and the last fit batsman, Shackleton, came out to join Allen. He remembers receiving no special instructions apart from the usual call of good luck as he left the rooms. This was not the last partnership, as Cowdrey—broken arm and all—had decided to bat if needed. He would bat one-handed, facing up as a left-hander, and had even had some practice in the dressing rooms in case he was required. In his autobiography he said that he felt confident of surviving a few overs if needed, although captain Dexter kept insisting he could go in only if the situation was desperate.

In addition to five overs and 15 runs there was now the added pressure of no wickets to spare, but the instructions from the captain were to keep pushing for the win. The light was also deteriorating, adding a further problem for the batsmen to contend with. Off the next four overs, six singles were scored, including a bye, and Worrell felt justified in not taking the new ball. This bye was quite an unusual one. A yorker from Griffith had struck the base of Shackleton's leg stump and gone to fine leg without disturbing the bails. Had they been disturbed Cowdrey would have had to come in and face a few deliveries.

When Hall began the last over England required eight runs, an unlikely scenario. The batsmen had decided that if either of them missed a ball they would try to run a bye to the keeper, who was standing a long way back. In Shackleton's words, 'Obviously we were trying to win the match, but we knew if either of us was out, Colin Cowdrey would have to bat with one arm'.

Shackleton played at the first delivery and missed, but he pushed

Colin Cowdrey, arm in plaster, walks out to bat. (Brian Bassano)

a single off the second. Allen glanced the third to fine leg, but with six runs needed from three balls, only a boundary would do.

Shackleton played and missed at the next delivery, and, as per instructions, Allen set off. Murray threw the ball at the striker's end stumps and missed. Worrell, at short leg, then grabbed the throw and set off in a race to beat Shackleton to the other end. Not prepared to let go of the ball and risk overthrows, he ran and flipped off the bails just before the batsman got home. Shackleton's view of the event is interesting. 'I set off to run and got tangled up in my pads and stumbled. Frank Worrell and I raced for the non-striker's end. As the wicket was broken I knew I was out. After the game, Frank said he dare not have thrown the ball as there was no one backing up.'

Nine wickets down, and out walked Colin Cowdrey, arm in plaster to help see England through. Thankfully, Allen was at the striker's end and it was decided during a long mid-pitch consultation that he would take the last two balls of an enthralling match. He remembered, 'The decision was left to me as to how to bat. If I received a bad ball I would go for victory'. Six runs off two deliveries from the West Indies fast bowler was not a real possibility. According to Allen, 'This was unlikely as Wes Hall had bowled well in the gathering gloom from the very dark background of the pavilion. In these situations the man in the middle is making the decisions, and it's actually more difficult watching from the pavilion.'

Cowdrey said that Allen was the calmest man on the ground as the West Indians sought to capture the last wicket.

Hall gave those last two balls everything he had, but Allen safely defended both and the match ended in a draw. His 45 minute innings of four not out had helped save the day for England. For all his preparedness to play, Cowdrey commented, 'I was relieved, however, that I didn't have to face Wes Hall flat out in the dark'.

If there was a hero on this extraordinary day, it was Hall. He had bowled unchanged for 200 minutes, broken only by the tea interval, and in the innings sent down 40 overs to take 4/93. J. S. Barker, in his book of the tour *Summer Spectacular*, called it 'a stupendous feat of endurance'. *The Times* said of his spell, ' His energy was astonishing, his stamina inexhaustible, his speed awesome, from the first ball to the last'. Interviewed recently about this performance Hall had no hesitation in calling it his finest hour. There would be few who would argue. Griffith also deserves praise. His 30 overs cost just 59 runs and he took three wickets, including the crucial one of Close.

Worrell had again proved the quality of his leadership under pressure. His side had not panicked. They had played to plan, and in doing so, had helped produce one of the great games of cricket. In the words of *The Times* correspondent, ' the game got the finish it deserved'.

The West Indian captain said, 'It was a great match and performance by both sides. It was a fitting end'. His England counterpart, Dexter, commented, 'Good going. I'm too hoarse to say anything else'. Most who witnessed it were adamant that it was the best game they had seen. The only ones who argued were those lucky enough to have seen the Brisbane tie.

England comfortably won the Third Test by 217 runs, thanks to a 12 wicket haul from Trueman, but the West Indies came back to win the last two by 221 runs and eight wickets to send Worrell into retirement with a 3–1 series victory.

If the series had not been quite as good as the one in Australia in 1960–61, there was still some memorable cricket played, including an unforgettable day at Lord's.

ENGLAND v WEST INDIES

Played at Lord's, London, on 20, 21, 22, 24, 25 June, 1963.
Toss: West Indies.

WEST INDIES

C. C. Hunte	c Close b Trueman	44	c Cowdrey b Shackleton	7
E. D. A. St J. McMorris	lbw b Trueman	16	c Cowdrey b Trueman	8
G. St A. Sobers	c Cowdrey b Allen	42	(5) c Parks b Trueman	8
R. B. Kanhai	c Edrich b Trueman	73	(3) c Cowdrey b Shackleton	21
B. F. Butcher	c Barrington b Trueman	14	(4) lbw b Shackleton	133
J. S. Solomon	lbw b Shackleton	56	c Stewart b Allen	5
F. M. M. Worrell *	b Trueman	0	c Stewart b Trueman	33
D. L. Murray +	c Cowdrey b Trueman	20	c Parks b Trueman	2
W. W. Hall	not out	25	c Parks b Trueman	2
C. C. Griffith	c Cowdrey b Shackleton	0	b Shackleton	1
L. R. Gibbs	c Stewart b Shackleton	0	not out	1
Extras	(B 10, LB 1)	11	(B 5, LB 2, NB 1)	8
Total		**301**		**229**

Fall: 51, 64, 127, 145, 219, 219, 263, 297, 297, 301.1   5, 15, 64, 84, 104, 214,224, 226, 228, 229.

Bowling

First Innings: Trueman 44–16–100–6, Shackleton 50.2–22–93–3, Dexter 20–6–41–0, Close 9–3–21–0, Allen 10–3–35–1.

Second Innings: Trueman 26–9–52–5, Shackleton 34–14–72–4, Allen 21–7–50–1, Titmus 17–3–47–0.

ENGLAND

M. J. Stewart	c Kanhai b Griffith	2	c Solomon b Hall	17
J. H. Edrich	c Murray b Griffith	0	c Murray b Hall	8
E. R. Dexter *	lbw b Sobers	70	b Gibbs	2
K. F. Barrington	c Sobers b Worrell	80	c Murray b Griffith	60
M. C. Cowdrey	b Gibbs	4	not out	19
D. B. Close	c Murray b Griffith	9	c Murray b Griffith	70
J. M. Parks +	b Worrell	35	lbw b Griffith	17
F. J. Titmus	not out	52	c McMorris b Hall	11
F. S. Trueman	b Hall	10	c Murray b Hall	0
D. A. Allen	lbw b Griffith	2	not out	4
D. Shackleton	b Griffith	8	run out (Worrell)	4
Extras	(B 8, LB 8, NB 9)	25	(B 5, LB 8, NB 3)	16
Total		**297**		**9/228**

Fall: 2, 20, 102, 115, 151, 206, 235, 271, 274, 297.   15, 27, 31, 130, 158, 203, 203, 219, 228.

Bowling

First Innings: Hall 18–2–65–1, Griffith 26–6–91–5, Sobers 18–4–45–1, Gibbs 27–9–59–1, Worrell 13–6–12–2.

Second Innings: Hall 40–9–93–4, Griffith 30–7–59–3, Sobers 4–1–4–0, Gibbs 17–7–56–1.

Match drawn

16

Pollock's Masterpiece

ENGLAND v SOUTH AFRICA

Trent Bridge, Nottingham
5 August, 1965 – Day One

T HE GREATEST tragedy for cricket lovers was South Africa's isolation from international competition from 1970 to 1992, which prevented them from seeing that country's players perform at the highest level. This was particularly disappointing as the Springboks could, at the time of their isolation, lay claim to being the best team in the world. However much we cricket lovers would like to keep sport and politics apart, there are bigger issues to consider. Happily, those issues have been resolved, and South Africa is now firmly back in the cricket spotlight. While all would rejoice at the changes which have taken place in that country, there remains the wish to have seen some more of those players whose international careers were ended in 1970. One of those was Graeme Pollock.

Pollock could lay a justifiable claim to being the game's finest left-hand batsman. In all the history of cricket, very few players have produced performances to rank comparison.

The South African began his Test career against Australia in 1963–64 at the age of just 19. He made 122 in his third game and 175 in his fourth, helping South Africa square the series, and drawing praise from no less a figure than Sir Donald Bradman. In his next series, at home against England in 1964–65, he batted consistently, scoring a century in the Fifth Test. That series was lost 1–0 after an England win in the first game.

When the South Africans visited England in 1965 for a three Test series they were eager to claim some revenge. Peter van der Merwe had a capable side, with the batting led by Pollock and opener Eddie Barlow. The bowling was spearheaded by the pace of Pollock's older brother, Peter, while in Colin Bland the Springboks possessed the finest fieldsman in the world.

England had comfortably won all three Tests of the series against New Zealand earlier in the summer, but there was the realisation for Mike Smith and his team that this would be a much tougher contest. This was immediately apparent when England just held on for a draw in the First Test. Set 191 in 235 minutes, they were 7/145 with John Edrich retired hurt after being struck on the head by a delivery from fast bowler Peter Pollock.

Coming to Trent Bridge, Nottingham, for the Second Test, England was forced to make a number of changes. Edrich was still unfit, so in came Middlesex batsman Peter Parfitt. Fast bowlers Fred Rumsey and David Brown were also unfit and were replaced by Sussex fast bowler John Snow and Warwickshire seam bowler Tom Cartwright. South Africa made one change, bringing in left arm spinner Atholl McKinnon for off spinner Harry Bromfield. According to all-rounder Richard Dumbrill, the Springboks were particularly confident after their moral victory in the First Test and some reasonable form in the first-class games.

Van der Merwe won the toss in front of 20,000 spectators and chose to bat on what appeared to be a damp and lifeless wicket, the result of recent heavy rain. Dumbrill remembers, 'Accumulated moisture and humidity would almost inevitably mean a fair amount of movement in the air and off the seam'. Van der Merwe made his decision to bat knowing that the conditions early in the day would most likely favour England's seam bowlers. There was an uncertain weather forecast, however, and he did not want his side to be caught in even worse conditions later in the game.

Openers Barlow and 'Tiger' Lance made a slow start, scoring just 16 runs in the first 52 minutes. The second ball from Northant's giant fast bowler, David Larter, had lifted at Barlow, but generally the attack was erratic and the batsmen were able to

Eddie Barlow is caught by Colin Cowdrey for 19 after the ball had hit the gloves of keeper Jim Parks. (Brian Bassano)

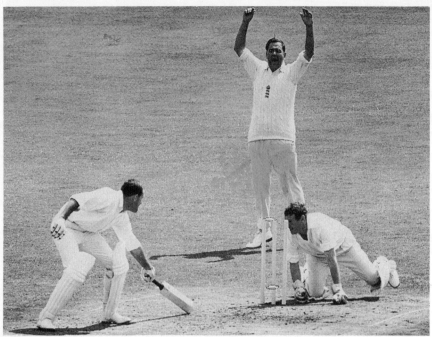

Colin Bland is stumped Parks, bowled off spinner Titmus for a duck. (Brian Bassano)

leave many deliveries alone. While Snow and Larter could make no impression, the introduction of Cartwright turned the game around. After two maidens he trapped Lance in front for seven with a ball which came in from the off. Then he had Denis Lindsay caught by keeper Jim Parks with one that went the other way, and the Springboks were 2/16.

Graeme Pollock came in and made a quiet start, endeavouring to build a recovery, but after he and Barlow had added 26, further disaster occurred. Barlow, who had fought it out for 90 minutes, edged a delivery from Cartwright. Parks dived, but could only knock the ball up into the air, and Colin Cowdrey at first slip completed the catch.

Bland (both a brilliant fieldsman and a very capable batsman) scored a single before he was out in rather unusual circumstances. Aiming a defensive shot at a delivery from off spinner Fred Titmus, he stunned the ball only to have it roll back towards the stumps where keeper Parks swept it into the wicket with Bland out of his ground. He departed, no doubt lamenting his bad luck, but his dismissal left South Africa in dire straits at 4/43. The pitch seemed to be behaving far worse than Van der Merwe had anticipated, but Pollock's response was to hit three spectacular fours.

Ali Bacher, a right-hand batsman playing in his first series, and a man who would do much to shape South African cricket for the rest of the century, was the next man in. The pair took the total to 76 without further loss and into the safety of the luncheon interval. Pollock was 34 not out. At the break,

With perfect precision Graeme Pollock drives through the covers. (Richard Dumbrill)

while the Springboks considered further recovery, England felt that a couple more wickets would put them in a winning position. Dumbrill remembers Pollock commenting that he noticed nothing spectacular about the bowling or the state of the pitch. Lesser mortals would have disagreed.

When Bacher was dismissed, dragging a ball from Snow into his stumps for 12, half the side was out for 80—'the verge of annihilation', according to Dumbrill—and England looked well on the way to victory. The only real obstacle was Pollock, and he decided that the best method of defence was to attack. Partnered by his skipper, the left-hander produced an onslaught the like of which has seldom been seen.

Cartwright, a bowler famed for his accuracy, was driven out of the attack for a time, as was the normally steady Titmus, who went for 12 in one over.

Pollock used a heavy bat, swinging it gracefully through the line and generating enormous power. He reached 50 after 95 minutes, with seven fours.

He then put the foot on the accelerator and the pace of scoring increased even more. By hitting a four and a single off Cartwright Pollock reached 90. He treated the leg spin of Barber in similar fashion in the next over.

On 95 he drove the first ball of the next over to the boundary, then pulled the following one to reach his century with his fifteenth four. Later in the over another delivery was dispatched to the ropes.

Having reached his milestone, Pollock showed no signs of letting up. He

Pollock's innings comes to a controversial end as Cowdrey takes the ball at slip. Note the lack of concern on the part of the batsman. (Brian Bassano)

struck two fours and a single off each of the next two overs he received from Cartwright and Barber.

Cartwright finally had his revenge, getting Pollock's wicket to a catch at first slip by Cowdrey. So complete was the batsman's control that his dismissal was totally unexpected. The young South African seemed surprised with the decision, believing he had hit the ground and not the ball. Dumbrill remembers Pollock's return to the pavilion. 'Graeme was no happy camper, believing he had struck the ground when driving at Cartwright and the ball had deviated off the bowler's footmarks. The eyes bore his anger.' The anger remained for some time, because had he batted the remainder of the day, almost anything would have seemed possible. 'Graeme recalls an elderly gentleman came up to congratulate him and his response was rather abrupt. After the well-wisher left Graeme castigated the room attendant for allowing in strangers.' He was mortified when he discovered the gentleman was the great batsman, Sir Leonard Hutton.

In bland statistics he scored 91 runs in the 70 minutes after lunch out of 102, with strokes of superb, effortless timing and placement. He brought up his century with a vicious pull to the boundary, but it was the crashing power of his off-side strokes—particularly those hit through the covers—

which remains most memorable. His second 50 had taken just 33 minutes and contained nine fours. In all he hit 21 fours in his 125 made in 145 minutes, and his ability to find the gaps defeated all the best intentions of Mike Smith. They were made out of 162 runs scored while he was at the wicket. It was the young man's fourth Test hundred and his 13th in first-class cricket, during which he became the youngest player at that time to score 1000 runs in Tests. Given the way he played, spectators could have been forgiven for thinking South Africa was in any trouble at all.

Commenting on this innings *The Times* correspondent remarked, 'It is a sure sign of greatness to stand alone as Pollock did. He held dominion where others floundered. It was inspiration as much as batting. The basic virtues were displayed to perfection; the top hand in control, the shoulder pointing the direction of the stroke, the ball timed not by effort so much as by instinct. The majority of his boundaries came from strokes through the covers, off front or back: strokes that were effortless and fluent. Comparisons with England's elegant left-hander Frank Woolley were widespread and inevitable. I can think of no innings played against England since the war which was so critical and commanding: I can think of none more beautifully played'.

John Woodcock, writing in *The Cricketer*, said, 'Not since Bradman's day could anyone recall having seen an England attack treated in such cavalier style. I think it was the ease with which Pollock batted which was more astounding than anything. It was this that will identify his innings as long as the memory of it endures'.

Peter West, in *Playfair Cricket Monthly*, commented on Pollock's achievement on a slow pitch, not conducive to playing strokes. The batsman's capacity to drive the ball 'on the up' was a thing to be wondered at.

Doyen of England's cricket writers, E. W. Swanton, thought it an innings fit to rank with any ever played, while J. L. Manning of the London *Daily Mail* went in search of metaphors. 'Pollock had rearranged the whole scene to his liking. He could walk on stage to play whatever matinee role he pleased... There was no thunder and lightning from Pollock. No fierce storm or hurricane blew... There was only the experience of a growing wonder that a man could bat so well.'

Pollock, himself, considered it his best innings, and he had plenty to choose from. In his autobiography, *Down the Wicket*, he said that everything he attempted came off.

Richie Benaud, who has seen more Test cricket than most, put his judgment on Pollock's innings with the comment that no one could ever have batted better.

For Dumbrill, sitting padded up in the pavilion, the innings had a tremendous effect. 'Waiting my turn at bat, I sat back and watched in awe as he carved up England's bowlers with one majestic stroke after another especially between mid-off and cover. With these strokes the shift in balance was powerful and dramatic in the extreme. To this day I still shake my head in amazement at this stupendous innings.'

Next man in, Dumbrill waited until Pollock left the field before he stepped out, not wanting to share the enormous ovation given by the crowd.

In a partnership of 98 with Pollock, Van der Merwe scored just seven, but it was batting of inestimable value. He allowed the young man to have his head, and when Pollock was dismissed he went on to partner Dumbrill in an important, but anticlimactic, stand of 43, assuming the role of the aggressor. His innings of 38 was of great value, a real captain's effort which ended in a terrible mix up when he was sent back to the non-striker's end and run out by Parfitt's throw from cover point. Dumbrill's knock of 30 was not as well played, but was extremely valuable in keeping up the momentum. He was particularly angry at getting out, citing impatience and miscalculation as the reasons. 'After Tom (Cartwright) stopped a snorter of a straight drive, critically damaging his hand in the process we learned later, I tried to lift his next ball to the long on boundary. I played the shot firm enough with good velocity only to find the ball had slowed down into the wind, enabling Peter Parfitt to latch onto a good catch over his right shoulder high above his head at wide mid-on.'

With ten from Botten in 40 minutes, 15 from Peter Pollock and eight not out from McKinnon, the South Africans' final total of 269 was far in excess of what they looked like achieving earlier in the day. The last five wickets had added an amazing 189 runs.

Cartwright used the damp pitch exceptionally well to take 6/94, wilting only under the incredible onslaught of Pollock. He stood head and shoulders over the rest of the attack, but even he was not sure what to do against Pollock's power. The batsman himself was warm in his praise of Cartwright's effort.

England now had the prospect of surviving a short, nasty period until stumps, a particularly annoying time on a day when the initiative had been taken away from them.

One Pollock had been responsible for putting his side back in the game, and the other now stepped in to drive home the advantage. In his first over Peter Pollock, the fastest bowler in England that summer, had Geoff Boycott caught by Lance at the second attempt, low down at second slip for no score. In the next Ken Barrington played on for one to have England 2/8. Barber and nightwatchman Titmus held on until stumps, although the latter must have been very close to leg before to a McKinnon delivery, but at 2/16 the South Africans were well on top.

Thanks to 105 from Cowdrey, 41 from Barber and 32 from Smith, England reached 240, conceding a lead of just 29. Peter Pollock bowled beautifully to take 5/53.

Batting a second time, South Africa overcame the loss of two early wickets to reach 289. The initial recovery was made by Barlow (76) and Pollock (59 in 85 minutes), and continued by Bacher who made 67. Larter (5/68) and Snow (3/83) were the most successful bowlers. Cartwright was unable to bowl in the second innings because of a broken thumb, courtesy of Dumbrill's drive on the first day.

Set 319 to win, England was dismissed for 224. A good recovery after being 4/13 gave South Africa a win by 94 runs. Only Parfitt (86) and Parks

Opener Geoff Boycott is caught by 'Tiger' Lance off Peter Pollock as England's first innings gets off to a bad start. (Brian Bassano)

(44 not out) made contributions as Pollock (5/34, giving him 10/87 for the match), and McKinnon (3/50) bowled their side to a famous victory. Peter Pollock continued to spearhead the Springbok attack until political isolation closed in during 1970. He ended his 28 Test career with 116 wickets at 24.18.

The Springboks were delighted with the victory and there were some unusual scenes at the end of the game. Richard Dumbrill remembers, 'No Test match has ever witnessed such exuberance as when many of the players led by Colin Bland and including Graeme Pollock stripped down to their underpants, left the dressing room and strode out to the middle, now mercifully devoid of spectators. With friendly help from the local constabulary we staged a pantomine cricket match using beer bottles as wickets. Captain Peter van der Merwe was helpless to intervene as he was handcuffed to a colleague in the dressing room. We ended by marching up and down the pitch, dousing it in cold South African beer before retiring shivering to the rooms to continue our celebration'.

A draw in the Third Test gave South Africa a series win in England for the second time, the first being exactly 30 years earlier.

It would be nearly another 30 years, 1994, before the two sides would meet again in a Test. For this 1965 South African side only two more series, both against Australia in 1966–67 and 1969–70, remained before the isolation set in. South Africa won both convincingly and Graeme Pollock continued to dominate bowlers. At the end of his Test career the left-hander had played 23 Tests in which he scored 2256 runs at 60.97 with seven centuries. His highest score of 274 is still the South African Test record. Pollock remained active in South African cricket and was still capable of taking centuries off the various 'rebel' attacks which toured there in the eighties, in spite of the fact that he was past 40.

In 1994–95 he played an exhibition game in Sydney and made a dazzling 80. For a man aged 50, it was an extraordinary display, serving once more to show the cricket world just what it had missed. If he was not, as one South African journalist said, 'the best since Bradman' then there were very few better.

ENGLAND v SOUTH AFRICA

Played at Trent Bridge, Nottingham, on 5, 6, 7, 9 August, 1965
Toss: South Africa.

SOUTH AFRICA

E. J. Barlow	c Cowdrey b Cartwright	19	(4) b Titmus		76
H. R. Lance	lbw b Cartwright	7	c Barber b Snow		0
D. T. Lindsay +	c Parks b Cartwright	0	(1) c Cowdrey b Larter		9
R. G. Pollock	c Cowdrey b Cartwright	125	(5) c Titmus b Larter		59
K. C. Bland	st Parks b Titmus	1	(6) b Snow		10
A. Bacher	b Snow	12	(3) lbw b Larter		67
P. L. van der Merwe *	run out	38	c Parfitt b Larter		4
R. Dumbrill	c Parfitt b Cartwright	30	b Snow		13
J. T. Botten	c Parks b Larter	10	b Larter		18
P. M. Pollock	c Larter b Cartwright	15	not out		12
A. H. McKinnon	not out	8	b Titmus		9
Extras	(LB 4)	4	(B 4, LB 5, NB 3)		12
Total		**269**			**289**

Fall: 16, 16, 42, 43, 80, 178, 221, 242, 252, 269. 2, 35, 134, 193, 228, 232, 243, 265, 269, 289.

Bowling:
First Innings: Larter 17–6–25–1, Snow 22–6–63–1, Cartwright 31.3–9–94–6, Titmus 22–8–44–1, Barber 9–3–39–0.
Second Innings: Larter 29–7–68–5, Snow 33–6–83–3, Titmus 19.4–5–46–2, Barber 3–0–20–0, Boycott 26–10–60–0.

ENGLAND

G. Boycott	c Lance b P. Pollock	0	b McKinnon		16
R. W. Barber	c Bacher b Dumbrill	41	c Lindsay b P. Pollock		1
K. F. Barrington	b P. Pollock	1	(5) c Lindsay b P. Pollock		1
F. J. Titmus	c G. Pollock b McKinnon	20	(3) c Lindsay b McKinnon		4
M. C. Cowdrey	c Lindsay b Botten	105	(6) st Lindsay b McKinnon		20
P. H. Parfitt	c Dumbrill b P. Pollock	18	(7) b P. Pollock		86
M. J. K. Smith *	b P. Pollock	32	(8) lbw G. Pollock		24
J. M. Parks +	c & b Botten	6	(9) not out		44
J. A. Snow	run out	3	(4) b Botten		0
J. D. F. Larter	b P. Pollock	2	(11) c van der Merwe b P. Pollock		10
T. W. Cartwright	not out	1	(10) lbw P. Pollock		0
Extras	(B 1, LB 3, W 1, NB 6)	11	(LB 5, W 2, NB 11)		18
Total		**240**			**224**

Fall: 0, 8, 63, 67, 133, 225, 229, 236, 238, 240. 1, 10, 10, 13, 41, 59, 114, 207, 207, 224.

Bowling
First Innings: P. Pollock 23.5–8–53–5, Botten 23–5–60–2, McKinnon 28–11–54–1, Dumbrill 18–3–60–1, G. Pollock 1–0–2–0.
Second Innings: P. Pollock 24–15–34–5, Botten 19–5–58–1, McKinnon 27–12–50–3, Dumbrill 16–4–40–0, G. Pollock 5–2–4–1, Barlow 7–1–20–0.

South Africa won by 94 runs

17

Walk Off

AUSTRALIA v ENGLAND

Sydney Cricket Ground
13 February, 1971 – Day Two

THE 1970–71 SERIES between England and Australia was expected to
be a close and exciting contest. Australia had held the Ashes since
1958–59, but had been thrashed by South Africa the previous season, and
was thought to be in decline, while England had been steadily building a strong
team under off spinner Ray Illingworth and was expected to offer a strong challenge. As the last few Ashes series had provided some rather dull, safety-first
play, and few highlights, many were hoping for an improvement.

Originally a six Test series, a total washout at Melbourne led to the
scheduling of a seventh game to make up for the one which was lost. As the
sides moved to Sydney for the final contest, a number of things became
apparent. England's batting, led by Geoff Boycott, John Edrich and Brian
Luckhurst, was immensely strong and the Australians had no bowler likely
to remove them cheaply. Graham McKenzie had been dropped, and the
Victorian Alan 'Froggy' Thomson was not successful. Only the raw talent of
a young fast bowler, Dennis Lillee, who took five wickets on debut in
Adelaide, looked to show some promise.

The Australian batting was also strong. Keith Stackpole's aggressive
opening was well supported by Ian Chappell, Ian Redpath and the young
Greg Chappell. New keeper Rod Marsh looked as if he could handle a bat,
too, and skipper Bill Lawry was still a hard man to move.

Although Australia's bowling had little to commend it, England did possess the one match-winning bowler in the series. Sussex pace man John Snow had bowled his side to victory in the first Sydney Test of the series, and always looked threatening. His pace and bounce had unsettled a number of the batsmen. The support for Snow had been steady, and England deserved their one nil lead as the sides prepared for Sydney.

Before the match the Australian selectors dropped a bombshell by replacing Bill Lawry as captain, and leaving him out of the side as well. Although he was not making runs in the quantity of previous seasons, he was still a good player. When Snow was on the rampage in Sydney, Lawry had carried his bat through the innings in making 60 not out. Ian Chappell, who was appointed captain, remains adamant that Lawry should have remained in the side. Chappell believes that had he been retained this series could have been squared and the 1972 one in England won. But the selectors, looking for something new, decided to dispense with a great servant of Australian cricket. A sad fact is that Lawry learned of his demise via team-mate Keith Stackpole, who heard it on the radio, an action which greatly coloured his successor's view of administrators, and made him determined that they would never have the chance to remove him in such a way.

Ian Chappell was given a new-look team for a game Australia had to win. In batting order it read Ken Eastwood, Keith Stackpole, Ian Chappell, Ian Redpath, Doug Walters, Greg Chappell, Rod Marsh, Kerry O'Keeffe, Terry Jenner, Dennis Lillee and Tony Dell. Eastwood (the 35-year-old Victorian and Lawry's replacement) and Queensland left-hand pace man Dell were making their debuts.

England, on the other hand, had a more settled and vastly more experienced combination, although an injury suffered by their leading batsman, Boycott, was a problem. In the series the Yorkshireman had scored 657 runs at 93.86, and it was thought that his presence in this final encounter would be sorely missed. The selectors chose John Edrich, Brian Luckhurst, Keith Fletcher, John Hampshire, Basil D'Oliveira, Ray Illingworth, Alan Knott, John Snow, Peter Lever, Derek Underwood and Bob Willis.

Chappell, having to win the game, took the aggressive option on winning the toss and sent the opposition in to bat. Only Percy McDonnell, George Giffen and Bob Simpson had done so in their first Test as captain.

The boldness paid off, as England collapsed to be all out for 184 before stumps on the first day. Illingworth top scored with 42, and Edrich (30) and Fletcher (33) got a start. The new look attack performed wonders. Leg spinners Jenner (3/42) and O'Keeffe (3/48) led the way, and Dell captured 2/32.

It was an excellent start, but how would the Australians fare against their nemesis, Snow, at the scene of his triumph earlier in the tour?

Thirty minutes' play remained before stumps for Stackpole and the 35-

year-old, crew-cut Eastwood to negotiate. It was really the worst possible start, as both openers were out for just 13 runs before stumps.

As the players walked onto the field for the second day's play, the game was evenly balanced. The two wickets lost the previous evening (particularly that of Stackpole) had taken much of the gloss from a very good Australian effort in the field.

Captain Ian Chappell and nightwatchman Rod Marsh resumed the innings, with the former hitting eight from medium pacer D'Olivera's first over. Disaster soon followed as Marsh swung at a leg side delivery from Lever and was brilliantly taken at leg gully by Willis. The Australian keeper played a good shot which flew only centimetres above the ground. Willis dived to his right, parallel to the ground in making the catch.

Chappell and the new batsman, Ian Redpath, began a recovery. The latter struck the first delivery he received through the covers for four, and Snow sent down four bouncers in an over to the former. This aroused the crowd of 29,000, who began booing the fast bowler.

The Australians proceeded slowly, but at 66 young Bob Willis, in his first Test series, bowled Chappell for 25, knocking his off stump out of the ground.

Four wickets down, and Doug Walters was on the way in. The dashing Walters had recently had a rough time against fast bowling, first in South Africa against Mike Procter and Peter Pollock, and in this series against Snow. He had begun with a century in Brisbane, but since then had looked increasingly fallible and uncomfortable against the short-pitched ball. On the other hand, Walters felt that some of the bowling in this game and the series was intimidatory, although he believes that is now a forgotten word.

Lever, keen to put some more pressure on in this area, gave Walters three bouncers in a row, but the batsmen survived to lunch, when the total stood at 4/84, still 100 runs behind.

Walters continued to live dangerously after the break, and when 16 was dropped by Fletcher off the left arm spin of Underwood. Redpath was playing with greater confidence, and took 18 from three Snow overs, an effort which brought up the 50 stand. Walters was again dropped, this time at third man by Underwood, when he slashed at a quicker delivery.

England was letting Australia back into the game, and 50 runs had been added in only 45 minutes since lunch.

With Australia only 37 behind Walters appeared to be well stumped by Knott, but Umpire Lou Rowan ruled not out. The England keeper looked shocked at the decision. Unfazed by his reprieve Walters tried a repeat shot and this time the umpire gave the decision in the fielding side's favour. Although he had plenty of luck, Walters made 42, adding 81 vital runs with Redpath.

Australia at 5/147 had its last two recognised batsmen in Redpath and Greg Chappell at the crease. The young Chappell had struck a glorious

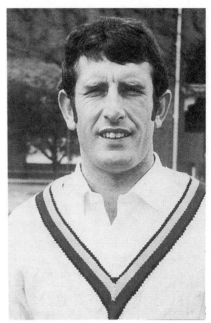

Left: Ray Illingworth was a tough, uncompromising and successful captain. (Moss Seigert)
Right: John Snow's pace bowling was Illingworth's main weapon in the 1970–71 series. (Moss Seigert)

hundred on debut in the Second Test in Perth, but had done little of note since. On this day, however, he began to play quite well and settled in with Redpath in an attempt to overhaul the England score.

This was not to be, because with the addition of just 15 runs to the total Redpath was deceived by Underwood's change of pace, and was caught and bowled for 59 made in 198 minutes with two fours.

A scoreline of 6/162 became 7/178 when all-rounder O'Keeffe was caught by Knott off Illingworth for three.

The final session of this day was to provide scenes not witnessed before in an Ashes Test. The new batsman, Jenner, was a capable player, but no great expert at dealing with short-pitched fast deliveries. However, he and Chappell kept the bowling out, and perhaps Illingworth and his team could see the game and the series slipping away from them. Before long, Jenner's stay at the crease resulted in the return of John Snow. The fast bowler quickly had the batsman in some discomfort, so much so that Illingworth himself moved to a position close on the leg side.

Snow let go a short ball, and Jenner, taking his eyes off the delivery, ducked into it and was struck on the back of the head. Snow described it as a shortish delivery, let go to remind the batsman that he could not just move onto the front foot. 'It would not have got above rib high if Jenner had not ducked into it.' With the batsman stunned and, after some minutes, helped off the ground bleeding from a head wound, umpire Rowan warned Snow,

139

Terry Jenner. (Moss Seigert)

telling him to ease up on the short deliveries. Those who have watched the barrage of short bowling from some players over recent years may find it slightly amusing that the bowler was in trouble after just one bumper.

(Rowan later wrote a book, *The Umpire's Story*, in which he gave his side of what happened. He denied that he acted in haste, and said that he had no regrets about the action he took. In his autobiography, *Cricket Rebel*, Snow described Rowan's account of the events as 'inventive'.)

This warning led to an argument between the umpire and the bowler. Snow, who admitted to losing his temper at this point, complained that he had bowled only one bumper.

Rowan then issued a warning for intimidation. He took this decision based on his assessment of the number nine batsman's ability, and the specific field placing used against him. The warning was issued as Snow was moving back to his mark. The fast bowler believed that the umpire should have done this sooner, rather than wait. Things had been settling down, but now they heated up again.

Illingworth, as captain, joined in. According to Rowan, the England captain raised his voice and threatened to report the umpire, while an angry Snow talked about cheating. When Illingworth waved an open hand at the umpire the booing and jeering began to hot up. This barracking continued through the remainder of Snow's over to the new batsman, Lillee. There were no further short-pitched deliveries. Rowan believed it was the reactions of the captain and fast bowler which really inflamed the crowd.

Illingworth felt that the umpire had behaved incorrectly, as Snow had bowled only one short-pitched delivery and Jenner was quite a useful batsman. According to Illingworth, the hand waving was simply him stressing that Snow had bowled just one short ball.

At the end of the over Snow moved off to his position at fine leg, while the booing continued. When he again moved towards the same position after the drinks break, a number of cans were thrown onto the field before he reached the fence. Seeing this, Illingworth called his men to the centre and they sat down, while amidst further booing the ground was cleared.

Illingworth, reclining on the ground, waits for the field to be cleared, shortly before taking his team off the S.C.G. (*The Age*)

When this had been done Illingworth sent his fieldsmen to their normal positions. This, of course, meant that Snow once more headed back towards fine leg. One spectator began hurling insults at the bowler, who kept walking towards the fence, and appeared to be answering the insults. Snow's autobiography makes no mention of this, but he does say that there was quite a bit of applause mingled with the booing.

Snow reached the fence, then turned back to the field. As he did this he was grabbed by the shirt by an older man wearing an orange T-shirt and a white floppy hat. A number of other spectators tried to pull the man away, but then more cans came onto the field.

Illingworth and some other players moved to help Snow, then as further cans came onto the field he ordered his side off. Not all of them seemed keen to go. Rowan considered both the sit down and the walk-off (as well as insisting that Snow field at fine leg) to be provocative actions on the part of the England captain.

Opposing captain, Ian Chappell, thought the walk-off a bit hasty—the sort of thing you might consider in India or the West Indies, but not Sydney.

Others have different views. R. S. Whitington, in his book on the tour, thought Illingworth behaved correctly throughout, except in ordering the

A spectator in a white towelling hat grabs Snow, an action which prompted the walk off. (ABC)

141

bouncer to be bowled at Jenner. Snow also said that Illingworth was calm and in control in ordering his side to leave the field. It was only in the dressing room, when manager David Clarke tried to get the players back onto the field, that Illingworth reacted angrily, insisting on the safety of his players.

The umpires and the batsmen stayed for a while until eventually the officials walked off. Rowan believed that at this moment he would have been well within his rights to have awarded the game to Australia. Illingworth had made no comment to the umpires concerning his actions and what he intended to do—something he regrets—so they decided to leave the ground.

This left the batsmen alone in the middle. Lillee did not have any idea what was going on, but both he and Chappell thought it wise to stay put rather than face their captain's wrath by walking off as well.

As Rowan and the other umpire, Tom Brooks, walked from the field the decision was made to give England an opportunity to resume. If they declined to do so, Australia would win by a forfeit. This was communicated to Illingworth and the manager in the dressing room by the umpires. Walters remembers the umpires informing the Australians that England had been given two minutes to get back on the field or the match was over.

Shortly afterwards, an announcement was made that the ground would be cleared and play resumed. Had England failed to return the match would have been awarded to Australia, and the series drawn. Rowan was convinced that Illingworth used the situation to get back at him because of the warning to Snow. Again, there is disagreement. Many thought it would be difficult to continue playing with cans coming onto the field. In fact, the sole casualty was a sightscreen attendant who was struck on the head by a can of beer, but had play continued there may have been further injuries.

When the players returned to the field, to the appreciation of the crowd, Snow again headed towards fine leg, but Willis chased after him and persuaded him to change places.

For the remainder of the day Chappell and Lillee held firm against an attack which contained no further short-pitched bowling.

The incident did provoke one amusing exchange. England batsman John Edrich said to Rowan, 'All this is caused through too much liquor', to which the umpire replied, ' Don't tell me your bowlers have been drinking!'

Rowan remained convinced that Illingworth and Snow provoked it all, while they, in turn, think that the umpire's unnecessary warning was the catalyst.

Just before stumps it was announced that Jenner had had one stitch inserted in his scalp and would be able to bat again.

The Australians batted through without further loss to be 7/235 at stumps with Chappell 62 and Lillee 6.

The next day Jenner did indeed bat again, and made 30 in Australia's 264. Chappell added only three to his overnight score. Lever (3/43) and Willis (3/58) were the most successful bowlers.

Thanks to 59 from Luckhurst, 57 from Edrich and 47 from D'Olivera, England reached 302 in the second innings, setting Australia 223 to win. O'Keeffe and Dell each took three wickets.

Australia was given an added bonus when Snow caught and broke a finger in the picket fence attempting to take a ball. However, the other bowlers, Illingworth (3/39), Underwood (2/28) and D'Oliveira (2/15) stepped into the breach and bowled Australia out for 160. Only Stackpole (67) and Greg Chappell (30) had any success with the bat.

There were no further dramas on the field, and England's 62 run victory confirmed them as the better side in the series. Much of the credit for their two nil victory goes to Snow, who captured 31 wickets in the series, and was always a hostile force. Australia had no bowler to equal him, and the local batsmen were often unable to counter him. After a long absence The Ashes returned to England in a series that belonged to the dark-haired fast bowling poet from Sussex.

Walters, who probably had more trouble with Snow than most, calls him the first of the modern day bowlers. 'He was accurate, didn't waste a delivery. Snow never bowled a bouncer a yard over your head. It was always at your head, and it came off a fair length, too.'

AUSTRALIA v ENGLAND

Played at Sydney Cricket Ground, on 12, 13, 14, 16, 17, February, 1971.
Toss: Australia.

ENGLAND

J. H. Edrich	c G.Chappell b Dell	30	c I.Chappell b O'Keeffe	57
B. W. Luckhurst	c Redpath b Walters	0	c Lillee b O'Keeffe	59
K. W. R. Fletcher	c Stackpole b O'Keeffe	33	c Stackpole b Eastwood	20
J. H. Hampshire	c Marsh b Lillee	10	c I.Chappell b O'Keeffe	24
B. L. D'Oliveira	b Dell	1	c I.Chappell b Lillee	47
R. Illingworth *	b Jenner	42	lbw b Lillee	29
A. P. E. Knott +	c Stackpole b O'Keeffe	27	b Dell	15
J. A. Snow	b Jenner	7	c Stackpole b Dell	20
P. Lever	c Jenner b O'Keeffe	4	c Redpath b Jenner	17
D. L. Underwood	not out	8	c Marsh b Dell	0
R. G. D. Willis	b Jenner	11	not out	2
Extras	(B 4, LB 4, W 1, NB 2)	11	(B 3, LB 3, NB 6)	12
Total		**184**		**302**

Fall: 5, 60, 68, 69, 98, 145, 156, 165, 165, 184.   94, 130, 158, 165, 234, 251, 276, 298, 299, 302.

Bowling

First Innings: Lillee 13–5–32–1, Dell 16–8–32–2, Walters 4–0–10–1, G.Chappell 3–0–9–0, Jenner 16–3–42–3, O'Keeffe 24–8–48–3.

Second Innings: Lillee 14–0–43–2, Dell 26.7–3–65–3, Walters 5–0–18–0, Jenner 21–5–39–1, O'Keeffe 26–8–96–3, Eastwood 5–0–21–1, Stackpole 3–1–8–0.

AUSTRALIA

K. H. Eastwood	c Knott b Lever	5	b Snow	0
K. R. Stackpole	b Snow	6	b Illingworth	67
R. W. Marsh +	c Willis b Lever	4	(7) b Underwood	16
I. M. Chappell *	b Willis	25	(3) c Knott b Lever	6
I. R. Redpath	c & b Underwood	59	(4) c Hampshire b Illingworth	14
K. D. Walters	st Knott b Underwood	42	(5) c D'Oliveira b Willis	1
G. S. Chappell	b Willis	65	(6) st Knott b Illingworth	30
K. J. O'Keeffe	c Knott b Illingworth	3	c sub b D'Oliveira	12
T. J. Jenner	b Lever	30	c Fletcher b Underwood	4
D. K. Lillee	c Knott b Willis	6	c Hampshire b D'Oliveira	0
A. R. Dell	not out	3	not out	3
Extras	(LB 5, W 1, NB 10)	16	(B 2, NB 5)	7
Total		**264**		**160**

Fall: 11, 13, 32, 66, 147, 162, 178, 235, 239, 264.   0, 22, 71, 82, 96, 131, 142, 154, 154, 160.

Bowling

First Innings: Snow 18–2–68–1, Lever 14.6–3–43–3, D'Oliveira 12–2–24–0, Willis 12–1–58–3, Underwood 16–3–39–2, Illingworth 11–3–16–1.

Second Innings: Snow 2–1–7–1, Lever 12–2–23–1, D'Oliveira 5–1–15–2, Willis 9–1–32–1, Underwood 13.6–5–28–2, Illingworth 20–7–39–3, Fletcher 1–0–9–0.

England won by 62 runs

18

Chandra

The Oval
23 August, 1971 – Day Four

BHAGWAT SUBRAMANYA CHANDRASEKHAR is an exotic name, in keeping with its possessor, who was one of Test cricket's most unusual players. The slightly built Indian bowled leg breaks with a right arm withered from polio. The quality which distinguished Chandrasekhar from all other leg spinners was the pace with which that right arm delivered the ball. Perhaps only the great Bill O'Reilly and England's Doug Wright bowled leg spin at something approaching Chandra's speed.

The injury to his right arm meant that he had to throw with his left when in the field, and his batting was of such number eleven status that for many years he held the record for the most ducks made in Test cricket.

But no matter what the other facets of his game, Chandrasekhar was a devastating leg spinner. In the Indian teams of his era, he made a striking contrast with the gentle, artful left arm flight of Bishen Bedi, the rotund off spinner Erapally Prasanna, and the quicker off breaks of Srinivas Venkataraghavan. While he was the most unpredictable in terms of form, Chandrasekhar was undoubtedly the one most likely to run through an opposing batting line up, and he was never more devastating than at The Oval in 1971.

This year was a crucial one for the leg spinner, as Chandra pointed out in a letter to the author. 'Ever since I returned home midway through the tour

Chandra bowling in the nets; a shot which clearly shows his withered right arm. (*The Age*)

of Australia in 1967–68 owing to a leg injury, I was driven into oblivion. I missed the home series against Graham Dowling's New Zealand and Bill Lawry's Australian sides. Then, despite a haul of 50 odd wickets in the domestic championship I was not considered for the tour of the West Indies in early '71. I thought, at the time, it was all over for me. Even when I got into the side for the trip to England, my selection was rated as a calculated risk by the chairman of the selection committee, Mr Vijay Merchant.' Under that sort of pressure 1971 was a critical point in Chandra's career.

In that year India made a three Test tour of England under the captaincy of left-hand batsman Ajit Wadekar. Previous tours of England had been strikingly unsuccessful, but there was a little more cause for optimism this time. Earlier in the year the Indians had defeated the West Indies 1–0 in the Caribbean, thanks to some excellent bowling from their spinners and brilliant batting from the tiny Sunil Gavaskar, who made over 700 runs in his first series. Perhaps this time they could make England struggle.

The home side was also on a wave of success, having just defeated Australia 2–0 to recover the Ashes. Captain Ray Illingworth had an experienced and capable side under his control, and in spite of the improvement of the Indians, it was odds on for an England win.

The first two Tests of the series were interrupted by rain. In the first India needed 38 runs with two wickets left at tea on the final day when rain ended the game. So, an enthralling finish was denied. In the second rain probably saved India from defeat. When the last day's play was washed out, India was 3/65 chasing 420 to win.

The Third Test arrived with the series all square. For this match England chose, in batting order, Brian Luckhurst, John Jameson, John Edrich, Keith Fletcher, Basil D'Oliveira, Alan Knott, Ray Illingworth, Richard Hutton, John Snow, Derek Underwood and John Price. The top order had not performed well so far in the series, and a better effort was required here. In the previous two Tests, the lower order had batted the side out of trouble. Perhaps it was asking a little much to hope that they could do it again.

The Indians, on the other hand, relied on the following to break the series deadlock: Sunil Gavaskar, Ashok Mankad, Ajit Wadekar, Dilip Sardesai, Gundappa Viswanath, Eknath Solkar, Farokh Engineer, Syed Abid Ali, Venkataraghavan, Bedi and Chandrasekhar. The attack relied heavily on the three spinners Venkat, Bedi and Chandra, supported by the medium pace of all-rounders Abid Ali and Solkar,

Srinivas Venkataraghavan's tight off spin helped keep the pressure on. (Brian Bassano)

while the batting, thanks to the presence of the all-rounders had some depth.

The Oval pitch looked in good condition as Illingworth won the toss and decided to bat. Burly Jameson struck 82, keeper Knott 90 and all-rounder Hutton 81 in a total of 355.

A number of Indian batsmen got a start, but no one really went on with it. Keeper Engineer top scored with 59, Sardesai made 54, Solkar 44 and Wadekar 48. The total reached 7/234 at stumps on the third day, the second having been lost to rain.

The fourth day's play began with Venkataraghavan and Abid Ali, the not out batsmen, determined to lift India's total past 300. Illingworth used the pace of Snow, his prime force in Australia, and Price for a few overs before turning to himself. The move looked to have backfired when the batsmen took 13 off one over, but from there the innings just faded away. The England captain bowled Abid Ali for 26, then had Bedi caught by D'Olivera for two, while left armer Underwood had Venkat leg before for 24. The innings closed at 284, giving England a useful lead of 71. Illingworth, with 5/70, had led from the front, varying his pace and flight and troubling all the batsmen. Sunil Gavaskar, writing in his book *Sunny Days*, thought England was well placed to drive home the advantage.

Those of us used to the more recent Indian attacks, which possessed some good seam bowlers, would find the attack of 1971 a strange sight. Medium pacers Abid Ali and Solkar were there only to take the shine off the ball before the spinners were swung into action. On this day Wadekar gave

Eknath Solkar, one of the game's finest close-to-the-wicket fieldsmen. (Brian Bassano)

them three overs each before bringing on Chandra and Venkat. For Chandra, who had done nothing startling on the tour, this was a 'now or never situation'.

Wadekar chose these two rather than Bedi, who, he felt, may have been a more expensive proposition. Chandra's bowling might get the wickets, while Venkat's accuracy would keep down the runs. England's lead meant that runs would also be vital.

Jameson had been severe on the spinners in the first innings, and he looked like doing so again when he drove Venkat straight to the boundary before he was dismissed in amazing fashion. Luckhurst hit a ball from Chandra hard back up the pitch, only to see it divert from the bowler's hand to the stumps with Jameson out of his ground. One for 23, and a very dangerous batsman run out for 16.

The new batsman, Edrich, played four balls, then was yorked by the fifth. This dismissal showed the unusual talents of Chandra as the batsman was not beaten by spin or flight, but more by the sheer pace of the delivery. The side's most dependable player out for nought, and the total 2/24.

With just a minute or two to go before lunch Fletcher came to the crease. His first ball from Chandra was a googly to which he pushed forward. It bounced a little more than he expected and took an edge, and Solkar—one of cricket's great close fieldsmen—dived forward from short leg and took a brilliant catch centimetres from the ground. The players walked off for lunch with England 3/24 and Chandra on a hat-trick. From looking for a win, England was now faced with a struggle to survive. Ajit Wadekar wrote in his autobiography, *My Cricketing Years*, that this was the moment when he believed his side would win. Chandra felt that these early wickets cheered the Indians, who had no specific plan, just a desire to do their best.

After the break the Indian captain crowded the batsman, D'Oliveira, but the hat-trick was denied when the ball struck the pads. It was almost three wickets in four balls though, as the next delivery was edged to slip where Sardesai missed a fast and difficult head-high chance. Three runs and a damaged hand to the fieldsman resulted. D'Oliveira was missed again two

overs later, by a diving Solkar at short leg. Perhaps he was the only fieldsman who could have got a hand to it.

Even though Solkar missed this chance his importance was noted in
Chandra's biography *The Winning Hand*. 'Then there was Solkar. I cannot
imagine how badly off we spin bowlers would have been without him. He
was just amazing. His very presence almost had the batsman thinking twice
about pushing forward.'

D'Oliveira had lived dangerously in compiling 17 runs, but fell when he
lofted Venkat to substitute fieldsman Jayantilal at long-on. His dismissal left
England 4/49. Wadekar had made the decision to use Venkat rather than the
left armer Bedi, because he felt the off spinner would restrict the runs while
Chandra attacked. It was an inspired decision.

The new batsman, Knott, was an extremely good player, and had been in
fine form, as shown by his first innings 90. He could be the man to support
Luckhurst in a rearguard action. There was also the thought that a lead of
over 200 might be too much for the Indians to chase in the last innings. But
those runs would take some making.

After the addition of just five runs, of which he scored a single, Knott
played Venkat towards the on side, only to see Solkar throw himself forward
and take the catch almost at the batsman's feet. As Chandra stated, so good
was his fielding that he was a vital part of the attack, as valuable as any
bowler. This was a perfect example.

With his side at 5/54 Illingworth joined Luckhurst. He made only four
before he drove a full toss back to Chandra and England was 6/65, and in
deep trouble. The lead was not enough and there was not a great deal of batting to come. At least the new man, Hutton, was a useful all-rounder, and
he too had made runs in the first innings.

From the beginning Luckhurst had played soundly. He had accumulated
33 runs out of 72 when he attempted to cut Chandra and was brilliantly
taken by Venkat at slip, getting the speeding ball in both hands moving to
his right. Chandra could not understand how the fieldsman saw the ball, let
alone caught it. Wadekar felt, at this moment, that England would do well
to exceed a hundred.

On the same score Chandra also removed Snow, caught and bowled, but
then Underwood and Hutton defended grimly for some time.

In an effort to break the deadlock, and not prepared to give England any
easy runs, Wadekar brought the left arm spin of Bedi on in place of Chandra,
and in his only over he removed Underwood, caught by Ashok Mankad off
an attempted sweep. The fieldsman had to run in some distance from deep
square leg, taking the ball at knee height on the run. The excellence of the
catching backed the bowling to perfection.

Chandra was then brought back into the attack, and trapped Price leg

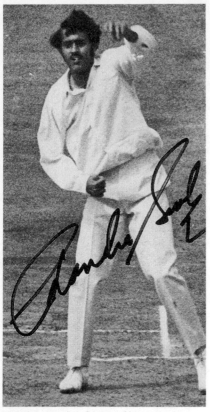

Chandra appealing for one of his six wickets at The Oval. (Brian Bassano)

before to end the innings at just 101. Not only was it England's lowest score against India—it was their lowest against anyone since being bowled out for 52 by Ray Lindwall and company in 1948. The architect of it all had been Chandrasekhar, who took 6/38 from 18.1 overs. Although it was undoubtedly the leg spinner's moment, Venkat had kept an end quiet, and captured 2/44 off his 20 overs.

Journalist E. W. Swanton commented on the lack of soundness in the England batting all summer, and this time the lower half of the order could not produce the necessary rescue act. The England collapse was, he thought, the result of 'high class spin bowling and spectacular catching'.

This was echoed by Chandra, who felt that there was nothing special in the pitch. 'We bowled to the field and the fielders did a remarkable job. Brilliant catches were taken which served to stimulate the bowlers. Though it may appear uncharitable to single out a fielder on that day, it is irresistible to say that Eknath Solkar, a wiry all-rounder with amazing reflex action, was the hero. He was a magnificent fielder. He possessed incredible talent to convert a half-chance into a successful catch. He was a source of inspiration to the bowlers.'

Chandra's demolition job meant that India needed 173 to beat England for the first time in England. It did not seem a lot of runs, and in truth it wasn't. The pitch was playing well and they had some good batsmen, but an early wicket or two could induce a collapse. The pressure would be applied by Illingworth, and sides before and since have faltered chasing scores of this size and less.

With two and a quarter hours remaining of this fourth day, the wonder boy Gavaskar and the more experienced Mankad went out to open the innings.

Snow gave England just the start they needed, trapping Gavaskar leg before in his second over without the batsman playing a shot. The batsman felt the ball had clearly pitched outside leg stump, and was disappointed with the decision. Nevertheless, India was 1/2 and a faint smell of panic could be detected in the air.

Mankad had made little impact so far in the series. In five previous innings his top score had been just ten, but now, joined by Wadekar, he managed to survive. In fact he did so well that his eleven runs occupied 75 minutes and 74 balls, before he fell to a catch by Hutton off Underwood. By then the total had reached 37, and the batting looked more composed. The threat of a sudden, early collapse had been avoided. Wadekar felt that as captain he had to set an example and stay there until stumps. This was a chance to take a series against England in England and he was not about to let the opportunity slip.

Shortly after Mankad's dismissal, Wadekar, on 22, swung at a ball which ballooned into the air for Edrich to run around from backward square leg to catch. On appeal, because the Indian captain had stood his ground, umpire Charlie Elliott ruled in the batsman's favour. This was a crucial decision, because if Wadekar had fallen the score would have been 3/38 and England may have had a chance.

There were no further opportunities for England before stumps. Wadekar played some neat strokes to reach 45 at the close, while his partner Sardesai, the other major success in the West Indies, had reached 13. At 2/76, just 99 runs were needed on the final day with eight wickets in hand. The Indians were well on the way to a historic victory.

That was achieved the next day, but not without a struggle. Wadekar fell without adding to his overnight score, but Sardesai (40), Viswanath (33) and Engineer (28 not out) took them there for the loss of six wickets, about an hour after lunch. Wadekar's dimissal may have prompted some panic, but the captain felt that his side had the talent and temperament to secure victory—so much so that he fell asleep on a couch, and missed the moment of victory. He was woken up by former England batsman, Ken Barrington, who told him he would have to go onto the balcony to receive the plaudits of the crowd. The reception accorded to Wadekar and his side moved the Indian captain to tears. It was an unforgettable experience, the finest of the Indian captain's career.

England had fought hard. Illingworth had not lost an official series since he became captain in 1969, but there were too few runs to chase. Chandra's extraordinary spell had seen to that. The leg spinner felt that there were many other occasions in his career when he bowled as well, but it was this game that assured him a permanent place in the side and lifted India to new heights in international cricket.

In a letter to the author Wadekar had some interesting points to make about Chandra's bowling. 'He wasn't a leg spinner in the real sense. He was a freak bowler and it was very difficult to read him. His faster one was faster

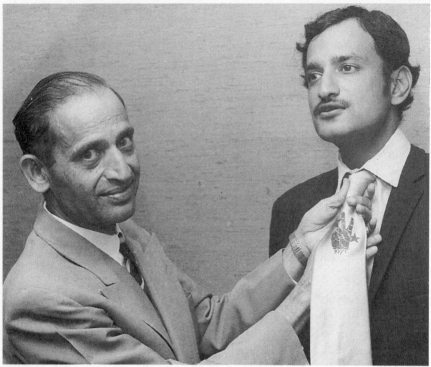

Indian manager Hemu Adhikari puts the victory tie around skipper Ajit Wadekar. (Brian Bassano)

than any of our medium pacers. The leg break hardly turned, except on a real turning track, but his googly was deceptive.' There was, however, a word of caution. 'If he didn't get an early wicket his bowling could go haywire. One had to handle him properly to get the best out of him.'

Although he would play Test cricket for many more years, and in 58 Tests take 242 wickets at 29.74, this was his finest moment—a performance which would forever change the perception of Indian cricket in England, and all though the courtesy of a right arm withered by polio.

The Indian public shared the cricketers' delight. The motorcade from Bombay airport to Brabourne Stadium held on the tourists' return remains a cherished memory. Chandra's final comment reflects his feelings at being a key participant in such an experience, 'The very thought of those passionate days of August 1971 makes me the proudest Indian. After all, we have written the most glittering pages in Indian cricket history. That I too had played a role in that triumph is a tale to tell my grandchildren'.

ENGLAND v INDIA

Played at Kennington Oval, London, on 19, 20, 21, 23, 24 August, 1971.
Toss: England.

ENGLAND

B. W. Luckhurst	c Gavaskar b Solkar	1	c Venkat b Chandrasekhar	33
J. A. Jameson	run out	82	run out	16
J. H. Edrich	c Engineer b Bedi	41	b Chandrasekhar	0
K. W. R. Fletcher	c Gavaskar b Bedi	1	c Solkar b Chandrasekhar	0
B. L. D'Oliveira	c Mankad b Chandrasekhar	2	c sub b Venkataraghavan	17
A. P. E. Knott +	c & b Solkar	90	c Solkar b Venkataraghavan	1
R. Illingworth *	b Chandrasekhar	11	c & b Chandrasekhar	4
R. A. Hutton	b Venkataraghavan	81	not out	13
J. A. Snow	c Engineer b Solkar	3	c & b Chandrasekhar	0
D. L. Underwood	c Wadekar b Venkat	22	c Mankad b Bedi	11
J. S. E. Price	not out	1	lbw Chandrasekhar	3
Extras	(B 4, LB 15, W 1)	20	(LB 3)	3
Total		**355**		**101**

Fall: 5, 111, 135, 139, 143, 175, 278, 284, 352, 355.   23, 24, 24, 49, 54, 65, 72, 72, 96, 101.

Bowling
First Innings: Abid Ali 12–2–47–0, Solkar 15–4–28–3, Gavaskar 1–0–1–0, Bedi 36–5–120–2, Chandrasekhar 24–6–76–2, Venkataraghavan 20.4–3–63–2.
Second Innings: Abid Ali 3–1–5–0, Solkar 3–1–10–0, Bedi 1–0–1–1, Chandrasekhar 18.1–3–38–6, Venkataraghavan 20–4–44–2.

INDIA

S. M. Gavaskar	b Snow	6	lbw b Snow	0
A. V. Mankad	b Price	10	c Hutton b Underwood	11
A. L. Wadekar *	c Hutton b Illingworth	48	run out	45
D. N. Sardesai	b Illingworth	54	c Knott b Underwood	40
G. R. Viswanath	b Illingworth	0	c Knott b Luckhurst	33
E. D. Solkar	c Fletcher b D'Oliveira	44	c & b Underwood	1
F. M. Engineer +	c Illingworth b Snow	59	not out	28
S. Abid Ali	b Illingworth	26	not out	4
S. Venkataraghavan	lbw b Underwood	24		
B. S. Bedi	c D'Oliveira b Illingworth	2		
B. S. Chandrasekhar	not out	0		
Extras	(B 6, LB 4, NB 1)	11	(B 6, LB 5, NB 1)	12
Total		**284**		**6/174**

Fall: 17, 21, 114, 118, 125, 222, 230, 278, 284, 284.   2, 37, 76, 124, 134, 170.

Bowling
First Innings: Snow 24–5–68–2, Price 15–2–51–1, Hutton 12–2–30–0, D;Oliveira 7–5–5–1, Illingworth 34.3–12–70–5, Underwood 25–6–49–1.
Second Innings: Snow 11–7–14–1, Price 5–0–10–0, D'Oliveira 9–3–17–0, Illingworth 36–15–40–0, Underwood 38–14–72–3, Luckhurst 2–0–9–1.

India won by 4 wickets

19

Dougie

AUSTRALIA v ENGLAND

WACA Ground, Perth
14 December, 1974 – Day Two

DOUG WALTERS was an extraordinary cricketer. He came from the New South Wales country town of Dungog to play Sheffield Shield cricket, and did so well that he made his Test debut against England in 1965–66 at the age of nineteen. The dashing right-hand batsman showed he possessed skills well above the ordinary by scoring hundreds in each of his first two Tests. In addition to his batting, he was a useful medium pace bowler and a brilliant fieldsman, particularly in close catching positions.

Walters's career was interrupted by two years' national service, but he returned to the Test team in 1968, and quickly re-established himself. His only real struggle came when confronted with English conditions. The seaming ball found holes in his slightly unorthodox technique, and in 1972, for the only time in his career, he was dropped from the team for the Fifth Test, after failing in the previous four. When England visited Australia next, in 1974–75, Walters was keen to banish any bad memories.

The English held the Ashes and were confident of retaining them, in spite of the absence of opening batsman, Geoff Boycott, who had exiled himself from the Test team. Even without him they brought a strong and experienced side captained by Mike Denness.

The Australians, on the other hand, were very much an unknown quantity. Although they had drawn the 1972 series two all, there had been some changes.

The valuable opening batsman Keith Stackpole had retired and the devastating swing bowler Bob Massie had faded from the scene. His partner, Dennis Lillee, was returning to the game after a serious back injury. No one was sure whether his body would stand up to the demands of fast bowling. So, there were concerns with batting and bowling.

However, the Australians had a secret weapon. Young fast bowler Jeff Thomson was said to have frightening pace. Thomson had played one Test against Pakistan two seasons earlier and taken 0/112, so the English were not impressed by his pedigree and saw little to worry about.

They quickly changed their minds. On a less than perfect pitch in Brisbane, Thomson bowled surely as fast as it is possible to bowl, taking nine wickets in the match. Lillee made a successful comeback, and England lost by 166 runs. In the process the pair, aided by the fast-medium Max Walker, unsettled a number of the English batsmen, who cannot have found any comfort in the fact that the Second Test would be played at the W.A.C.A. in Perth, the fastest pitch in the world.

Doug Walters – a unique cricketing talent. (Brian Bassano)

Injuries to the England batsmen necessitated flying in a replacement. The man chosen was 42-year-old Colin Cowdrey, nominated by the players because of his technique against fast bowling. The Kent right-hander had first toured Australia in 1954–55, and, fine player that he still was, many were worried about his ability to deal with such speed.

For the Perth Test England chose David Lloyd, Brian Luckhurst, Colin Cowdrey, Tony Greig, Keith Fletcher, Mike Denness, Alan Knott, Fred Titmus, Chris Old, Geoff Arnold and Bob Willis. There were five changes from the losing side in Brisbane, but most were due to injury, and the rest to illness.

The Australians selected Ian Redpath, Wally Edwards, Ian Chappell, Greg Chappell, Ross Edwards, Doug Walters, Rod Marsh, Max Walker, Dennis Lillee, Ashley Mallett and Jeff Thomson. The only change from the winning side of the previous Test was the inclusion of off spinner and brilliant gully fieldsman Mallett in place of leg spinner Terry Jenner.

Ever aggressive, and keen to exploit the psychological advances won by his bowlers in Brisbane, Ian Chappell sent England in to bat on winning the toss. Lillee, Thomson, Walker and Walters took two wickets each, and England

155

was out for 208 just before stumps. Lloyd made 49, wicketkeeper Knott 51, and Cowdrey fought it out for just over two hours in making 22. At one stage they were comfortably placed at 1/99, but the fast bowlers just blew the middle order away.

The highlight of the innings was the brilliance of the Australian fielding, which missed nothing, and caught some that no one had a right to see, let alone catch. Seven wickets fell to catches in the area between slip and gully.

The day had one more unpleasant surprise in store for England. Fletcher dropped Redpath in the slips off Willis. A quick wicket would have buoyed the spirits for the next day.

More than 23,000 people attended the ground for the second day, and they were all given something to remember for the rest of their lives.

Perfect weather and excellent batting conditions highlighted the value of winning the toss, as Redpath and West Australian Wally Edwards came out to resume the innings.

Willis bowled a very hostile first over, hitting Edwards on the back and appealing for a catch behind against Redpath. In the following over, from Arnold, a leg before appeal was turned down. Early on the batsmen looked vulnerable, but the bowlers were unable to break through.

Edwards then began to play a mixture of good and rash strokes. The left-hander had made a substantial impact in the previous season for his State, and it was to be hoped that he would be the opener the Australians had been looking for. He had reached 30, and the stand 64, when he drove a wide half-volley from Greig to cover for Lloyd to take the catch.

Australian captain Ian Chappell immediately launched into Greig's medium pace, hitting him to the boundary five times. Four overs from the tall all-rounder went for 31 runs, plus four byes when a beamer flew over the keeper's head to the fence.

With the score reaching 100 at better than a run a minute, Greig was replaced by veteran off spinner, Titmus. Bowling into the breeze, he put the brakes on the scoring. Then he went one better, luring Redpath forward into the drive, beating him in flight for Knott to complete the stumping. The ball glanced off the batsman's boot, but the Kent keeper took it with nonchalant ease. Redpath was out for 41 and the score 2/101. Old supported Titmus with eight overs for just 16 runs.

The Chappell brothers did not have time to build a partnership, as shortly after lunch Ian was beautifully caught down the leg side by Knott off Arnold for 25. With Australia 3/113 England had a glimmer of a chance. A couple more wickets and the Australians could be prevented from taking a substantial lead. It almost came about when Knott dived forward to a delivery from Titmus and appealed for a bat-pad catch against Greg Chappell. Many of the fieldsmen were convinced it was out, but the umpire was not.

The small hope of further quick wickets was snuffed out by a solid partnership between Chappell and West Australian Ross Edwards. While Chappell played his elegant drives, Edwards took runs when they were presented and played well within his limitations. This was a typically valuable innings, with Edwards applying the sheet anchor for his more gifted team-mates.

Chappell had made a century in his previous Test in Perth against England—his debut innings—and looked like repeating it, until he cut a short ball from Willis to Cowdrey in the gully. The fieldsman did not take the ball cleanly, but deflected it to Greig, who completed the catch.

Ross Edwards. (Brian Bassano)

Chappell was out for 62, and with Australia 4/192 England had an opportunity to take some more wickets and restrict the first innings lead. The visitors must have fancied their chances of doing this when they saw Doug Walters walking in to bat. He had enjoyed two not particularly successful series against them, and the bowlers felt they had his measure. Walters said he had no special instructions. 'In a Test team everyone knows what to do. You don't have to be told.' The outgoing batsman may have had some premonition of what was about to happen. As he passed Walters, the normally quiet Chappell said, 'It's set up for you to get a hundred in the last session'.

A further pressure was that only a few minutes remained until tea. The batsman survived to make three runs before the break.

When the players returned Walters opened the floodgates. He wanted to attack, and nothing appeared likely to stop him. Old and Greig, whose four overs cost 31, were repeatedly dispatched to the fence as 50 runs came in eight overs, 43 of them to Walters. The 50 partnership took 38 minutes. Titmus returned, but his introduction made no difference, 10 coming in his first over, nine of them to Walters, whose seven boundaries saw him reach a 48 minute 50. With that milestone passed, he showed no sign of slowing up. The century partnership was reached in 85 minutes, and then Edwards, almost unnoticed, reached his half century. If it was quieter, it was a no less valuable innings, but it paled beside the fireworks taking place at the other end.

Pulls, drives, cuts—Walters unloaded every shot in the book and a few others of his own invention. The crowd responded with thunderous applause as the batsman continued to do what he wanted with the bowling. At the beginning of his career, Walters had been given the unwanted title of 'another Bradman'. No one can live up to that for very long, but on this day, and in the presence of the Don himself, he made the comparison at least reasonable.

In the hour since tea 75 had been added, 66 of them to Walters. At the drinks break he had visions of being about 140 at stumps, such was his command of the bowling. However, at this point, Walters became upset at his partner. 'Roscoe was a handy cricketer, but he got a bit too defensive, got singles four overs in a row to keep pinching the strike from me. If that hadn't happened I would have got a lot more.'

There was no question of any strike manipulation on the part of Edwards. It was just the way it happened, but it certainly frustrated the in-form Walters. At this stage Edwards was actually outscoring his partner.

As the day drew to a close, interest centred on whether Walters could reach a hundred in the session. At drinks this had seemed a certainty, but losing the strike now put it in doubt. He had achieved this against the West Indies in Port-of-Spain in 1972–73; could he do it again?

Willis began the final over of the day to Edwards, who took a two off the first ball and three off the next. Walters, who was on 93, now had six balls to get seven runs for his century and ten for 100 in the session. Two gullies and two men out on the leg side confronted the batsman. The inevitable bouncer was skied over the keeper to the sightscreen for four, one of the very few false strokes in the innings. This was not a convincing stroke. Walters felt that Willis would bowl another. 'He was sending down three or four short ones each over, and had two men on the fence behind square. I knew there'd be another one, especially after the way I played the first. It was a matter of waiting.'

The bowler fought back, preventing a run being taken until the final ball was reached. Walters needed three for his century and six for a hundred in the session, and remembers being well aware of these statisitics. Would he play safe for the next day, or would he go for it?

There was really only one answer for Walters. Willis finally dropped it short, and the batsman smashed the ball high over mid wicket for six to achieve both his goals.

To the applause of the crowd, many of whom had run onto the field, Walters fought his way into the dressing room where he expected a great welcome. Sensing the chance to get one back on a great practical joker, the entire Australian team went and hid in the showers.

Walters charged into an empty room. When the players emerged, Ian Chappell gave the batsman a 'serve'. 'Don't tell me you got out off the last ball!'

'No Bertie,' said Walters, 'I hit it for six and got a hundred in the session.'

Doug Walters smashes the final ball of the day for six to reach his century and a hundred runs in the session. Bob Willis is the bowler. (Patrick Eagar)

'Rubbish', or some similar word, replied Chappell.

It took Walters some time to pick the joke.

Despite the joke it had been an extraordinary innings. The England bowlers had been put to the sword, and Australia would gain a substantial lead and be well on the way towards going two up in the series.

To emphasise his unpredictability, Walters was out in the first over next morning, for 103.

It really did not matter. Edwards went on to make 115 and the Australian total of 481 gave Ian Chappell the lead he needed. Another five wicket haul to Thomson, and two each to Lillee and Mallett, removed England for 293. Australia lost one wicket in scoring the 23 needed to win.

A draw in Melbourne was followed by Australian victories in Sydney and Adelaide. England had a consolation win in the final Test in Melbourne, but that was when both Lillee and Thomson were out injured.

It was a convincing series win to Australia based on the fast bowling of Lillee and Thomson, well supported by Max Walker and Ashley Mallett, some solid batting against a far from brilliant attack, and some wonderful fielding. Although the ferocious Australian bowling was certainly a high-light, was there a better moment than Walters's magic in Perth? The player himself considers this as technically the best innings he ever played. 'It was just

159

a magical day where the bowlers just kept aiming at the middle of the bat.'

Walters retired from first class cricket in 1981, after failing to win a place in the team to England. His past record and his age no doubt told against him, but he had been in the Australian team all summer and had played well. He left the game after 74 Tests in which he scored 5357 runs at 48.26 with 15 centuries. In addition, his medium pacers captured 49 wickets and his fielding 43 catches.

It was not the number of runs, but the manner in which they were scored, that made Doug Walters a cricketing legend. He could turn a game in a short space of time, and it was this capacity which Ian Chappell praised so highly. Walters won games for his side. He created winning positions.

Who knows? Half an hour of Walters at Headingley in 1981 may have produced an Australian victory.

AUSTRALIA v ENGLAND

Played at WACA Ground, Perth, on 13, 14, 15, 17 December, 1974.
Toss: Australia.

ENGLAND

D. Lloyd	c G. Chappell b Thomson	49	c G. Chappell b Walker	35
B. W. Luckhurst	c Mallett b Walker	27	(7) c Mallett b Lillee	23
M. C. Cowdrey	b Thomson	22	(2) lbw b Thomson	41
A. W. Greig	c Mallett b Walker	23	c G. Chappell b Thomson	32
K. W. R. Fletcher	c Redpath b Lillee	4	c Marsh b Thomson	0
M. H. Denness *	c G. Chappell b Lillee	2	(3) c Redpath b Thomson	20
A. P. E. Knott +	c Redpath b Walters	51	(6) c G. Chappell b Lillee	18
F. J. Titmus	c Redpath b Walters	10	c G. Chappell b Mallett	61
C. M. Old	c G. Chappell b I. Chappell	7	c Thomson b Mallett	43
G. G. Arnold	run out	1	c Mallett b Thomson	4
R. G. D. Willis	not out	4	not out	0
Extras	(W 3, NB 5)	8	(LB 4, W 1, NB 11)	16
Total		**208**		**293**

Fall: 44, 99, 119, 128, 132, 132, 194, 201, 202, 208.   62, 106, 124, 124, 154, 156, 219, 285, 293, 293.

Bowling

First Innings: Lillee 16–4–48–2, Thomson 15–6–45–2, Walker 20–5–49–2, Mallett 10–3–35–0, Walters 2.3–0–13–2, I.Chappell 2–0–10–1.

Second Innings: Lillee 22–5–59–2, Thomson 25–4–93–5, Walker 24–7–76–1, Mallett 11.1–4–32–2, Walters 9–4–17–0.

AUSTRALIA

I. R. Redpath	st Knott b Titmus	41	not out	12
W. J. Edwards	c Lloyd b Greig	30	lbw b Arnold	0
I. M. Chappell *	c Knott b Arnold	25	not out	11
G. S. Chappell	c Greig b Willis	62		
R. Edwards	b Arnold	115		
K. D. Walters	c Fletcher b Willis	103		
R. W. Marsh +	c Lloyd b Titmus	41		
M. H. N. Walker	c Knott b Old	19		
D. K. Lillee	b Old	11		
A. A. Mallett	c Knott b Old	0		
J. R. Thomson	not out	11		
Extras	(B 7, LB 14, NB 2)	23		0
Total		**481**		**1/23**

Fall: 64, 101, 113, 192, 362, 416, 449, 462, 462, 481.   4.

Bowling

First Innings: Willis 22–0–91–2, Arnold 27–1–129–2, Old 22.6–3–85–3, Greig 9–0–69–1, Titmus 28–3–84–2.

Second Innings: Willis 2–0–8–0, Arnold 1.7–0–15–1.

Australia won by 9 wickets

Breaking the Ice

NEW ZEALAND v ENGLAND

Basin Reserve, Wellington
14 February, 1978 – Day Four

NEW ZEALAND played its first Test against the English in 1929–30, and by the start of the 1977–78 season had yet to win a game against them. Of 47 Tests played, 23 had been lost and the rest drawn. Indeed, Test victories for the Kiwis had been few and far between. They had not won a game at all until they defeated the West Indies in 1956 and they had failed to win a series until their success against Pakistan on the subcontinent in 1969. There had been a meritorious two all draw in South Africa in 1961–62, but generally there had been precious little to show for all the hard work.

The optimists hoped that things would be different as the England side arrived in New Zealand to play a three Test series, following a similar one held in Pakistan. As England had played reasonably well there, and at home had easily accounted for Australia, only an optimist would have given the New Zealanders a chance of winning a game, let alone the series.

One point in the home side's favour was that England would be without its successful and highly regarded captain, Mike Brearley, who had suffered a broken arm in Pakistan. The skipper for the New Zealand tour would be the captain of Yorkshire and one of cricket's most controversial personalities, Geoff Boycott. It would be fair to say that Boycott had been disappointed that players with what he regarded as less ability than he had been given the opportunity to lead England before him. His chance had now come, and many waited to see how he would perform. A number of critics—and Boycott had many during his career—felt that he was too introspective, too caught up in his own game, to be a good leader. Here was the opportunity to prove them wrong.

Also in New Zealand's favour, the opposition's batting did not look strong, with all-rounder Geoff Miller listed at number three, although the bowling looked very competent.

Boycott made a bold beginning when he won the toss and sent New Zealand in to bat. No doubt he thought the conditions would help his quicker bowlers, and this proved to be the case when the Kiwis could muster only 228. John Wright, playing in his first Test, top scored with 55 in 348 minutes, although he was lucky to survive an appeal for a catch behind the wicket off his first ball. Veteran Bevan Congdon, with 44, made the only other substantial contribution. Chris Old took 6/54 and Bob Willis and Ian Botham captured two wickets each.

Unfortunately for Boycott his batsmen could do no better in the conditions, making 215. The captain ground it out for 442 minutes to get 77, but the next best was Graham Roope with 37. In fact it was slow going all round, as the innings lasted 504 minutes. Richard Hadlee (4/74), left armer Richard Collinge (3/42) and medium pacer Congdon (2/14), had used the conditions just as well as the English attack.

New Zealand's openers, Wright and Robert Anderson, had time to score 12 runs before stumps on the third day.

The game, which had staggered along at an almost funereal pace, roared into life on the fourth day—a day New Zealand cricket will never forget.

When play began, Anderson and Wright were intent in building on their team's slender first innings lead, and for most of the pre-lunch session they did just that. Their partnership had reached 54 when Anderson fell leg before to Old for 26. He had batted 105 minutes and hit four boundaries.

Partnered by Geoff Howarth, Wright continued his dogged defiance, and the pair took the total to 75 at the luncheon interval. With just one wicket down and the lead approaching 100, the New Zealanders were beginning to think about what sort of score they could set England in the last innings.

Seven runs had been added to the total when Wright was caught by Roope in the slips off Willis for 19. He batted 165 minutes on this occasion, completing a very promising debut. There was much praise for the young man's application on a difficult pitch in his first game. According to Wright, conditions for batting were far from easy. 'It was a dog of a wicket: two-paced and inconsistent. You could never settle in on it, as the odd delivery went through the top of the pitch.'

Further disaster followed 20 minutes later when Howarth was caught by Phil Edmonds off Willis for 21. He received probably the nastiest delivery of

Robert Anderson holds a chance from Geoff Miller. Richard Hadlee and skipper Mark Burgess share the joy. (*Evening Post*)

the whole match. His dismissal sparked an avalanche of wickets, which resulted in the innings reaching only 123.

It was an extraordinary collapse. Willis, bowling fast and straight, captured five wickets in seven overs. With his height he was making the ball lift uncomfortably into the batsmen's ribs and no one seemed to have any answer to him. 'Bloody quick', was John Wright's comment. Of those remaining, only keeper Warren Lees, with eleven, passed double figures. Extras, with 26, was equal top score with Anderson. Hendrick and Botham also used the conditions well, each capturing two wickets.

Perhaps there was some defence; the conditions were far from ideal, and Howarth, Burgess, Parker and Richard Hadlee were all victims of the pitch as Willis exploited the worn and rough patches superbly. Sir Richard Hadlee described the conditions. 'Batting wasn't easy. The pitch had variable bounce and at times a little dust puffed when the ball hit the pitch. It was two-paced and if bowlers could maintain good line and length and consistency, batsmen would be tested, exposed and eventually beaten.'

With the fall of the last New Zealand wicket, tea was taken, and the Kiwis were left to contemplate the fact that they had thrown away a winning position. Between lunch and tea, nine wickets had fallen for just 48 runs, and England now had eight hours in which to make 137 to win. In spite of the pitch, it seemed an easy enough task.

In a letter to the author, Sir Richard Hadlee had this to say about the situation: '137 should have been an easy target for England to achieve victory. All it needed was someone to take the initiative and dominate from the outset. We probably felt that we had blown the match, but Richard Collinge and myself talked about a sensation and making some-thing happen'. He also remembered some unkind remarks from spectators as he walked down the steps and out onto the field.

John Wright, along with most of his team-mates, felt that the target was not enough.

New Zealand had two hours in which to give it everything they had. They were able to attack without the worry of conserving themselves, and see if they could use the worn

Opening batsman Brian Rose turns his back on a Richard Hadlee delivery and is struck on the arm. Rose was forced to retire hurt, further adding to England's troubles. *(Evening Post)*

patches and bowlers' footmarks as well as Willis had. They also believed that, Boycott aside, the batting wasn't too strong, particularly with an all-rounder like Geoff Miller at number three. Team manager and Test selector, Frank Cameron, felt that his side had a chance if they could get Boycott early.

All optimism aside, it seemed only a miracle could prevent an England victory, and it occurred in Collinge's second over, when he yorked Boycott for a single. It was the bowler's five hundredth first-class wicket, and he never took a better one. Wright was fielding at mid-on and had a perfect view. 'Boycott just played across a full length ball on middle and leg. With him out, we thought we might just have a chance.' The sight of Boycott's shattered stumps remains Wright's most vivid memory of the day. 'It was beautiful.'

In Collinge's next over, one took off from short of a length and Miller could only touch it to Anderson in the slips. With the total on 14 Rose was struck on the arm by a very fast delivery from Hadlee, bowling around the wicket at the left-hander, and had to retire hurt. The batsman ducked into a delivery which did not rise as much as he expected.

Collinge's third over produced another body blow for England when Derek Randall was trapped in front for nine. At 3/18, England's target of 137 was looking a long way away. Richard Hadlee, bowling with great pace, now joined the party as Roope was well caught by keeper Lees for no score. The Surrey right-hander looked very uncomfortable in his short stay, and, in the words of journalist Romanos, 'looked almost relieved to get out'. By this time the crowd, which seemed to be getting bigger every minute, chanted, cheered and willed their heroes on to what was looking increasingly like an astonishing victory. John Wright now considered New Zealand 'a real big show'.

The dismissal of Roope brought the dangerous Ian Botham to the crease. Even at this early stage of his career, he was a player capable of mauling an attack. One hour, or even less, of the young Somerset all-rounder could tilt the balance of the game. He adopted the expected approach and began to hit out. Joined by keeper Bob Taylor, Botham struck three boundaries, adding 20 runs in just 25 minutes, but then both fell with the total on 38. Botham was caught by Steve Boock behind square leg, attempting to hook Hadlee, for 19, and from the next ball Taylor was run out by a throw (also from Boock) without scoring. Old played the ball behind square leg and the fieldsman ran back from the bat-pad position, picked up the ball, threw on the turn and hit the single stump he had to aim at.

With the total on 6/38, and 99 still needed, England seemed headed for defeat. Old and Edmonds attempted to stop the rot and added 15 runs for the seventh wicket before two more batsmen fell on the same score. Old was leg before for nine, then Hendrick was caught at the second attempt by John Parker, without scoring. Hadlee claimed both wickets, punching the air with delight.

Edmonds and Willis held out until stumps, with the total a highly unhealthy 8/53 and Rose retired hurt. Even if he could bat on the next day, a miracle of major proportions would be required for England to get anywhere near the target of 137. 'Our boys didn't bat too well', was the understated comment from coach and former Test batsman, Ken Barrington.

It was the end of a day of incredible excitement. In the four hours since lunch 17 wickets had fallen for 101 runs. While it might have been poor batting, it was great entertainment, and the New Zealand fairytale looked like coming true. Collinge and Hadlee had maintained their stamina for two hours in hot conditions to give Basin Reserve its finest cricketing moment. Sir Richard Hadlee commented on the tremendous atmosphere, the crowd coming alive and the siren sounding each time an English wicket fell. 'It was inspired, sensational cricket.'

On the fifth day, with some 2000 people in attendance, it looked as though England's miracle might just occur as misty drizzle and low cloud delayed play for 41 minutes. However, justice would not have been done if the New Zealanders hadn't been given the opportunity to end the match. In 49 minutes they took the last two wickets, bowling England out for 64 and winning by 72 runs. Hadlee took those wickets, giving him 6/26 for the innings and ten for the match. Although he was an established member of the team, a great bowler had now emerged, and in this moment of triumph he remembered his father, former captain Walter Hadlee, who had tried for many years to do what his son had accomplished. 'This win was important to me because my father had played for and captained New Zealand, been an administrator, selector and chairman, and had never seen New Zealand beat England in the nearly 50 years of his involvement. It was a pleasing moment to see a dream of Dad's fulfilled.'

If Richard Hadlee had the figures, then Collinge's 3/35 should not be forgotten. He struck the first three blows, including the vital wicket of Boycott for just one. Those early wickets gave the fielding side confidence and made the modest target assume much larger proportions.

Mark Burgess led New Zealand to the country's first Test win against England. (Brian Bassano)

Writing in *The Cricket Player*, Brian Turner was keen to point out that the New Zealanders should not be over-praised (basically, that one swallow does not make a summer), and that people should not expect Mark Burgess to lead New Zealand out of the wilderness. They were prophetic words, as the period of fruition came later with the leadership of Geoff Howarth and then Jeremy Coney, and the teams they built under them.

Boycott's side came back to win the Second Test and gain a draw in the series, but the Yorkshireman never had another opportunity to captain England. In a career of great personal achievement and pride, that must have been an abiding disappointment.

In his editorial in *The Cricket Player*, Don Cameron said, 'New Zealand won because they were a team, a band of men obviously all aiming in the same direction, and in some way or another all eleven contributed something substantial to the victory'. Cameron was also lavish in his praise for the bowling of Hadlee and Collinge. 'I do not think I have ever seen a bowling attack so carefully controlled, the batsmen put under such consistent pressure, so few loose balls giving the batsmen easy runs with which to break the bowler's grip.'

Captain Mark Burgess, leading the side for the first time, believed the selectors had picked the right players with the right attitude, and the spirit followed from there.

Henry Blofeld, in *The Guardian*, thought that the win was important for New Zealand cricket, lifting it above the challenge of other summer sports, giving it a bigger impact in the country, and making potential sponsors more aware of its commercial possibilities.

Not all were overwhelming in their congratulations. Christopher Martin-Jenkins pointed out that New Zealand had been untouched by World Series Cricket, while England had lost a number of players. Batsman Glenn Turner, who was in England arranging his county benefit, said that wins against the West Indies in 1969 and Australia in 1974 were better because they were against stronger teams. He believed that England should complain only about their own performance. 'After all, 130-odd shouldn't be hard to get, even on a tricky pitch', he said at the time.

Turner may well have been correct, but it was New Zealand's first win over England in 47 years of trying, it was achieved in the most sensational manner, and it was the first step in a process along a path to the country's most successful decade, the 1980s. To Sir Richard Hadlee this was a significant win because it gave the basically amateur New Zealanders the confidence that they could compete with and defeat the best. It was, according to journalist Cameron, 'the end of a long, long trail'. Those points alone will ensure that this day will never be forgotten as long as the Kiwis play cricket.

NEW ZEALAND v ENGLAND

Played at Basin Reserve, Wellington, on 10, 11, 12, 14, 15 February, 1978
Toss: England.

NEW ZEALAND

J. G. Wright	lbw b Botham	55	c Roope b Willis	19
R. W. Anderson	c Taylor b Old	28	lbw b Old	26
G. P. Howarth	c Botham b Old	13	c Edmonds b Willis	21
M. G. Burgess *	b Willis	9	c Boycott b Botham	6
B. E. Congdon	c Taylor b Old	44	c Roope b Willis	0
J. M. Parker	c Rose b Willis	16	c Edmonds b Willis	4
W. K. Lees +	c Taylor b Old	1	lbw b Hendrick	11
R. J. Hadlee	not out	27	c Boycott b Willis	2
D. R. Hadlee	c Taylor b Old	1	c Roope b Botham	2
R. O. Collinge	b Old	1	c Edmonds b Hendrick	6
S. L. Boock	b Botham	4	not out	0
Extras	(B 12, LB 3, W 1, NB 13)	29	(B 2, LB 9, W 2, NB 13)	26
Total		**228**		**123**

Fall: 42, 96, 114, 152, 191, 193, 194, 196, 208, 228.

54, 82, 93, 93, 98, 99, 104, 116, 123, 123.

Bowling

First Innings: Willis 25–7–65–2, Hendrick 17–2–46–0, Old 30–11–54–6, Edmonds 3–1–7–0, Botham 12.6–2–27–2.

Second Innings: Willis 15–2–32–5, Hendrick 10–2–16–2, Old 9–2–32–1, Edmonds 1–0–4–0, Botham 9.3–3–13–2.

ENGLAND

B. C. Rose	c Lees b Collinge	21	not out	5
G. Boycott *	c Congdon b Collinge	77	b Collinge	1
G. Miller	b Boock	24	c Anderson b Collinge	4
R. W. Taylor +	c & b Collinge	8	(7) run out	0
D. W. Randall	c Burgess b R. Hadlee	4	(4) lbw b Collinge	9
G. R. J. Roope	c Lees b R. Hadlee	37	(5) c Lees b R. Hadlee	0
I. T. Botham	c Burgess b R. Hadlee	7	(6) c Boock b R. Hadlee	19
C. M. Old	b R. Hadlee	10	lbw R. Hadlee	9
P. H. Edmonds	lbw b Congdon	4	c Parker b R. Hadlee	11
M. Hendrick	lbw b Congdon	0	c Parker b R. Hadlee	0
R. G. D. Willis	not out	6	c Howarth b R. Hadlee	3
Extras	(LB 4, NB 13)	17	(NB 3)	3
Total		**215**		**64**

Fall: 39, 89, 108, 126, 183, 188, 203, 205, 206, 215.

2, 8, 18, 18, 38, 38, 53, 53, 63, 64.

Bowling

First Innings: R. Hadlee 28–5–74–4, Collinge 18–5–42–3, D. Hadlee 21–5–47–0, Boock 10–5–21–1, Congdon 17.4–11–14–2.

Second Innings: R. Hadlee 13.3–4–26–6, Collinge 13–5–35–3, D. Hadlee 1–1–0–0.

New Zealand won by 72 runs

21

Sarfraz's Miracle

AUSTRALIA v PAKISTAN

Melbourne Cricket Ground
15 March, 1979 – Day Five

THE 1978–79 season had been a particularly disappointing one for the official Australian team. The second year of World Series Cricket had been much more successful, while the fortunes of the inexperienced Board side had plummeted. Mike Brearley's men had administered a 5–1 thumping, and while the Australians had had their moments, they were unable to make anything substantial of them.

Then, as if to add insult to injury, Graham Yallop's team was to play two Tests against Pakistan before the end of the season. The Australians were given little chance as the visitors had included all of their World Series players— the first and only time this occurred in official Tests in Australia. When this had happened in the West Indies the previous season, the Australians had been thrashed. While the full strength Pakistan side was not as powerful as the West Indians, it was generally accepted that they would be too good for what was really a third Australian eleven.

Vice-captain Kim Hughes conceded that relationships between the two sides were not that good, although the young Australians were thrilled to be playing against the best and eager to prove they were up to the challenge.

Yallop's team did its very best to be competitive in the first four days of the First Test at Melbourne.

Mushtaq Mohammad won the toss and batted, only to see his strong side dismissed for 196. No batsman managed to reach 40, as Rodney Hogg and Alan Hurst continued their fine form of the summer with 4/49 and 3/55 respectively.

The Australian batting, as it had all summer, failed to take advantage of the situation, collapsing for just 168. Sri Lankan-born Victorian batsman Dav Whatmore made 43. Imran Khan (4/26), Sarfraz Nawaz (2/39) and leg spinner Wasim Raja (2/23) did the damage.

Led by 108 from opening batsman Majid Khan, Pakistan did much better in the second innings, reaching 9/353 before Mushtaq declared. Zaheer Abbas (59) and Asif Iqbal (44) also made some runs. Hogg (3/75) and Hurst (3/115) again carried the attack, and a young man named Allan Border took 2/35 with his left arm spinners.

Mushtaq's declaration left Australia a target of 382 to win. There was nothing to suggest that they would get even remotely close. Like Pakistan, they made a much better fist of things second time around, and reached 2/117 at stumps. Those dismissed were openers Dav Whatmore for 15 and Andrew Hilditch for a fine 62. Border was 25 not out and captain Yallop 3 not out at stumps. So Australia needed 265 on the last day with eight wickets in hand. The belief remained that Pakistan would be comfortable winners.

Matters turned more in Pakistan's favour early on the final day, when after the addition of eleven runs, Yallop was run out for eight. He pushed a delivery from Imran behind square leg and called for a single. When he saw Asif Iqbal getting to the ball he changed the call. However, Border had failed to hear, and so Yallop took off in a vain attempt to make his ground. He got about half-way. The Australians had suffered from run outs all season, and this was another crucial one. The captain had been his side's most successful batsman in the recent Ashes series, and his loss was a cruel blow.

The new player was the blond-haired West Australian Kim Hughes. A player of great talent, Hughes was a frustrating mixture. He could tear apart any bowler in the world, but he could also lose his wicket when seemingly in total control. On his day, however, there were few better sights in cricket.

Allan Border hits Imran Khan to square leg for four during the left-hander's maiden Test century. *(The Age)*

Left: Sarfraz Nawaz, whose 9/86 turned certain defeat into a miracle win. (Brian Bassano)
Right: The Pakistanis celebrate as Sarfraz claims another wicket. (Ken Piesse)

This day, he was immediately in form, and joined Border in an excellent partnership of 177. It was a stand which featured some good running between the wickets—something of a rarity for the Australians in this summer—and effective treatment of any loose bowling. Border reached his maiden Test century off the last ball before tea, and Hughes had helped him keep the score moving. Imran and Sarfraz did most of the bowling, but although they did a solid job they could not make the breakthrough. As the score mounted an Australian victory started to seem a possibility.

According to Hughes the pitch was a difficult one to bat on, but not impossible. 'It was hard for a new batsman coming in. However, once you became settled you could score runs.'

At the start of the last session 98 runs were needed, and by 4.30 on that last afternoon the score stood at 3/305. Only 77 runs were required with seven wickets in hand, and it was now the Pakistanis who were looking defeat in the face as 30 minutes plus 15 overs still remained. Enter Sarfraz to produce the required miracle. Sarfraz was a tall, well-built right arm fast-medium bowler with a stiff–backed approach to the wicket. He was an extremely combative character, and his never-say-die attitude was just what was required. He had bowled well thoughout the game, and now he secured the vital wicket, bowling Border for 105, made in 373 minutes. The left-hander tried to hit a delivery to the leg side and succeeded only in playing the ball onto his leg stump.

Sarfraz leads his jubilant team-mates from the field. (Ken Piesse)

As Hughes watched from the other end, Sarfraz produced an amazing transformation. 'The ball suddenly started swinging "Irish"—the first time I'd come across this. I couldn't believe how much and how late it was swinging.'

Graeme Wood came in at number six. He had dropped down the order as a result of an injured wrist (sustained in a collision with his batting partner Hilditch in the first innings), which had caused him to retire hurt. It was impossible to tell whether the injury would trouble his batting as he attempted to cut his first delivery from Sarfraz and edged it to keeper Wasim Bari. It was a ball he could well have left alone.

Now 5/305, the pressure was back on the inexperienced Australians, as Test debutant South Australian Peter Sleep walked out to bat. The hat-trick was avoided, but with the fourth ball of his next over Sarfraz bowled Sleep for no score.

Australia's chances now hinged on the ability of Kim Hughes to take control of the situation. This he attempted to do, but succeeded only in hitting a catch to Mohsin Khan at mid-off. It looked like the shot of a frustrated man. Hughes's 84 had been an excellent innings, but his dismissal left Australia 7/308, and it was hard to see where the runs would come from now. In his book *Lambs to the Slaughter*, Yallop described this wicket as the end of any chance of victory, calling the shot an indiscreet one.

It was even harder one run and two balls later when Sarfraz bowled Wayne Clark with one which kept a little low. Another run and Hogg was struck on the pads by Sarfraz. Umpire Harvey pondered the screaming appeal for some time before raising his finger to send the batsman on his way.

Last man Alan Hurst was nobody's idea of a batsman. He survived just two balls before edging a Sarfraz delivery low towards the slips. Realising it would not carry, Wasim Bari dived across and took a magnificent catch to complete one of the game's most amazing comebacks. It was the perfect end to Pakistan's 100th Test. Keeper Kevin Wright was left one not out, having watched most of the carnage from the other end.

Australian captain Graham Yallop was shattered by his team's collapse. It was Yallop's last Test as captain. (Doug Crampton)

Sarfraz had taken a phenomenal seven wickets in 33 deliveries for just one run. His final analysis of 9/86 was, at the time, the fifth best in all Tests. Leg spinner Abdul Qadir with 9/56 against England at Lahore in 1987–88 is still the only Pakistani to have improved on Sarfraz's figures. It was an extraordinary performance. Mushtaq Mohammad called it his country's finest performance in Australia. He confessed that he believed the game to have been lost when the players left the field at tea. 'After the break we were just trying to contain Border and Hughes', he said later.

The Australians were left to ponder just how they had managed to let the match slip from their grasp. 'Shocked', was Yallop's description. He felt that throughout the summer the Australians showed a lack of experience in stopping a collapse. It had cost them dearly in the Ashes series, and this was another, if more spectacular, example. Hughes also pointed out what the lack of experience meant to a young side. 'We had no one to learn from, no one to talk us through. We were in a winning situation and we didn't know how to finish it off.'

The Australians did, however, have the satisfaction of winning the Second Test in Perth and drawing the series—a tremendous result considering the relative strengths and experience of the two sides. This was no comfort to Yallop, who was out with a torn calf muscle. Kim Hughes led the side, and although Yallop returned to play some fine innings in Test cricket, he never again led his country.

Even the loss in Perth, however, could not detract from Sarfraz's miracle at Melbourne. The big Pakistani pace man continued to play for his country until 1984. In 55 Tests he took 177 wickets at 32.75, and as a useful tailender scored 1045 runs at 17.71. An innings of 90 was the highest of his four fifties and he took 26 catches. Melbourne 1979 was indeed his finest hour, when in the space of a few balls, he turned a game and won a match which, by all rights, should have been lost.

AUSTRALIA v PAKISTAN

Played at Melbourne Cricket Ground, on 10, 11, 12, 14, 15 March, 1979.
Toss: Australia.

PAKISTAN

Majid Khan	c Wright b Hogg	1	b Border	108
Mohsin Khan	c Hilditch b Hogg	14	c & b Hogg	14
Zaheer Abbas	b Hogg	11	b Hogg	59
Javed Miandad	b Hogg	19	c Wright b Border	16
Asif Iqbal	c Wright b Clark	9	lbw b Hogg	44
Mushtaq Mohammad *	c Wright b Hurst	36	c sub (J.Higgs) b Sleep	28
Wasim Raja	b Hurst	13	c Wright b Hurst	28
Imran Khan	c Wright b Hurst	33	c Clark b Hurst	28
Sarfraz Nawaz	c Wright b Sleep	35	lbw b Hurst	1
Wasim Bari +	run out	0	not out	8
Sikander Bakht	not out	5		
Extras	(B 2, LB 7, W 1, NB 10)	20	(B 4, LB 6, NB 9)	19
Total		**196**		**9/353**

Fall: 2, 22, 28, 40, 83, 99, 122, 173, 177, 196.

30, 165, 204, 209, 261, 299, 330, 332, 353.

Bowling
First Innings: Hogg 17–4–49–4, Hurst 20–4–55–3, Clark 17–4–56–1, Sleep 7.7–2–16–1.
Second Innings: Hogg 19–2–75–3, Hurst 19.5–1–115–3, Clark 21–6–47–0, Sleep 8–0–62–1, Border 14–5–35–2.

AUSTRALIA

G. M. Wood	not out	5	(6) c Bari b Sarfraz	0
A. M. J. Hilditch	c Miandad b Imran	3	b Sarfraz	62
A. R. Border	b Imran	20	b Sarfraz	105
G. N. Yallop *	b Imran	25	run out	8
K. J. Hughes	run out	19	c Mohsin b Sarfraz	84
D. F. Whatmore	lbw b Sarfraz	43	(1) b Sarfraz	15
P. R. Sleep	c Bari b Imran	10	b Sarfraz	0
K. J. Wright +	c Imran b Raja	9	not out	1
W. M. Clark	c Mushtaq b Raja	9	b Sarfraz	0
R. M. Hogg	run out	9	lbw b Sarfraz	0
A. G. Hurst	c & b Sarfraz	0	c Bari b Sarfraz	0
Extras	(B 1, LB 5, W 2, NB 8)	16	(B 13, LB 13, NB 9)	35
Total		**168**		**310**

Fall: 11, 53, 63, 97, 109, 140, 152, 167, 167, 168.

49, 109, 128, 305, 305, 306, 308, 309, 310, 310.

Bowling
First Innings: Imran 18–8–26–4, Sarfraz 21.6–6–39–2, Sikander 10–1–29–0, Mushtaq 7–0–35–0, Wasim Raja 5–0–23–2.
Second Innings: Imran 27–9–73–0, Sarfraz 35.4–7–86–9, Sikander 7–0–29–0, Mushtaq 11–0–42–0, Wasim Raja 3–0–11–0, Majid 9–1–34–0.

Pakistan won by 71 runs

22

500 to 1

Headingley, Leeds
21 July, 1981 – Day Five

IF EVER THE term 'miracle win' could be applied to a game of cricket, this was the one. At Headingley, Leeds, in the Third Test of the 1981 series, England were so far gone that bookmakers were offering 500 to one on them winning the game. Coming back almost from beyond the grave, they confounded the critics, threw all logic out the door, and perhaps even suprised themselves.

Until this game 1981 had been a disappointing year for England. Under new captain Ian Botham, they had been easily defeated on tour in the West Indies, and had performed little better in the early part of the series at home against Australia. They had lost the First Test by four wickets, and managed to salvage a draw in the second. Their performances had been uninspiring, and worse than that, Botham, the star player—the great all-rounder— seemed to have lost form completely. In the Second Test at Lord's, he had been dismissed for a pair. The situation drove him to resign the captaincy, apparently shortly before he was to be sacked, if other sources are to be believed.

How could England resurrect itself and turn the series around? First the selectors made the decision to return Mike Brearley to the captaincy. The Middlesex batsman had created a reputation as one of his country's great leaders. His understanding of tactics and his players stood him in good stead as he led the side successfully through the period of World Series Cricket.

Although Australians respected Brearley for those skills, they really didn't think much of him as a cricketer. To them, his batting was not up to Test standard, and his wins as skipper had come against teams weakened by World Series Cricket. He had never led a team against the West Indies in a Test, and his only series against a full strength Australian side, in 1979–80, had resulted in a 3–0 loss. There seemed little to fear. In addition to Brearley, the selectors brought in fast medium-bowler Chris Old, and left out spinner John Emburey and batsman Bob Woolmer.

Australia played a team unchanged from the side which performed well at Lord's.

In the early stages there seemed little reason to think that anything England could do would alter the situation. Kim Hughes, the Australian skipper, won the toss and decided to bat. His side took the advantage and scored 401. Opener John Dyson made 102, Hughes 89 and Graham Yallop 58. The only bright spot for England was the return to form of Botham the bowler. He captured 6/95.

Faced with chasing a huge score, England's batting capitulated for 174. Dennis Lillee (4/49), Terry Alderman (3/59) and Geoff Lawson (3/32) were simply too good. Again Botham showed a glimmer of form, top scoring with 50.

Presented with a huge first innings lead, Hughes enforced the follow-on, hoping for a similar burst from his bowlers. If they could produce it, the series could well be all over. Once again, they looked like doing just that, as England sunk rapidly to 7/135. It was about this time that the bookmakers put the 500–1 odds on the board. At that point it even seemed a generous gesture. This was the moment a couple of Australians decided that they would have a little piece of those incredible odds.

Enter Ian Botham to play one of the great Test innings. He slaughtered the bowling, reaching 100 in just 87 balls, and at stumps had taken his score to 145. In doing so he became only the second player after Australian Jack Gregory to score a century and take five wickets in an Ashes Test. It was the fourth time the Somerset all-rounder had completed the feat in Tests. Botham was ably supported by fast bowlers Graham Dilley and Chris Old, who made 56 and 29 respectively. At stumps on the fourth day England was 9/351, a slender lead—not enough to win, but some pride regained. If Brearley did nothing else, his rejuvenation of Botham had paid the cost of his recall.

Hughes was criticised in some circles for his overuse of Alderman and Lillee and for ignoring the left arm spin of Ray Bright. With the side just a wicket away from certain victory, and the feeling that Botham's luck must run out, Hughes may have been justified in staying with his two strike bowlers. The Australian captain was also critical of the make-up of his side. 'I would have liked opening batsman Bruce Laird and off spinner Bruce Yardley in the touring party, but I had no say in selection.' Hughes is convinced that Yardley would have given Botham something to think about, and that the gritty Laird would have resisted the English bowling with far more success than some of the players who were selected.

When play resumed on the final day, England's supporters were no doubt hoping that Willis might hang around while Botham slogged another 50 or so, giving the bowlers some sort of score to defend. For Australia, a quick end, and the fewer runs to chase the better.

After a single to Willis and a boundary to Botham, Alderman had the former caught by Border to end the innings at 356. The two fast bowlers had persevered in the face of Botham's incredible batting, Alderman capturing 6/135 and Lillee 3/94.

The early end to England's innings meant that Australia had most of the day to score 130 to win the game and take a 2–0 lead in the series.

Brearley was not entirely dismayed. In his book of the series, *Phoenix from the Ashes*, he repeated his words to his team, 'More aggression, more adrenalin, more encouragement for the bowlers. The Australians will be nervous now'.

Dyson and Graeme Wood opened the batting to the bowling of Botham and Dilley. Most were surprised that Brearley did not use Willis, but as the pair had batted so well together he was keen to see if they could repeat their domination. Lightning failed to strike twice and Dilley was removed after two poor overs.

Botham, however, did produce a breakthrough when he had Wood caught behind in his second over for ten. It did not look likely initially, as the left-hander had dispatched the first two deliveries from Botham, a long hop and a half-volley, to the boundary. Australia's 1/13 was gradually improved by Dyson and the new batsman Trevor Chappell.

Willis was brought into the attack from the football stand end, into the breeze, and he appeared to be struggling as he had in the first innings. Half an hour before lunch Brearley produced the masterstroke and switched the fast bowler to the Kirkstall Lane end with the wind at his back. Many may have wondered why the fast bowler didn't begin from that end, but Botham wanted it because he thought it might help swing the ball. When that wasn't really happening the switch was made.

Suddenly, the game changed. Not only was Willis bowling fast, but he was making the ball lift as well, though Australia at 1/48 looked to be heading for victory.

With the score on 56 Willis made one lift alarmingly at Chappell, who could only cock it up into the air for keeper Taylor to take the catch. Two runs later Hughes was well caught at second slip to his left by Botham for no score, and then Yallop could not keep the ball down, stabbing it to Mike Gatting at short leg, who dived forward to take the catch. Another batsman on his way for nought, and Australia 4/58 and looking worried.

Left: Rod Marsh watches anxiously as the ball heads towards Graham Dilley, who took the catch. (Brian Bassano) *Right:* Bob Willis starts to celebrate as Geoff Lawson edges a delivery to keeper Bob Taylor. (Brian Bassano)

Brearley said that a few minutes earlier he was discussing the view that Australia would win the game by four or five wickets. He had been far from optimistic, but now, as they say, things had changed.

Lunch was taken at the fall of Yallop's wicket, and it was a nervous interval for both sides before Willis returned to the attack. It is unlikely that he ever bowled faster, digging the ball in and making it rear at the batsmen. During the interval the England players tried to analyse how the remaining batsmen would play.

Seven runs were added before Old claimed the vital wicket of Allan Border, knocking over his leg stump. With half the side gone for 65—half the runs—an England win was now a possibility. Three runs later this became more distinct when Dyson, on 34, hooked at Willis only to glove the ball to Taylor. This was a crucial wicket, as Dyson had been holding the side together with his solid defence, but had not missed any opportunity to score runs. He was a little unlucky, as he had hooked Willis to the fence in the previous over, but this time he was through the shot too soon.

England hadn't won yet, not while the stocky figure of Rod Marsh was at the crease. The Australian keeper was a strong hitter of the ball, and a few well-timed blows could swing the balance of the game. It was not to be his day, however, as he hooked Willis to fine leg, where Dilley made a difficult and important catch look easy. Willis was warned by the umpire

Bob Willis, whose 8/43 was his greatest performance. (Moss Seigert)

not to bounce the new batsman, Geoff Lawson. He didn't need to. One run later, Lawson edged Wills to Taylor, and Australia, incredibly, was 8/75. This catch was the keeper's 1271st, a world first class record. Willis had taken six wickets in six overs, and Australia had lost 7/19 in 58 minutes.

Ray Bright and Dennis Lillee were better known for their bowling skills, but both could bat to some extent, in particular Bright, who had a first-class century to his credit. The pair decided that there was nothing to be gained by mere survival, and that they would play some shots. They would either die fighting, or score runs and put the pressure back on England.

Their tactic looked like working as the pair added 35 in four overs. Lillee played some unusual strokes, stepping back and lifting Willis over the slips, and flicking him away on the leg side. It was, however, too good to last. Willis fired in another fast, short ball at Lillee, who went for the hook. He mistimed the stroke and the ball went high into the air. Gatting had a lot of ground to cover running in from mid-on, but he got there and—more importantly—held on to the ball. There was relief at this dismissal, as the aggressive tactics of the batsmen had reduced the target to 20. Now there was just Terry Alderman to remove.

Brearley brought Botham back in place of Old, no doubt hoping that it would be a fitting end if the all-rounder could take the last wicket. He nearly did. Alderman edged a delivery to Old at third slip, who dropped it.

The miss was not crucial. In the next over Willis yorked Bright for 19 and the match was won by 18 runs. Willis ran from the ground with 8/43 beside his name—the bowling performance of his life. Writing in *The Times*, John Woodcock was glowing in his praise of Willis's courage and determination. He had flown home injured from the West Indies a few months previously, and there were doubts that he would play for England again. In fact there was some thought that he would be omitted from the side for this game, because of his indifferent recent performances.

Ray Bright is bowled by Willis and England has won. (Brian Bassano)

When remembering this game, most attention focuses on Botham's century, and certainly it gave the side heart and a score to bowl at. But in spite of his heroics Australia still should have made the runs. It was Willis, charging in from the Kirkstall Lane end, who made the win a reality.

England had won a famous victory. Brearley's team was only the second side to follow on in a Test and win. They had previously accomplished the feat way back in 1894–95 under the captaincy of A. E. Stoddart.

Botham had risen like Lazarus and Brearley had returned like a prophet to breathe life into English cricket and the series. For Australia, this was an unmitigated disaster. How could such a game have been lost? Kim Hughes was gracious in defeat, but the hurt was there.

In a recent interview with the author Hughes explained Headingley as he saw it. 'There are wickets where luck plays a part. We batted with a lot of luck in the first innings. Then we played and missed; this time we nicked them. Botham rode his luck and we couldn't get him out. It was a wicket that you were never in on, no matter how many you scored. In the first innings they missed catches—even Botham and Gower dropped them—but in the second they held everything. I'd seen Bob Willis bowl just as well at other times and not take nearly as many wickets.'

The win had boosted England to such an extent that it won the next two games and drew the last to win the series 3–1. Those other victories contained more heroics from Botham. In the next Test Australia was 3/96; Botham took 5/1 in 28 balls and England won by 29 runs. It was another shattering defeat. At Old Trafford the all-rounder scored a century off just 86 balls and hit six sixes to set up another win. The last game was drawn, but the series and the efforts of Botham, Willis and Brearley were consigned to cricket legend. 'Those two (Botham and Willis) made Brearley look like the Messiah', was Hughes' comment.

For Australia, this Headingley game also became part of legend, and many believed its effects were long-lasting and are still felt to this day. In its report on the game, *The Times* said that Allan Border was seen with his head buried in his hands after his dismissal. How much Headingley 1981 remained in his mind will never be known, but from that day, every time the Australians struggled in pursuit of a small target, the spectre of Headingley seemed to be looking over their shoulders. One of Border's better memories must have been to win there at the start of the successful 1989 Ashes campaign.

ENGLAND v AUSTRALIA

Played at Headingley, Leeds, on 16, 17, 18, 20, 21 July, 1981.
Toss: Australia.

AUSTRALIA

J. Dyson	b Dilley	102	c Taylor b Willis	34
G. M. Wood	lbw b Botham	34	c Taylor b Botham	10
T. M. Chappell	c Taylor b Willey	27	c Taylor b Willis	8
K. J. Hughes *	c & b Botham	89	c Botham b Willis	0
R. J. Bright	b Dilley	7	(8) b Willis	19
G. N. Yallop	c Taylor b Botham	58	(5) c Gatting b Willis	0
A. R. Border	lbw b Botham	8	(6) b Old	0
R. W. Marsh +	b Botham	28	(7) c Dilley b Willis	4
G. F. Lawson	c Taylor b Botham	13	c Taylor b Willis	1
D. K. Lillee	not out	3	c Gatting b Willis	17
T. M. Alderman	not out	0	not out	0
Extras	(B 4, LB 13, W 3, NB 12)	32	(LB 3, W 1, NB 14)	18
Total		**9/401**		**111**

Fall: 55, 149, 196, 220, 332, 354,357, 396, 401.

13, 56, 58, 58, 65, 68, 74, 75, 110, 111.

Bowling

First Innings: Willis 30–8–72–0, Old 43–14–91–0, Dilley 27–4–78–2, Botham 39.2–11–95–6, Willey 13–2–31–1, Boycott 3–2–2–0.

Second Innings: Botham 7–3–14–1, Dilley 2–0–11–0, Willis 15.1–3–43–8, Old 9–1–21–1, Willey 3–1–4–0.

ENGLAND

G. A. Gooch	lbw b Alderman	2	c Alderman b Lillee	0
G. Boycott	b Lawson	12	lbw b Alderman	46
J. M. Brearley *	c Marsh b Alderman	10	c Alderman b Lillee	14
D. I. Gower	c Marsh b Lawson	24	c Border b Alderman	9
M. W. Gatting	lbw b Lillee	15	lbw b Alderman	1
P. Willey	b Lawson	8	c Dyson b Lillee	33
I. T. Botham	c Marsh b Lillee	50	not out	149
R. W. Taylor +	c Marsh b Lillee	5	c Bright b Alderman	1
G. R. Dilley	c & b Lillee	13	b Alderman	56
C. M. Old	c Border b Alderman	0	b Lawson	29
R. G. D. Willis	not out	1	c Border b Alderman	2
Extras	(B 6, LB 11, W 6, NB 11)	34	(B 5, LB 3, W 3, NB 5)	16
Total		**174**		**356**

Fall: 12, 40, 42, 84, 87, 112, 148, 166, 167, 174.

0, 18, 37, 41, 105, 133, 135, 252, 319, 356.

Bowling

First Innings: Lillee 18.5–7–49–4, Alderman 19–4–59–3, Lawson 13–3–32–3.

Second Innings: Lillee 25–6–94–3, Alderman 35.3–6–135–6, Lawson 23–4–96–1, Bright 4–0–15–0.

England won by 18 runs

23

Kim and Dennis

Melbourne Cricket Ground
26 December, 1981 – Day One

THE AUSTRALIANS had returned from the 1981 tour of England in a rather downcast frame of mind. The recall of Mike Brearley to lead the England team had coincided with an astonishing return to form of Ian Botham, and Kim Hughes's team had lost a series which they seemed certain to win.

The 1981–82 summer would offer little respite, with the visit of the all-powerful West Indians, preceded by three Tests against the strong Pakistani side. The Australians had comfortably won the first two of these games, but lost the final one by an innings. This last game was played at the Melbourne Cricket Ground, and the pitch there had been a source of some criticism. The First Test against the West Indies would be played on this ground, starting on Boxing Day.

For the locals, there were some differences from the 1981 tour. Greg Chappell had returned to the captaincy, but his batting had lacked consistency. Nevertheless, his mere presence was a positive influence on the team. The other plus was the emergence of Bruce Yardley as a top class off spinner, giving the attack the variety it lacked in England.

In spite of this, the West Indian opposition was expected to dominate. The batting of Des Haynes, Viv Richards, captain Clive Lloyd and Larry Gomes was a brilliant mixture of solidity and aggression, while to back them up was an awesome quartet of fast bowlers. Michael Holding, Andy

Roberts, Colin Croft and Joel Garner were universally accepted as the strongest of the West Indies pace batteries because each offered such a different threat.

Holding was the fastest, gliding to the wicket with the grace of an athlete, but lightning fast—'Whispering Death' was an appropriate nickname. Roberts was the most experienced, a bowler capable of pace and movement with two bouncers: the slower sucker ball and the quicker killer blow. Croft was a giant of a man, who bowled the ball from very wide on the return crease, angling in at the batsman and repeatedly lifting the ball into the rib cage area. He gave the impression that he didn't mind hitting the batsman either. Garner was even taller than Croft. With the ball being delivered from such a great height the batsman had trouble picking up the length of the delivery. The bouncer and particularly the yorker were his weapons. All were different, all were lethally fast. There was no respite.

Dennis Lillee was in no doubt about the quality of the quartet. 'This was the best West Indies pace attack I ever played against. They all offered a different threat.' Australian batsman Kim Hughes thought Croft was the most awkward of the four, while Roberts was the closest to Lillee with his mean attitude towards batsmen.

When the sides inspected the pitch for the opening Test there was a feeling that runs would be at a premium, and that conditions would deteriorate as the game progressed. Chappell won the toss and decided to bat, no doubt hoping that things would be at their best on the first day or so. This had been the case in the recent game against Pakistan, when the toss proved decisive.

Bruce Laird and Graeme Wood opened the batting to the bowling of Holding and Roberts, but sensations were not far away. Laird, a tough little West Australian, was a fine player of fast bowling and a man whose wicket the West Indians prized. He had made all four of Australia's runs when he edged a ball from Holding to keeper David Murray.

Things were immediately made worse as Chappell was caught first ball by Murray, his fourth consecutive duck in international cricket. It was a fast, lifting delivery moving away from the batsman. In going across to cover the movement, Chappell could only edge the ball to the keeper, putting Holding on a hat-trick. This was avoided by Allan Border, but only just, as he allowed a ball to lift dangerously over his off stump.

Four runs later Wood went to the first ball of Roberts's sixth over, edging another catch to Murray. Australia was in deep trouble at 3/8.

Border had been badly out of form this summer, and his innings on this day was typical of that. He struggled for just over an hour in making four runs, and lost his wicket when he pushed a slower full toss back to the bowler Holding.

With the total 4/26, Kim Hughes, now partnered by the inexperienced Dirk Wellham, decided that attack was the only way to go. This admirable

Left: Keeper David Murray, who took five catches in Australia's first innings. (Brian Bassano)
Right: Kim Hughes, who regards this innings as the best he ever played. (Moss Seigert)

tactic almost backfired, as he was dropped on more than one occasion, and with his score on 13 must have been close to lbw to Garner. Still, the pair survived and went to lunch with the total on 4/44. Not good, but better than it had been, and Hughes was beginning to settle down after his early recklessness.

With 15 runs added after the break, Hughes lost Wellham, caught by substitute fieldsman Gus Logie off Croft for 17. As only keeper Rod Marsh and the bowlers remained, the West Indians must have been hoping to end the innings for under a hundred. However, Marsh proved a valuable ally, scoring 21 in a partnership of 56 for the sixth wicket, before being caught by Richards in the slips off Garner.

Although Bruce Yardley was more highly regarded for his off spin bowling, he was quite a capable lower order batsman. He favoured aggression, and could destroy a bowling attack in a short space of time. On this day, he decided that his natural game was still the best option. In 17 balls, he hit 21 runs, including two boundaries, and 34 runs came in just 35 minutes. Unfortunately, it couldn't last, as Garner fired one through Yardley's defence and into his stumps. A scoreline of 7/149 was far from healthy, but it was infinitely better than it looked like being earlier in the day. If the remaining batsman could just hold on and let Hughes continue on his way, then a total of over 200 was a possibility. The blond West Australian had found better form in the afternoon session, hitting 50 of the 101 runs made.

The quick dismissals of Lillee for one and Geoff Lawson for two appeared to signal the imminent end of the Australian innings. Holding claimed them both, the first caught by Gomes and the second bowled, to give him five for the innings. Australia, 9/155, had only Terry Alderman to partner Hughes (71) towards his century. With Alderman's limited batting skills, it seemed unlikely that he would get anywhere near it. Lloyd made the task more difficult by setting ultra-defensive fields when Hughes was on strike.

The Australian vice-captain, battered and bruised by the pace barrage, his hands aching from the constant jarring, decided to make

Kim Hughes hooks the ball to the boundary. (*The Age*)

one last effort. He tore into the bowling, particularly that of Garner, traditionally the hardest of the quartet to score from. Anything within reach went, mostly through point and extra cover. In the latter stages of this innings he had been missed at 66 and 76, giving sharp chances off the bowling of Garner, but fortune continued to favour the brave.

Greg Chappell believed Hughes's innings to be worth 200 in the conditions. Writing in *Wisden Cricket Monthly* Peter McFarline thought it was 'one of the finest batting performances by an Australian in international cricket'. This day, like the whole match, was 'a privilege to watch'.

Alderman held on, even on driving Croft to the boundary. But this brought a quick retaliation: a short ball which struck the batsman on the arm. Garner hit Alderman on the helmet when he ducked into an attempted bouncer which did not lift as much as the batsman thought it would. Most considered the assault on the Australian number eleven to be intimidatory, but the umpires issued no warnings.

Hughes moved into the nineties, occasionally taking one hand off the bat in dealing with some of the short-pitched bowling. He cut Garner for two, then square drove him through point to the fence to reach his century. The ovation from the crowd of 39,046 was tremendous. A couple of fieldsmen said, 'Well played', the only comment Hughes can remember from the opposition throughout his innings.

Alderman, his job done, was caught by Murray off Croft for ten, and the innings ended at 198. It was the keeper's fifth catch of the innings. Hughes remained 100 not out. He had defied the most fearsome pace attack the game had ever seen for 266 minutes and struck eleven fours. Dennis Lillee would not rate as Kim Hughes's number one admirer, but he was lavish in his praise of this innings. 'It was a dangerous wicket and he decided to take them on—get as many as possible as quickly as possible. In the circumstances it was a great innings, I think the best Hughes ever played, especially considering the state of the game and the quality of the opposition.' Hughes himself rates this as the best innings he ever played.

In an interview with the author the Australian batsman described the difficulties of the Melbourne pitch. 'It was uneven with a little grass and quite moist. For the first session it was a minefield with the ball holding and jumping, then later it flattened out a bit before keeping very low later in the game. You couldn't duck in case one ran along the deck. They had you buggered, so I just decided to play every shot I could. Sooner or later they would get you. I was going to try to get a few before they did.'

Hughes comments about the pace attack are also interesting. 'Three or four out of every six would be at your chest or head. It wasn't pleasant. They would just wear you down. It was worse than Bodyline because they were so different in size and because there were four of them they never got tired. When they were on top it was difficult to come in and get in the groove. There was always a screaming bouncer and you never got an easy start. A side was always prone to collapse.'

While lauding Hughes, a number of critics were unimpressed by the efforts of the other Australian batsmen. Brian Mossop in the *Sun-Herald* wrote, 'In the light of the day's events, Hughes' century stood out like a beacon. He was under pressure from the moment he went in, but he showed maturity and a remarkable calm in the crisis... It was an innings to savour amid the feeble attempts by the rest of the team to come to terms with the West Indian pace'.

The other star performer was Holding, who finished with 5/45. Garner and Croft picked up two wickets each, and Roberts took the other one.

After being 3/8 and then 4/26, the recovery to make 198 was a boost to the Australians. In the dressing room, the bowlers were fired up by Hughes's innings, and were keen to get at the batsmen in the hope of picking up a wicket or two in the 35 minutes remaining until stumps.

What occurred must have exceeded their wildest dreams. Alderman made the break, having opener Faoud Bacchus caught at third slip by Wood for one in his first over. The West Indies were 1/3 and nightwatchman Croft came in to partner Desmond Haynes.

Then enter Lillee. Bowling as fast as he had all summer, he had Haynes caught by Border at second slip for one, then trapped Croft in front for no score. At 3/6 the West Indies were exactly where Australia had been nearly six hours earlier.

The key figure now was Viv Richards. A man capable of destroying any attack, the Australians had to get him quickly. The batsman did look a little nervous, attempting and missing two hook shots, one of which went dangerously close to his gloves. But Lillee was not to be denied. With the final ball of the day he captured the vital wicket of Richards. The batsman aimed a drive at one which came in from outside the off stump, and took an inside edge before hitting the wicket. Richards was out for two, and the West Indies were 4/10 at stumps. Lillee had taken 3/3 in 11 balls, and he was particularly delighted with the wicket of Richards. 'I'd like to say that I clean bowled Viv, but he did

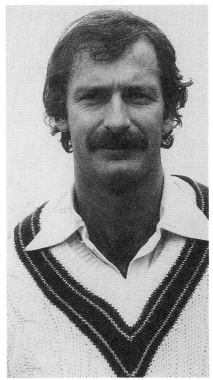

Lillee, whose devastating spell had the West Indies 4/10 at stumps. (Doug Crampton)

get an inside edge. When it happened the crowd erupted. It was unbelievable. We had nothing to lose and hoped we could get one or two wickets before stumps. We didn't consider four, but fortune went our way. It set us up for the rest of the match.'

Kim Hughes remembers 40,000 hands going up as Richards was dismissed and Lillee came screaming down the pitch. 'It was sensational; something only great bowlers can create.'

Hughes's positive tactics drew comparison with the assault by Stan McCabe on Bodyline nearly 50 years earlier, but even that great player might have struggled against these bowlers on this pitch. Hughes's comments on this subject are recorded above.

With the day ending on such a dramatic note, the crowd went crazy. They stood, cheered, yelled and screamed, and the chant of 'Lillee, Lillee, Lillee' followed the Australians into the pavilion. The reaction of the crowd took some time in wearing off. Lillee remembers, 'About 25 minutes after play ended I was going upstairs, and I looked out and there were still thousands of people sitting there. They just couldn't believe it'.

Lillee was right in saying that it did set Australia up for the rest of the game. The West Indies recovered somewhat to score 201, thanks to Gomes (55),

Dennis Lillee screams his delight as Viv Richards is bowled off the last ball of a dramatic day. West Indies' captain Clive Lloyd looks on. (Ken Piesse)

newcomer Jeff Dujon (41) and Murray (32). Lillee continued his dynamic form, capturing his Test best 7/83; the wicket of Gomes, caught at slip by Chappell, gave the great fast bowler the then record number of Test wickets. 'Was it that game?' asked Lillee when questioned, 'I wouldn't have remembered that'. Records were not imprinted on the memory as much as the sight of seeing Richards's stumps shattered.

The Australians fought hard in their second innings to reach 223. Border returned to form with 66, Laird made 64 and Wood 46. Holding was again the destroyer with 6/62, and Garner captured 3/37.

Set 220 to win, Alderman took two wickets in his first over, including Richards for nought, and the West Indies never recovered. They were dismissed for 161 to give Australia a 58 run win. Only Dujon with 43 made any substantial contribution with the bat. Yardley (4/38) and Lillee (3/44) finished what Alderman had started.

The Second Test was drawn, but the West Indies won the third to draw the series. The Australians fought to the bitter end, but the aggression of Lloyd and a little luck took the visitors home by five wickets.

Although a drawn series was the result, the memory will remain of this dazzling Boxing Day in Melbourne, when two vastly different players set up a win against all the odds. Hughes had played the innings of his life, an amazing display touched by genius, and Lillee had proved yet again that he was the greatest of fast bowlers—a man capable of turning a game in the space of a few deliveries.

Kim Hughes was adamant that this was the greatest day's cricket he ever took part in. 'We beat them in conditions which suited them. It was a day people will remember for the rest of their lives, and such things come along very rarely.'

The Boxing Day of a Melbourne Test is a special event. It has an atmosphere all of its own, and it has seen some great days of cricket, but was any one day ever better than this?

AUSTRALIA v WEST INDIES

Played at Melbourne Cricket Ground, on 26, 27, 28, 29, 30 December, 1981.
Toss: Australia.

AUSTRALIA

Batsman	First Innings		Second Innings	
B. M. Laird	c Murray b Holding	4	lbw b Croft	64
G. M. Wood	c Murray b Roberts	3	c Murray b Garner	46
G. S. Chappell *	c Murray b Holding	0	c Murray b Garner	6
A. R. Border	c Murray b Holding	4	b Holding	66
K. J. Hughes	not out	100	b Holding	8
D. M. Wellham	c sub (A.Logie) b Croft	17	lbw b Holding	2
R. W. Marsh +	c Richards b Garner	21	c Murray b Holding	2
B. Yardley	b Garner	21	b Garner	13
D. K. Lillee	c Gomes b Holding	1	c Murray b Holding	0
G. F. Lawson	b Holding	2	not out	0
T. M. Alderman	c Murray b Croft	10	b Holding	1
Extras	(B 1, LB 6, NB 8)	15	(B 5, LB 4, W 1, NB 4)	14
Total		**198**		**223**

Fall: 4, 4, 8, 26, 59, 115, 149, 153, 155, 198.

82, 106, 139, 184, 190, 199, 215, 218, 220, 222.

Bowling

First Innings: Holding 17–3–45–5, Roberts 15–6–40–1, Garner 20–6–59–2, Croft 16.1–3–39–2.
Second Innings: Holding 21.3–5–62–6, Roberts 18–4–31–0, Garner 18–5–37–3, Croft 20–2–61–1, Richards 5–0–17–0.

WEST INDIES

Batsman	First Innings		Second Innings	
D. L. Haynes	c Border b Lillee	1	c Lillee b Yardley	28
S. F. A. F. Bacchus	c Wood b Alderman	1	lbw b Alderman	0
C. E. H. Croft	lbw b Lillee	0	(11) not out	0
I. V. A. Richards	b Lillee	2	(3) b Alderman	0
C. H. Lloyd *	c Alderman b Yardley	29	(4) c Border b Lawson	19
H. A. Gomes	c Chappell b Lillee	55	(5) b Yardley	24
P. J. L. Dujon	c Hughes b Lillee	41	(6) c Marsh b Yardley	43
D. A. Murray +	not out	32	(7) c Marsh b Yardley	10
A. M. E. Roberts	c Marsh b Lillee	18	(8) lbw b Lillee	10
M. A. Holding	c & b Alderman	2	(9) lbw b Lillee	7
J. Garner	c Laird b Lillee	7	(10) lbw b Lillee	0
Extras	(B 1, LB 3, NB 9)	13	(B 1, LB 10, NB 9)	20
Total		**201**		**161**

Fall: 3, 5, 6, 10, 62, 134, 147, 174, 183, 201.

4, 4, 38, 80, 88, 116, 150, 154, 154, 161.

Bowling

First Innings: Lillee 26.3–3–83–7, Alderman 18–3–54–2, Lawson 9–2–28–0, Chappell 2–2–0–0, Yardley 7–2–23–1.
Second Innings: Lillee 27.3–8–44–3, Alderman 9–3–23–2, Lawson 17–3–36–1, Yardley 21–7–38–4.

Australia won by 58 runs

24

The Lion's First Roar

SRI LANKA v PAKISTAN

Saravanamuttu Stadium, Colombo
11 September, 1985 – Day Five

S RI LANKA'S admission to Test status in 1981, after a ten year struggle, gave the cricketers of this island nation the opportunity to pit their skills against the game's best. Between their initial Test, against England at Colombo in 1981–82, and the visit of a strong Indian side in 1985–86, certain qualities had been noticed about Sri Lankan cricket. The most prominent of these was that the batting far exceeded the bowling in terms of skills and effectiveness.

Players like Sidath Wettimuny, Roy Dias and Ranjan Madugalle impressed watchers with their wristy elegance, while rotund Duleep Mendis could devastate bowlers with his unorthodox technique and powerful hitting. Bowling, however, was a different matter. Asantha de Mel and Ravi Ratnayeke were steady medium pacers, but unlikely to destroy batting line-ups. Leg spinner Somachandra de Silva was a potential matchwinner, but was in the veteran category when Test cricket came along, and played only a couple of seasons before retiring.

It is an adage that in Test cricket bowlers win matches, and until Sri Lanka found some, victories would be difficult to achieve. In spite of this,

Left: Dulip Mendis, Sri Lanka's successful captain. (Doug Crampton) *Right:* Asantha de Mel, the most experienced of the Sri Lankan pace attack. (Doug Crampton)

there had been moments when victory was a possibility, according to Mendis. 'In a game against Pakistan we dropped Javed Miandad and that cost us a chance, and we could nearly have beaten England at Lord's in 1984.'

The country's introduction to Test cricket was also complicated by the decision of a number of their top players, including their first captain Bandula Warnapura, to accept an offer to tour South Africa, earning themselves a ban in the process. The loss of so many meant that pressure was put on second string and younger players before some were ready or capable of dealing with it.

There was every reason to believe that when India arrived for a three Test series in September 1985, they would easily account for the newcomers. The visitors were particularly strong in batting with players like Kris Srikkanth, Sunil Gavaskar, Mohammad Azharuddin, Dilip Vengsarkar and Mohinder Amarnath. To further strengthen the batting were all-rounders Ravi Shastri and Kapil Dev. It was difficult to see how the Sri Lankans were going to bowl them out. This opinion was not shared by captain Mendis, who was confident of winning at least one of the games.

Predicting cricket is a dangerous business, because in the First Test India were bowled out twice and Sri Lanka needed 123 off eleven overs to win. They finished at 4/61 and the game was drawn. The batting had looked good, and the bowling, led by de Mel, young fast-medium bowlers Rumesh Ratnayake and debutant Saliya Ahangama, had given the Indians plenty of trouble. Ratnayake was a particularly interesting character. A right-hand fast-medium bowler with a slinging action who could also swing the ball, he had 'roughed up' the West Indies in a one day game in Australia the previous season, and was a player with some potential. Sri Lanka could move on to the Second Test with some confidence.

Mendis achieved the perfect start by winning the toss and batting, and his team did not let him down. Wicketkeeper and opening batsman Amal Silva made 111, being given six lives, and he was well supported by Dias (95), Madugalle (54) and Mendis (51). Fast-medium Chetan Sharma (5/118) was the most effective bowler, but 385 was an excellent total.

India collapsed to 5/88, but recovered to 244 through Srikkanth (64), Gavaskar (52) and Amarnath (60). The pace bowlers de Mel (2/63), Ratnayake (4/76) and Ahangama (3/59) had once again caused concern among the visiting batsmen.

In a second time and with a good lead of 141, the Sri Lankans went after quick runs, declaring at 3/206 shortly before stumps on the fourth day. Dias (60 not out) and Aravinda de Silva (73) were the top scorers. Faced with getting 348 in 393 minutes Lalchand Rajput and Srikkanth scored 16 of them by stumps. It was certainly a reasonable declaration given the strength of the Indian batting, and skipper Kapil Dev expressed the opinion that his side could win. Sri Lankan pace bowler Asantha de Mel was confident of a victory, 'While the pitch was still good for batting, there was a bit in it for the bowler and we were able to move the ball in the air and off the seam'.

The next day the pair took the score to 39 before de Mel trapped Rajput in front for 12. Two deliveries later Ratnayake accounted for Srikkanth (25) in identical fashion. Two further runs were added before Vengsarkar, on nought, edged a delivery from Ratnayake and Silva took the catch, although there was some thought that it might have flicked his pad, rather than his bat. India had plummeted to 3/41.

Azharuddin and Gavaskar, batting in the middle order instead of opening, combined to reach lunch without further loss. They went on to add 43 before disaster struck again. Both went within nine balls—Gavaskar courtesy of a catch by Silva off Ratnayake for 19 attempting a glance and Azharuddin, aiming a careless hook, to another catch by the keeper, this time off de Mel.

Amarnath and Shastri now attempted to stem the tide, but after adding 14 both fell with the total on 98, the third double blow in the innings. Shastri was out to a wonderful catch at forward short leg by de Silva off Ahangama, and Amarnath gave Silva his fourth catch of the innings when he edged a delivery from Ratnayake. De Mel saw the cheap dismissal of Amarnath as the turning point which put Sri Lanka on the road to recovery.

At 7/98 India looked dead and buried, but Kapil Dev attempted to breathe some life back into the body. Partnered by leg spinner Laxman

Kapil Dev. The Indian all-rounder made a determined bid to stave off defeat with a bold 78. (Doug Crampton)

Sivaramakrishnan, he went on the attack. The pair added 70 in 85 minutes, causing the Sri Lankans to experience some nervous flutters. However, de Mel at last found the edge of Sivaramakrishnan's bat and Silva had his fifth catch of the innings. The leg spinner's 21 had been a useful innings, and if keeper Sadanand Viswanath could do the same, India might still escape. He lasted just three balls before Ahangama had him leg before.

Last man Chetan Sharma was also a useful player, and he defended while Kapil continued to go for his strokes. 'We were struggling a little to get the final wicket', remembers Mendis. But the Sri Lankans would not be denied. In the first over of the final hour, and after adding 29 runs, Kapil, on 78, hit a return catch to Ratnayake, who dived to his right and gleefully took the ball, his fifth wicket, and Sri Lanka's first Test win, by the impressive margin of 149 runs. 'We were able to surprise the Indian batsmen', commented de Mel. Ratnayake (5/49), de Mel (3/64) and Ahangama (2/56) had been too good for the batting once again. Mendis was high in his praise of the bowlers, who had used a pitch which seamed a little to perfection.

For de Mel, and all the other Sri Lankan's, this dismissal remains the day's most vivid memory.

The ecstatic crowd swarmed onto the field and lifted Ratnayake into the air. Chanting and celebrations continued well into the night. The President was present and he declared a national holiday in honour of the win.

At the time Mendis was quoted as saying, 'This is the finest hour of my cricketing career. It is a dream come true'. Reflecting on that some ten years later, he still thinks it is the case, although he puts his innings of 111 and 94 against England at Lord's in 1984 along with it. 'That game was important, too, because it made people in England take us seriously', he said in an interview with the author.

De Mel's assessment of the match is worth reading. 'Winning this match was very important to us. In the past we had come close to winning, but

Rumesh Ratnayake, with 5/49, spearheaded his side to victory.

missed out. This was a major breakthrough and all our supporters were very happy.'

Kapil Dev congratulated the Sri Lankans, saying that they had outplayed his side. He was particularly disappointed with the Indian fielding, which had seven catches dropped on the first day. The visitors were very distressed at losing this game and a few were critical of some umpiring decisions, but the winners had played the better cricket. Mendis believes there will always be decisions to argue about, but that his side simply outplayed the opposition.

India tried manfully to square the series in the final Test, but centuries on the last day by Dias and Mendis denied them. The captain's and vice-captain's performances meant that Sri Lanka's first Test win would be their first series win as well.

The three bowlers who spearheaded the win had different futures in store. Ahangama, the least experienced of the trio, took 18 wickets at 19.33, but never played Test cricket again. Given his results he certainly deserved another chance. Asantha de Mel captured 59 wickets at 36.95 in his 17 Tests, the last of which was played against India in 1986–87. Rumesh Ratnayake continued to be a valuable bowler for his country, capturing 73 wickets at 35.10 in 23 Tests. He seemed certain to be the first Sri Lankan to reach 100 Test wickets, but his career was sadly interrupted by a serious shoulder injury. The popular Ratnayake enjoyed a wonderful series, snaring 20 wickets at 22.95, with his performance in this game the highlight. There were other fine moments in his career, none better than his 6/66 against a strong Australian side at Hobart in 1989–90.

Some ten years after their maiden win the Sri Lankans have indeed achieved the cricketing recognition Mendis was seeking in 1985. In recent times they have defeated New Zealand and Pakistan on tour, won the tournament in Sharjah by beating the West Indies and recently won the World Cup. There are still wristy, elegant batsmen, but there are now bowlers capable of dismissing Test sides. And watching it all with great pride and enjoyment is the man who set it all going, the current manager, Duleep Mendis.

SRI LANKA v INDIA

Played at P. Saravanamuttu Stadium, Colombo, on 6, 7, 8, 10, 11 September, 1985.
Toss: Sri Lanka.

SRI LANKA

S. Wettimuny	run out	19	c Rajput b Sharma	32
S. A. R. Silva +	c Viswanath b Shastri	111	c Vengsarkar b Kapil Dev	11
R. S. Madugalle	lbw b Sharma	54		
R. L. Dias	c Viswanath b Sharma	95	not out	60
L. R. D. Mendis *	c Shastri b Amarnath	51	not out	13
A. Ranatunga	lbw b Sharma	21		
P. A. de Silva	c Azharuddin b Sharma	2	(3) b Shastri	75
A. L. F. de Mel	lbw b Shastri	0		
R. J. Ratnayake	c Sivaramakrishnan b Shastri	7		
C. D. U. S. Weerasinghe	b Sharma	3		
F. S. Ahangama	not out	0		
Extras	(LB 3, W 4, NB 15)	22	(B 4, LB 6, NB 5)	15
Total		**385**		**3/206**

Fall: 74, 169, 229, 328, 368, 372, 375, 375, 379, 385.   46, 48, 180.

Bowling

First Innings: Kapil Dev 32–10–69–0, Sharma 33–3–118–5, Shastri 45.3–11–74–3, Sivaramakrishnan 31–4–90–0, Amarnath 15–2–31–1.
Second Innings: Kapil Dev 20–4–73–1, Sharma 13–1–55–1, Shastri 13–4–41–1, Sivaramakrishnan 7–1–27–0.

INDIA

L. S. Rajput	c Silva b De Mel	0	lbw b De Mel	12
K. Srikkanth	c Mendis b Ahangama	64	lbw b Ratnayake	25
M. Azharuddin	c Silva b Ratnayake	0	c Silva b De Mel	25
D. B. Vengsarkar	c Ranantunga b Ratnayake	1	c Silva b Ratnayake	0
L. Sivaramakrishnan	c Wettimuny b Ratnayake	18	(9) c Silva b De Mel	21
S. M. Gavaskar	st Silva b Ranatunga	52	(5) c Silva b Ratnayake	19
M. Amarnath	c Ahangama b De Mel	60	(6) c De Silva b Ratnayake	10
R. J. Shastri	c Silva b Ahangama	17	(7) c Silva b Ahangama	4
Kapil Dev *	c Ratnayake b Ahangama	6	(8) c & b Ratnayake	78
S. Viswanath +	c Wettimuny b Ratnayake	7	lbw b Ahangama	0
C. Sharma	not out	4	not out	4
Extras	(B 4, LB 6, W 1, NB 4)	15	(LB 2, NB 2)	4
Total		**244**		**198**

Fall: 0, 1, 3, 79, 88, 178, 218, 229, 238, 244.   39, 39, 41, 84, 84, 98, 98, 168, 169, 198.

Bowling

First Innings: De Mel 31–8–63–2, Ratnayake 25.1–5–76–4, Ahangama 18–3–59–3, Weerasinghe 16–7–28–0, Ranatunga 5–1–8–1.
Second Innings: De Mel 22–4–64–3, Ratnayake 23.2–6–49–5, Ahangama 14–3–56–2, Weerasinghe 3–1–8–0, Ranatunga 4–0–19–0.

Sri Lanka won by 149 runs

25

Madras Tie

INDIA v AUSTRALIA

Chidambaram Stadium, Chepauk, Madras
22 September, 1986 – Day Five

WHEN THE Australian team visited India at the start of the 1986–87 season there were question marks hanging over the side. The previous summer had been extremely disappointing. Following an unsuccessful tour of England in 1985, Australia had been comprehensively outplayed at home and away by New Zealand, and could only draw a home series with India. By the season's end, captain Allan Border had become so frustrated that he threatened to resign unless there was some improvement. This visit to India would be the first opportunity to see if Border's words had been heeded.

The first game of the three Test series was to be played at Chepauk Stadium, Madras, one of Test cricket's least pleasant venues. In addition to the smell of an open sewerage canal next to the ground, the players had to contend with various other problems. According to David Boon, 'It was pretty tough. The dressing rooms were not what we were used to, and the ground was rough. Then there was the climate. The first day was something like 44 degrees and about 100 per cent humidity, and it dropped by about one degree per day. Very hot and humid, and hygiene was also a problem. You had to be very careful where things came from, which meant you had to rely much more on your off–field support'. Greg Matthews remembers the conditions being very oppressive, particularly for bowling.

All in all, it was far from an ideal venue, but the Australians made the most

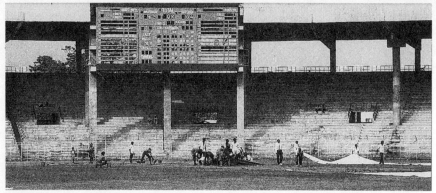

Chepauk Stadium, Madras—one of the game's less pleasant venues. (Gulu Ezekiel)

of it. Border won the toss and batted, and his players responded. Boon began with 122, then Dean Jones played one of the most heroic innings of all time. He made 210, and in the process ended up in hospital on a saline drip. Border made 106 and was able to declare at a healthy 7/574.

India was perilously close to following on, and was only saved by a dashing 119 from all-rounder Kapil Dev which saw them to 397. Off spinner Greg Matthews was the best of the bowlers with 5/103.

Batting in their second innings, and with a substantial lead, the Australians reached 5/170 at stumps on the fourth day.

Twelfth man Dave Gilbert remembers that the Australian captain wanted to bat on a little on the last day, but coach Bob Simpson was keen to declare. The coach must have put some persuasive arguments because Border declared overnight, leaving India 348, from what ended up being 87 overs, to make on the last day. Vice-captain Boon described the thinking behind the decision. 'We had been on top and we thought we could win, even though the track was very easy to bat on. We were confident just because of how many India had to make. Not many sides made that many on the last day to win a game. The problem was that the wicket was like a road, really flat. So what we were going to rely on was the pressure of batting out a whole day and us bowling really well. That was the theory behind it, and we thought we were a fair chance of winning.'

Cricket, though, does have a habit of upsetting theories. Kris Srikkanth began with an aggressive 39 in an opening partnership of 55 with Sunil Gavaskar, before he attempted to hit Matthews over the sightscreen and fell to a catch by Steve Waugh at long-on. The fieldsman sprinted some 25 metres to take the ball. Joined by veteran Mohinder Amarnath, Gavaskar moved up a gear, and the pair added 103 for the second wicket. The Indians were looking in ominous control when Amarnath departed to a catch by Boon at forward short leg, again off a well-flighted Matthews delivery for 51, made off 113 balls with eight boundaries.

With Mohammad Azharuddin as his partner, Gavaskar went on the attack, with 31 runs coming off five overs. The little opener moved towards another Test century, but fell ten runs short, when he was caught in the covers by Jones off the left arm spin of Ray Bright. It was a fine innings by the 'little master' and had taken the team to 3/204. In all, Gavaskar batted 259 minutes, faced 170 balls and hit 12 fours and a six.

Journalist Mike Coward, who watched the match, commented that following Gavaskar's dismissal the mood of the game changed as tensions and frustrations reached boiling point. At one stage he considered physical violence on the field a possibility.

Throughout the day the Australians had remained in a positive frame of mind, but by tea they were getting agitated. Having made all the running, they felt that things were in danger of slipping away. The heat was having an effect, too. According to Gilbert, 'Bright became so distressed that he retired to the dressing room with about 40 overs to go and asked me to ask Border if he wanted him back out there again. Border's reply was to tell his spinner "to get his arse out there as soon as possible"'.

At tea, when India needed 118 off 20 overs with wickets in hand, Border began to wonder if he 'had made the worst decision of all time' in declaring overnight. The possibility of defeat never entered the mind of Matthews as he continued what seemed an endless spell of bowling, although the Indians were now sure they would win.

The pressure was maintained by Azharuddin, who scored 42 before being caught by Greg Ritchie in the deep, and Chandra Pandit (39). Kapil Dev failed, caught second ball at square leg by Bright off Matthews for a single, attempting an ambitious cross batted stroke. Pandit's dismissal, playing on to Matthews, left India 6/291, needing just 57 for victory with Shastri batting very well. At this time a dreadful possibility began to dawn on the Australians, among them David Boon: 'About half way through the last session we thought we were going to lose. Shastri was batting exceptionally well, and they were cruising'.

Watching from the dressing room Dave Gilbert thought the Australians were in trouble. 'India paced their run chase extremely well, but they still managed to lose a wicket every now and then which kept us in the game. Shastri's innings was the one which looked like swinging the game India's way.'

Shastri now found a willing partner in Chetan Sharma. Better known as a fast-medium bowler, Sharma was a useful lower order batsman, and he conspired to give the Australians some more worries. He made 23 in adding 40 for the seventh wicket to take India to the brink of victory, and Australia to the edge of defeat. During this partnership Sharma clashed verbally several times with keeper Tim Zoehrer. On one occasion the Australian turned away and pointed his backside at the batsman. Zoehrer was con-

Ravi Shastri almost carried his team to victory, but was left 48 not out. (Gulu Ezekiel)

vinced he had stumped Sharma off Matthews and pointed the batsman towards the pavilion when he was dismissed shortly afterwards. During the exchange with Zoehrer, Sharma had complained to the umpire that the Australian had called him 'dirty names'.

Matthews had also had some discussions with Pandit while the Indian was at the crease, and during the drinks break they were yelling at each other. The Indian batsman had to be dragged away by the twelfth man. When Pandit was dismissed Matthews pointed him in the direction of the dressing room. In fact, it would be fair to say that relationships between the sides were not good at this time.

In this last part of the game the Australians ran into some trouble with the umpires, in particular Dotiwalla. Vice-captain Boon said, 'We got into the last hour where we had to bowl a certain number of overs, and with it getting very tight, A. B. was taking a reasonable amount of time. We had to guard against bowling any more than we had to. Then it got tighter. The cut-off time of 5.30 had come about and we still had about five or six overs to bowl. That's when A. B. said, "The time's up. It doesn't matter how long it takes us now." There was still plenty of light left, but the umpire started telling us to get on with it. He got quite shirty about it. A. B. in his typical manner told him it was our job and the overs would get bowled and to stop panicking. Then the umpire tried to threaten that he would send AB off the ground. A. B. was pretty fired up at this stage, as was everybody. He turned to me and said, "Well, he can't send me off, can he?" and I said, "Buggered if I know. I s'pose not". I had no idea'.

Border decided not to push the issue, things settled down enough to allow the game to finish, and cricket history missed the sight of an umpire attempting to send a Test captain from the field. Quoted in the press afterwards, Border was critical of the 'niggly nature' of the umpires where certain things were concerned, but he praised them for their courage in giving leg before decisions against the home side.

In spite of the disputes, manager Alan Crompton decided to take no action against any of his players, preferring to put their behaviour down to the appalling heat and humidity as well as the pressure they were under during that last afternoon. He did concede, however, that some things might not have been acceptable at other times and in other places.

With Shastri and Sharma well in command, India appeared headed for victory when Bright struck three crucial blows. First he had Sharma caught at deep mid-on by McDermott, then three runs later he trapped Kiran More in front for no score. Off spinner Shivlal Yadav made eight in a ten run partnership for the ninth wicket before he lunged forward at Bright, missed and was bowled off his pads. The tailender had looked very dangerous, hitting Matthews for six high over long-on in the previous over.

India at 9/344 were four runs from victory and Australia one wicket as the final over began. Greg Matthews had been bowling virtually all day and Border entrusted him with the task. With Shastri on strike most thought the odds favoured India. He defended the first ball, then played the next off an inside edge to Steve Waugh, who fumbled it forward of square leg, and they ran two. Boon remembered what happened next. 'Shastri hit one down to long-on and took one. He left Maninder Singh on strike for the last few balls. (In a letter to the author the Indian spinner said that he and Shastri had decided to go for the win.) Maninder was hit on the pads by the first delivery from Matthews, but the umpire turned it down. The wicket by this time was turning appreciably and everyone had come in. Then Greg bowled

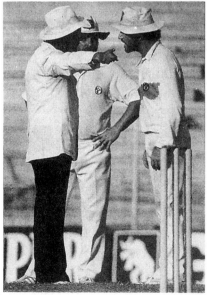

Left: Allan Border and the umpire exchange heated words as the game nears its climax. Vice-captain David Boon looks on. (Gulu Ezekiel) *Right:* The umpire points towards the boundary, threatening to send Border off. (Gulu Ezekiel)

The Australians run to celebrate as Maninder falls leg before and the game is a tie. (Gulu Ezekiel)

and hit him on the pads, and the umpire was up with us. There are photos where Greg is starting to appeal and the umpire's finger is already up. Whether he wanted to be part of history or not, I don't know.'

Maninder stood and pointed at his bat. Boon believed the batsman had missed it, and other Australians—including short leg fieldsman Geoff Marsh—supported Boon's claim, although Allan Border and Tim Zoehrer were not so sure. The Indians, on the other hand, were adamant that Maninder did hit it. His partner Shastri was quoted as saying, 'I have no doubt he nicked the ball'. Journalist Trevor Grant described it this way: 'The Indian left arm spinner patted the first ball back but with the next, pitched right in line with the stumps, he shuffled across and back, misread the line and was plumb lbw'.

Perhaps the best person to ask is the batsman himself. According to Maninder Singh, 'I did play the ball. I felt shattered when the umpire lifted his finger, but then the umpire's decision is final. I will have to live with this disappointment all my life even though the Test is a part of cricket history. I would have preferred not to be made out to be the cause of this history. The rising finger of that umpire is my most vivid memory of that day'.

Shastri remained 48 not out—an innings which contained three fours and two sixes. The last four wickets had fallen for 16 runs in just 22 balls, when India had been cruising towards victory.

The wicket ended India's innings at 347, creating Test cricket's second tie, and, as in 1960–61, which also finished on the second last ball of the game, there was some confusion about the result. Boon thought Australia had won. 'My immediate reaction was that we'd won. It wasn't until five minutes later when everything had calmed down a bit that we realised it was a tie, according to the scoreboard.'

The aftermath. An exhausted Greg Matthews is congratulated by Dean Jones, while Border seems to want to know just what happened. (Gulu Ezekiel)

This last comment was expanded upon. 'There were stories that when the sheets came back to Australia they didn't add up and that we'd won by 4 runs. These sorts of things were floating around, but I don't give any pertinence to them.'

Whatever may or may not have gone on with the scores, the official result was a tie, and the Australians had much to thank their spinners for. Matthews bowled 39.5 overs to take 5/146 and ten wickets in the match for the first time in his Test career, and Bright took 5/94 off 25 overs. Boon is high in his praise of both: 'I don't know whether that's the best Greg's ever bowled, but if you take into account the conditions and the situation he did an exceptional job. Brighty did too, for a guy with a lot more years than Greg. He started to get tired a long time before Greg, but Greg was able to push through it'. Bright had been battling illness and had done a wonderful job just to keep going.

Matthews did not regard it as the high point of his career at the time, simply because Australia failed to win. On the other hand, it was a relief not to lose. In a letter to the author he admitted to feeling great satisfaction at the result and believed his performance in the match was certainly up there with his best.

At the end of the game Gilbert sprinted onto the field and embraced his friend Matthews, who had careered out to square leg after taking the wicket. 'The release of tension was immense. You would have thought we had just won an Ashes decider. I remember Allan Border giving the ball to Matthews. He had picked it up at the fall of the last wicket.'

A famous scoreboard. (Gulu Ezekiel)

As the Australians ran from the field, they were greeted by their coach, Bob Simpson, who had taken part in Test cricket's only other tie, and was one of very few privileged to have seen them both. 'Being coach was worse. There is nothing you can do. You just have to sit there, and it was agony. The day seemed to go on forever and everything was drained out of you by the end. I was initially disappointed with the result because we had made all the running and really deserved to win.'

Zoehrer, in his controversial autobiography, felt the Australians should have won, citing a number of decisions which went against them throughout the final day.

Gilbert also found the day a strain: 'It was nerve–wracking stuff. I lost count of the number of times I ran errands onto the field, such were the demands of the players to cope with the situation. There was just a feeling of helplessness sitting and watching as you felt the tension, but could do little about it, other than yelling encouragement and attending to player needs.'

For Boon, the aftermath remains hazy. 'It's hard to remember because I think we were in such a state of mind, playing five days in that heat. Jonesy was still crook and I'd been throwing up for for three days. It's all a bit of a daze really. But you look at it now, and for cricket, and for us to be involved, it was one hell of a day.'

Amen to that!

INDIA v AUSTRALIA

Played at Chidambaram Stadium, Madras, on 18, 19, 20, 21, 22 September, 1986.
Toss: Australia.

AUSTRALIA

D.C. Boon	c Kapil Dev b Sharma	122	lbw Maninder	49
G.R. Marsh	c Kapil Dev b Yadav	22	b Shastri	11
D.M. Jones	b Yadav	210	c Azharuddin b Maninder	24
R.J. Bright	c Shastri b Yadav	30		
A.R. Border *	c Gavaskar b Shastri	106	(4) b Maninder	27
G.M. Ritchie	run out	13	(5) c Pandit b Shastri	28
G.R.J. Matthews	c Pandit b Yadav	44	(6) not out	27
S.R. Waugh	not out	12	(7) not out	2
T.J. Zoehrer +				
C.J. McDermott				
B.A. Reid				
Extras	(B 1, LB 7, W 1, NB 6)	15	(LB 1, NB 1)	2
Total		**7/574**		**5/170**

Fall: 48, 206, 282, 460, 481, 544, 573.   31, 81, 94, 125, 165.

Bowling

First Innings: Kapil Dev 18–5–52–0, Sharma 16–1–70–1, Maninder 39–8–135–0 Yadav
49.5–9–142–4, Shastri 47–8–161–1, Srikkanth 1–0–6–0.

Second Innings: Kapil Dev 1–0–5–0, Sharma 6–0–19–0, Maninder 19–2–60–3, Yadav
9–0–35–0, Shastri 14–2–50–2.

INDIA

S.M. Gavaskar	c & b Matthews	8	c Jones b Bright	90
K. Srikkanth	c Ritchie b Matthews	53	c Waugh b Matthews	39
M. Amarnath	run out	1	c Boon b Matthews	51
M. Azharuddin	c & b Bright	50	c Ritchie b Bright	42
R.J. Shastri	c Zoehrer b Matthews	62	(7) not out	48
C.S. Pandit	c Waugh b Matthews	35	(5) b Matthews	39
Kapil Dev *	c Border b Matthews	119	(6) c Bright b Matthews	1
K.S. More +	c Zoehrer b Waugh	4	(9) lbw b Bright	0
C. Sharma	c Zoehrer b Reid	30	(8) c McDermott b Bright	23
N.S. Yadav	c Border b Bright	19	b Bright	8
Maninder Singh	not out	0	lbw b Matthews	0
Extras	(B 1, LB 9, NB 6)	16	(B 1, LB 3, NB 2)	6
Total		**397**		**347**

Fall: 62, 65, 65, 142, 206, 220, 245, 330, 387, 397.   55, 158, 204, 251, 253, 291,
331, 334, 344, 347.

Bowling

First Innings: McDermott 14–2–59–0, Reid 18–4–93–1, Matthews 28.2–3–103–5,
Bright 23–3–88–2, Waugh 11–2–44–1.

Second Innings: McDermott 5–0–27–0, Reid 10–2–48–0, Matthews 39.5–7–146–5,
Bright 25–3–94–5, Waugh 4–1–16–0, Border 3–0–12–0.

Match tied

26

Just One Run

AUSTRALIA v WEST INDIES

Adelaide Oval
26 January, 1993 – Day Four

A LLAN BORDER achieved almost everything he could have wished for in his long and distinguished Test career. More Test appearances, runs and catches than anyone else deservedly put him at the pinnacle of the game's achievement. However, in all that cricket, one thing eluded him: a series victory against the West Indies. Border's career coincided with the Caribbean team's domination of the game. A seemingly endless array of fast bowlers meant that it was an achievement to win a match, let alone a series. Border had been involved in a few of these victories, including one in Sydney when he captured eleven wickets with his gentle left arm spinners. No player had resisted the pace blitz with more courage, but as the years and series went by, time to climb this last peak looked to be running out. The Tests to be played in Australia in 1992–93 would be the last chance.

Coming into this series the home side had more reason to be confident than for many years. The West Indies pace attack was good, but did not seem as formidable as before, and the retirements of Viv Richards, Gordon Greenidge and Jeff Dujon left the batting a little weaker. Border, on the other hand, had been building a useful team. He had a balanced attack with the pace of Craig McDermott, Bruce Reid (if he could stay fit) and Merv Hughes, blended with the leg spin of Shane Warne and the off spin of Tim May or Greg Matthews. The Australian batting, led by Mark Taylor and David

Boon, contained the Waugh twins and Border, with Ian Healy a good competitor in the lower order.

The confidence seemed to be well placed as the series unfolded. In Brisbane, the West Indies were teetering on the brink of defeat at 8/133 when stumps were drawn on the last day. Moving on to Melbourne, Shane Warne was included in the side and took 7/52 to send the visitors crashing to a 139 run defeat. The West Indies could obtain only a draw in Sydney, in spite of the magnificence of Brian Lara's 277.

Between the third and fourth games, the West Indies had started to run into some form, winning the one day series, but it looked a tall order to take the Test series with just two games to go.

Richie Richardson started on the right note in Adelaide by winning the toss and batting. However, his batsmen failed to take the advantage, making only 252. Desmond Haynes and Phil Simmons made 45 and 46 respectively, getting the side away to an 84 run start, but after that only Lara (52) and keeper Junior Murray (49 not out) got past 20. Merv Hughes (5/64) and Tim May (2/41) led the bowling.

The Australians were unable to gain a first innings lead as Curtly Ambrose (6/74) dismissed them for 213. Hughes top scored with 43, Steve Waugh made 42 and David Boon made 39 not out, after having to retire hurt, courtesy of a vicious blow on the arm from an Ambrose delivery.

With a small but possibly significant lead of 39, the West Indian batsmen were hoping for more success the second time around. It was not to be, as they were dismissed for just 146, of which skipper Richardson made 72. Tim May produced the astonishing figures of 5/9 in 6.5 overs to sweep away the lower order.

Border's dream was 186 runs away from coming true, and two days were available in which to get them. But there was some work to do before it happened. The West Indians had not lost a series to Australia since 1975–76 and had not lost one at all since 1979–80. They would not surrender that record easily.

'We'd been batting quite well,' remembers David Boon, 'scoring a lot of runs, so we were confident, but you always know that the West Indies are capable of going through you.'

How tough it was going to be was quickly seen early on the fourth day, when Ambrose trapped Boon in front with one which kept a little low for no score. The solid Tasmanian had been Australia's best batsman in the series, and his dismissal put more pressure on the other players.

Over the years Boon has been in a unique position to discuss the West Indies pace attack. He had these thoughts about dealing with Ambrose, Walsh and Bishop: 'Curtly is just a non–relenting bowler and quick. He makes you play nine out of ten. Walsh is more variable. He'll vary his pace and length a lot more. Curtly hates getting hit for runs; Walsh does too, but he's not afraid to try a few things if he can get you out. Ian Bishop is also a good bowler, more a taller version of Malcolm Marshall, but he was quick and could swing it'.

Mark Taylor had been having a poor series, and he had reached seven after 50 minutes of struggle, when he edged one to keeper Murray from the bowling of Kenny Benjamin, the fourth member of the pace attack. At 2/15 things were now looking decidedly shakey. The Australians did not have a good record of chasing small targets in the fourth innings and the thought was there that it could happen again.

The advent of Mark Waugh to the crease seemed to settle things down, and with debutant Justin Langer he took the total past 50.

Just when the Australians were beginning to relax a little, all hell broke loose as wickets tumbled with alarming rapidity. Having made 26 out of 54, Waugh edged a delivery to Carl Hooper at second slip, giving Courtney Walsh his first wicket of the innings. Australia went to lunch an uneasy 3/64.

Steve Waugh had made just four when he drove the first ball after the break to cover, where Keith Arthurton juggled then held the catch—and Ambrose had another wicket.

It was up to the captain to provide the lead, but Ambrose had the answer: a wicked lifting delivery hitting the glove and carrying to Haynes at short leg. The score was a sorry 5/72 and Border out for a single.

Ian Healy has made valuable runs for Australia on many occasions, but not this day. He played on to Walsh, giving the pace man his 1000th first-class wicket. The keeper was gone for nought and the score 6/73.

Merv Hughes had made runs in the first innings, but Ambrose trapped the big fellow in front for one—the Antiguan fast bowler's 10th wicket of the match.

From 7/74 it was surely asking too much from Langer playing in his first Test, partnered by the tail, to make the 112 runs needed for victory. A West Indian win looked a certainty, but this game was a long way from finished.

Leg spinner Shane Warne is more noted for his bowling than batting, but he is quite a capable player, and he held on, making a run here and there while Langer gradually built the score. The hundred was reached with the pair still together, but shortly afterwards Bishop had Warne leg before for nine after 72 minutes at the crease.

Tim May's 5/9 the previous day had given his team a reachable score, but now, on his 31st birthday, he would have to score runs as well if victory was to be achieved. The South Australian off spinner was not an entirely useless proposition with the bat, having a first-class century to his credit. However, that was against the far more gentle Tasmanian attack in a Sheffield Shield game.

Right from the first moment, May was in line behind the ball. He never took a backward step, and scored runs whenever the opportunity presented

itself. With Langer accumulating at
the other end, the score gradually
mounted. The Western Australian
left-hander reached 50 in his maiden
Test, and it is debatable if anyone in
the history of the game has received
a tougher baptism. Battered and
bruised, he held on, and frustration
started to creep into the West Indians'
game. After having Australia 7/74
they couldn't lose, could they?

Both Ambrose and Bishop were
warned by the umpires for intimidation as they fired in short deliveries,
hoping to unsettle the batsmen.

After adding 42 with May for the
ninth wicket, Langer went to swing
a delivery from Bishop down the leg
side, but got a bottom edge and
keeper Murray took the catch. The
young left-hander had batted 253

Justin Langer, who endured one of Test cricket's
toughest debuts to score 54 in Australia's
second innings. (Moss Seigert)

minutes and faced 146 balls for his 54 runs. Every minute of his innings was
played under intense pressure, every run had to be earned. As he walked off
he could have been forgiven for wondering how anyone survived Test cricket
if this was what it was like.

Justin Langer remembered Steve Waugh saying to him during one of the
breaks that it would never get any harder than this. 'It was certainly a lot
tougher than anything I had played before. The thing that stood out was
the increase in intensity. There was constant pressure, and that made the
experience a tough, but enjoyable one. I probably regret playing that pull
shot, but to tell the truth things still looked pretty hopeless at that stage.'

The Test debutant had earned the respect of noted tough man David
Boon. 'The West Indies gave him a hard time, but the little fellow's got heaps
of it. He kept hanging in there. In the first innings he'd been hit a couple of
times and he was starting to feel a bit wobbly. He pulled away at one stage
and they gave him absolute Hell. I remember going down to him and saying,
"Look mate, if you can't see it, if you start going wobbly don't worry about
what these guys say to you, just face up when you're ready". Then as soon
as I got hit he came down and said the same to me. It's probably the luck of
the draw that he hasn't played more, and he was a bit unlucky in getting a pair
in New Zealand, but he's got heaps of guts and he gave it everything he had.'

Langer's dismissal left McDermott and May to make 42 to win for the

Left: Craig McDermott turns to see keeper Junior Murray take the catch that will win the game by just one run. (Nicholas Wilson/*The Advertiser*) *Right:* Craig McDermott, who was reduced to tears in the rooms after his dismissal. (Moss Seigert)

last wicket. The Queensland pace bowler was once thought of as a potential all-rounder, but after some confrontations with the West Indies' pace attacks he showed a distinct dislike of the short ball. The fast bowlers were sure they had his measure. In fact, they believed his courage was decidedly lacking.

Inspired, perhaps, by the efforts of May and Langer, McDermott forced himself to get behind the line most of the time and concentrated furiously to keep the bowlers out. By now May was assuming the role of a batsman, even having the audacity to drive through the covers for four.

Gradually, as the number of runs required came down, the Australians started to wonder if the pair just might do it. Each run was greeted by wild cheering from a crowd which was steadily growing. With about 20 to go Boon and the other Australian players began to think they had a chance.

With five needed, Richardson dived and almost caught McDermott at mid-off. Perhaps, more importantly, he saved some runs as well. In the dressing room things were really getting tense.

Then with just two required McDermott whipped the ball off his legs, only to see Haynes make the save at short leg. Boon remembered the moment. 'Everybody was off their seats. "Billy" hit it towards mid wicket and Desmond Haynes stuck his foot out. It would have won us the game as

Courtney Walsh, who took the final wicket, is hugged by Phil Simmons as Keith Arthurton runs to join in the celebrations. (Ken Piesse)

there was no one behind him. We needed two and it would probably have gone for four. Just hit him on the foot, pure arse.'

The last wicket pair had held out for 88 minutes and 40 runs when Walsh bowled a short ball, the last delivery of his 19th over. McDermott, on 18, tried to get out of the way, but the ball clipped his glove, then helmet, before going through to keeper Murray. 'It just touched the end of his glove', said a dejected Border. 'Technically it was out, but it was a brave decision.' Boon agreed, 'You can look at the replay and it's very hard to tell, although Craig said later that he did hit it'.

'I knew that ball was going to get a wicket', Richardson said afterwards.

A jubilant Walsh embraced his team-mates as the West Indies won by a run, the narrowest margin in Test history. The Australians stood in disappointment, then trudged off with the realisation that they had come so close only to fail. May, 42 not out in 135 minutes, had played the innings of his life, but to no avail. Common sense might say that, after being 7/74, Australia did well to get so close. Such things were small compensation for the batsmen, who having got this far could not really understand how they had lost. 'Two measly runs' was the comment in one press report.

In the Australian rooms, the players were devastated. As Boon remembered, 'Everyone just went flat, but we tried to lift when Craig and Tim came in to give them some encouragement for the effort they'd made'. The two batsmen had differing responses. 'Craig was visibly upset. He cried. When the emotion came he just lost it for a few moments. That doesn't show weakness, but strength and pride in performing for Australia. Maysie just couldn't speak.'

Australian coach Bob Simpson said that he felt as bad as at any moment in his entire cricket career, and that Border was as disappointed as he'd ever seen him. Langer said that he would always remember the look on Allan Border's face when McDermott was dismissed. Boon later took particular pride in having Border join the team's celebrations at the end of the successful 1994–95 series. 'He was as happy as anyone, but if we could have won that game it would have capped off everything for him. But I suppose that's cricket.'

Writing in *Wisden Cricket Monthly*, editor David Frith felt that one day cricket might be in danger of losing its appeal if more games like this occurred. Peter McFarline of *Cricketer* called it 'one of the most extraordinary and gripping Test finishes of the modern era'. Former England player and columnist for *The Guardian*, Mike Selvey, wrote, 'Can there ever have been a better or more tense Test than this? No side in history has got so close to victory and lost, and certainly people who saw the tied Tests of Brisbane and Madras say this one loses nothing by comparison'. Justin Langer's comments on this game are worth recalling: 'My most vivid memory was the incredible mixed feeling of the experience. I was disappointed that we had lost, but I was in awe of the situation. It was my first Test match, and I was thrilled to have been part of such a magnificent game of cricket'.

As buoyed by their victory as their opponents were demoralised, the West Indies thrashed Australia by an innings in Perth to take the series 2–1, and for the final time deny Allan Border the only thing he did not achieve in Test cricket.

AUSTRALIA v WEST INDIES

Played at Adelaide Oval on 23, 24, 25, 26 January, 1993.
Toss: West Indies.

WEST INDIES

D. L. Haynes	st Healy b May	45	c Healy b McDermott		11
P. V. Simmons	c Hughes b S. Waugh	46	b McDermott		10
R. B. Richardson *	lbw b Hughes	2	c Healy b Warne		72
B. C. Lara	c Healy b McDermott	52	c S. Waugh b Hughes		7
K. L. T. Arthurton	c S. Waugh b May	0	c Healy b McDermott		0
C. L. Hooper	c Healy b Hughes	2	c Hughes b May		25
J. R. Murray +	not out	49	c M. Waugh b May		0
I. R. Bishop	c M. Waugh b Hughes	13	c M. Waugh b May		6
C. E. L. Ambrose	c Healy b Hughes	0	st Healy b May		1
K. C. G. Benjamin	b M. Waugh	15	c Warne b May		0
C. A. Walsh	lbw Hughes	5	not out		0
Extras	(LB 11, NB 12)	23	(LB 2, NB 12)		14
Total		**252**			**146**

Fall: 84, 99, 129, 130, 134, 189, 206, 206, 247, 252. 14, 49, 63, 65, 124, 137, 145, 146, 146, 146.

Bowling

First Innings: McDermott 16–1–85–1, Hughes 21.3–3–64–5, S. Waugh 13–4–37–1, May 14–1–41–2, Warne 2–0–11–0, M. Waugh 1–0–3–1.

Second Innings: McDermott 11–0–66–3, Hughes 13–1–43–1, S. Waugh 5–1–8–0, May 6.5–3–9–5, Warne 6–2–18–1.

AUSTRALIA

M. A. Taylor	c Hooper b Bishop	1	(2) c Murray b Benjamin		7
D. C. Boon	not out	39	(1) lbw b Ambrose		0
J. L. Langer	c Murray b Benjamin	20	c Murray b Bishop		54
M. E. Waugh	c Simmons b Ambrose	0	c Hooper b Walsh		26
S. R. Waugh	c Murray b Ambrose	42	c Arthurton b Ambrose		4
A. R. Border *	c Hooper b Ambrose	19	c Haynes b Ambrose		1
I. A. Healy +	c Hooper b Ambrose	0	b Walsh		0
M. G. Hughes	c Murray b Hooper	43	lbw b Ambrose		1
S. K. Warne	lbw b Hooper	0	lbw b Bishop		9
T. B. A. May	c Murray b Ambrose	6	not out		42
C. J. McDermott	b Ambrose	14	c Murray b Walsh		18
Extras	(B 7, LB 3, NB 19)	29	(B 1, LB 8, NB 13)		22
Total		**213**			**184**

Fall: 1, 16, 46, 108, 108, 112, 181, 181, 197, 213. 5, 16, 54, 64, 72, 73, 74, 102, 144, 184.

Bowling

First Innings: Ambrose 28.2–6–74–6, Bishop 18–3–48–1, Benjamin 6–0–22–1, Walsh 10–3–34–0, Hooper 13–4–25–2.

Second Innings: Ambrose 26–5–46–4, Bishop 17–3–41–2, Benjamin 12–2–32–1, Walsh 19–4–44–3, Hooper 5–1–12–0.

West Indies won by 1 run

27

The First Step

ZIMBABWE v PAKISTAN

Harare Sports Club
4 February, 1995 – Day Four

WHEN ZIMBABWE was elevated to Test level in 1992 not all were pleased with the decision. A country with only 100,000 whites and a black population which had as yet not taken to the game seemed to offer little chance of producing enough talented players and to have too small a population base to ensure a healthy survival. This would be especially true if it was confronted by the giants of Test cricket.

When Zimbabwe was admitted as a Test playing nation, *Wisden Cricket Monthly* produced an editorial headed, 'Come in, dear weaklings', in which grave doubt was cast on the African nation's ability to match it with the powers of the game.

The Zimbabwe Cricket Union and the players disagreed, certain in the belief they would be competitive. From their first Test, against India in October 1992, they have managed to be just that.

By the start of the 1994–95 series against Pakistan, they had played eleven Tests. Although they had failed to win a game, they were seldom outclassed, and on occasions—particularly on tour in Pakistan—they could well have won at least one Test. While in the initial stages there was not a great depth of players, some talented cricketers were produced.

Before the series against Pakistan, the Zimbabwe team had visited Australia to compete in the one day World Series Cup. The experience gained there had been of benefit, particularly to younger players like fast bowler Heath Streak and leg spinner Paul Strang. A defeat of England was a highlight, and the side returned home, convinced they could give the Pakistanis a run for their money.

Pakistan, one of the world's most unpredictable sides, had just completed a disappointing tour of South Africa, and the series against Zimbabwe would be an opportunity to regain some pride. Captained by Salim Malik, the visitors possessed a strong pace attack, containing Wasim Akram, Waqar Younis and Aqib Javed. In addition to Malik, Inzamam-ul-Haq, Aamir Sohail, Saeed Anwar and Ijaz Ahmed formed a solid core of batsmen.

Andy Flower, who had the honour of leading Zimbabwe to its first Test win. (Moss Seigert)

For the First Test of the series, to be played at the Harare Sports Club, Waqar Younis was absent, but all the others were available. To oppose them captain Andy Flower had Mark Dekker, Grant Flower, Alistair Campbell, Dave Houghton, Guy Whittall, Stuart Carlisle, Paul Strang, Heath Streak, David Brain and Henry Olonga. Carlisle and Olonga were making their debuts. The last named was of particular interest. Born in Zambia, but with a Kenyan passport, the 18-year-old fast bowler was the first of the indigenous population to represent Zimbabwe. His success could pave the way for the surge of interest which could really establish the game among the blacks, where soccer was the number one choice.

Flower won the toss and decided to bat, but his side was in immediate trouble with the loss of three early wickets for 42 runs. The situation was saved by an astonishing partnership of 269 between the Flower brothers. When Andy was dismissed for 156, Guy Whittall joined Grant Flower in another double century stand. When Grant reached his double century, the declaration was made with the total an impressive 4/544. Whittall remained 113 not out. The pitch had played well and there was nothing to suggest that the strong Pakistani line-up could not save the game. Such a total, however, would allow Andy Flower to support his bowlers with attacking fields.

After some excellent fast bowling from Streak and superb catching, Pakistan struggled to 7/271 at stumps on the third day with Inzamam 53 not out.

Heath Streak, the young pace bowler who shattered the strong Pakistani batting. (Moss Seigert)

Streak was initially disappointed when play resumed, as Inzamam was twice dropped off his bowling, first by Whittall at second slip on 59 and then by Olonga at fine leg ten runs later. In the fifteenth over of the morning Wasim Akram was taken at short leg by Carlisle, his third catch of the innings, for 27. Four overs later Inzamam fell to a brilliant gully catch by Grant Flower for 71, made in 257 minutes with seven fours. He had been so hampered by his injured shoulder that he was forced to play some shots one-handed. Aqib Javed was leg before for nought and Streak had captured the final three wickets to finish with 6/90, the best figures for Zimbabwe in Tests. With a score of 322, Pakistan finished 23 short of avoiding the follow-on.

The only real problem for Zimbabwe was the calling of Olonga by umpire Ian Robinson for throwing. This event, plus a side strain, limited his contribution to just ten overs in the first innings and none in the second. Olonga has since spent some time with Dennis Lillee, and the problems with his action have been sorted out. Streak compares the young man's pace with that of South African 'White Lightning' Alan Donald and believes he has a major part to play in Zimbabwe's cricket future.

In spite of being a bowler short, Andy Flower enforced the follow-on, seeing it as the only way in which his side could force a win. The openers Sohail and Anwar had wiped off eleven of the 222 run deficit by lunch.

What happened after the break must have surprised even the most ardent Zimbabwean supporters. Medium pacer Guy Whittall trapped Saeed Anwar in front for seven. The dangerous Aamir Sohail went to another fantastic catch, this time by Campbell in the covers off left arm quick David Brain for five. Brain then bowled Asif Mujtaba for four, had captain Salim Malik caught behind for six, and—to complete an amazing session—caught Ijaz Ahmed at fine leg off Streak for two. Incredibly, Pakistan was 5/35 and well on the road to defeat.

Inzamam and keeper Rashid Latif added some much needed fight in a partnership of 96 for the sixth wicket. If they could wipe off the deficit and

Left: Inzamam-ul-Haq was the only Pakistani to come to terms with Zimbabwe's bowlers.
Right: Controversial Pakistani Salim Malik endured his worst moment as captain when Zimbabwe thrashed his side by an innings.

set some sort of target on the last day Pakistan could well be back in the match. But Whittall broke the stand when he removed Inzamam, caught by keeper Andy Flower for 65 flashing at a wide ball. This wicket signalled the end of any real resistance.

Rashid was superbly caught by Houghton in the slips off Whittall for 38. Wasim Akram clubbed 19, then holed out to leg spinner Strang, before Streak returned fittingly to capture the final two wickets, bowling Kabir Khan for nought and Aqib for two. Pakistan's total of 158 gave Zimbabwe an emphatic innings and a 64 run victory.

Streak took 3/15, giving him 9/105 for the match, and was well supported by Brain (3/50), Whittall (3/58) and Strang (1/35).

Both Andy Flower and Heath Streak insisted that the pitch was quite a good one, and it is hard to be critical of a surface on which one team scores 4/544. Streak thought that the Pakistanis bowled far too short and wasted any movement there might have been in the surface. The Zimbabweans, on the other hand, kept the ball up, made the batsmen come forward, and picked up a number of catches in the slip and gully area.

For Zimbabwe coach and former England batsman John Hampshire, the moment was one to savour. 'It was one of the best days I've ever had in cricket. Coming into the fourth day I was sure we'd win, but I didn't think we'd do it on that day. I didn't think our win would be as pronounced as it was.' Hampshire also paid tribute to the fantastic catching, and the bowling of Streak. He felt too, that the Pakistanis had been demoralised by how well his team had played. It was also no secret that the visitors had some problems within their team, and were far from united.

This victory was the first step along Zimbabwe's road to recognition. Hampshire felt that some teams looked to games against the Test newcomers as ones in which to build averages and aggregates. 'They're going to have to think again', was the coach's warning.

For captain Andy Flower the win was most important. 'We wondered when that first win would come and whether we would have to wait months or even years. It was a great relief for us and a great boost to the whole country.' The Zimbabwe skipper was also high in his praise of Streak's fast bowling. 'He is very mature for such a young man. In the last year he has increased his pace, swings it away and is pretty quick too. That combination, plus a good head on his shoulders makes him a player with great potential.'

Andy Flower did not think the game would be wrapped up on the fourth day. 'I thought we'd get six or seven, then have to finish them off on the last day and chase a small total to win.' He sounded out his country's desire for the future: 'We want more experience, particularly against the powerful nations. That's the only way we'll keep improving'.

The last point is one also made by Heath Streak. 'We bowled well and forced errors because they tried to play shots which weren't on. On their day Pakistan can be invincible, but they weren't prepared for what came.'

The Pakistanis regained their pride and reputation by winning the remaining two Tests, one of them on a dreadful pitch in Bulawayo, to take the series. But no matter what the final result, the series will always be remembered for Zimbabwe's historic first Test victory, a major step along the path to Test cricket prowess.

ZIMBABWE v PAKISTAN

Played at Harare Sports Club, on 31 January, 1, 2, 4 February, 1995.
Toss: Zimbabwe.

ZIMBABWE

M.H. Dekker	c Rashid b Aqib	2
G.W. Flower	not out	201
A.D.R. Campbell	lbw b Wasim	1
D.L. Houghton	c Sohail b Aqib	23
A. Flower *+	c Wasim b Kabir	156
G.J. Whittall	not out	113
S.V. Carlisle		
H.H. Streak		
P.A. Strang		
D.H. Brain		
H.K. Olonga		
Extras	(B 4, LB 19, W 3, NB 22)	48
Total	**4/544**	

Fall: 4, 9, 42, 311.

Bowling:
Wasim Akram 39.5–12–95–1, Aqib Javed 34.1–8–73–2, Kabir Khan 35–5–142–1, Salim Malik 9–0–42–0, Akram Raza 34–6–112–0, Asif Mujtaba 7–0–30–0, Aamir Sohail 6–1–27–0.

PAKISTAN

Aamir Sohail	c Houghton b Brain	61	c Campbell b Brain	5
Saeed Anwar	c A. Flower b Olonga	8	lbw b Whittall	7
Akram Raza	c Whittall b Streak	19	(9) not out	2
Asif Mujtaba	c Carlisle b Streak	2	(3) b Brain	4
Salim Malik *	c Carlisle b Whittall	32	(4) c A. Flower b Brain	6
Ijaz Ahmed	c G. Flower b Streak	65	(5) c Brain b Streak	2
Rashid Latif +	c Campbell b Whittall	6	c Houghton b Whittall	38
Inzamam-ul-Haq	c G. Flower b Streak	71	(6) c A. Flower b Whittall	65
Wasim Akram	c Carlisle b Streak	27	(8) c Dekker b Strang	19
Kabir Khan	not out	2	b Streak	0
Aqib Javed	lbw b Streak	0	b Streak	2
Extras	(B 3, LB 4, W 9, NB 13)	29	(W 2, NB 6)	8
Total		**322**		**158**

Fall: 36, 82, 88, 131, 135, 151, 271, 317, 322, 322. 13, 16, 26, 29, 35, 131, 142, 156, 156, 158.

Bowling:
First Innings: Streak 39–11–90–6, Brain 27–4–94–1, Olonga 10–0–27–1, Whittall 29–10–49–2, Strang 15–5–45–0, Dekker 4–1–10–0.
Second Innings: Streak 11–4–15–3, Brain 16–4–50–3, Whittall 16–3–58–3, Strang 19–7–35–1.

Zimbabwe won by an innings and 64 runs

28

Hat-tricks and Hundreds

ENGLAND v WEST INDIES

Old Trafford, Manchester
30 July, 1995 – Day Four

ALMOST SINCE Test cricket began, back in 1877, critics have been pre-dicting its demise, but in spite of its occasional flat spots and lacklustre games, it has the pleasant knack of producing the unexpected, of creating classic moments and nail-biting tension. This was such a time.

When the West Indies came to England in 1995, they had much to prove. Earlier in the year they had been comfortably outplayed at home by Mark Taylor's Australians, losing a series in the Caribbean for the first time since 1972–73. The batting looked decidedly fragile, the bowling lacked its usual menace, and to all intents and purposes they appeared to be a team in decline.

For England too, there were questions to be answered. Their recent tour of Australia had been disappointing in the extreme. The coach, Keith Fletcher, had been sacked, and questions were raised about the suitability of Mike Atherton's leadership. A decent performance at home against Richie Richardson's team would be crucial in re-establishing some pride in English cricket. The summer of 1995 would be an important one.

The West Indies struck first with a comfortable victory in the First Test, and the scene looked depressingly familiar to English followers. However, with fast-medium bowler Dominic Cork capturing eleven wickets in his first Test, England levelled the series at Lord's. England's batting failed once again in the Third Test, and the West Indies came to Old Trafford for the fourth game of the series, leading 2–1. Would England be able to fight back again?

It certainly looked as though they could, after they bowled the visitors out for 218 on the first day. Only the wonderful Brian Lara, with 87, could get past 30, as Angus Fraser and Cork each captured four wickets, and debutant off spinner Mike Watkinson, two.

The fightback was well and truly on as England then replied with 437. Graham Thorpe made a brave 94, but many others contributed. Cork made 56, a maiden half-cen-

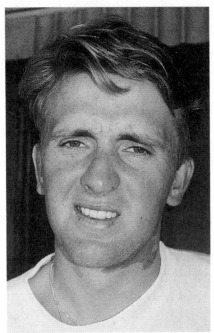

Dominic Cork, whose fine bowling in his maiden Test series enabled England to square the rubber. (Moss Seigert)

tury, underlining the fact that he was a potentially fine all-rounder. Atherton (47), Robin Smith (44), Jack Russell (35) and Watkinson (37) also helped, as did the record 64 extras conceded by the West Indies. Courtney Walsh, with four wickets, was the most successful of the bowlers.

So the West Indies went into bat a second time, faced with a deficit of 221. Some seriously good batting would need to take place if they were to set England a target on the last day. The situation was further compounded by an injury to Carl Hooper. He had broken a bone in his hand and was unable to open the innings with Sherwin Campbell. At the end of the third day England had moved closer to victory by dismissing Arthurton, Campbell and Adams for 97, before the threatening Lara and the out-of-form Richardson had taken them through to stumps and a total of 161.

As the fourth day began, most thought that the West Indies' hope stood or fell with the partnership between the side's two best batsmen. England, on the other hand, required a quick breakthrough, and Cork gave it to them in what just might be the most sensational first over of a day's play ever delivered. Unfortunately, about half the crowd were still coming into the ground and missed what was about to transpire in a first over which lasted eleven minutes.

To the fourth delivery Richardson offered no stroke to a ball which clipped the pad and hit the stumps via the inside edge of the bat. The bowler and

Dominic Cork falls to his knees as Carl Hooper is given out leg before to complete the hat-trick. (Patrick Eagar)

fieldsmen were jubilant. It was the perfect start. Junior Murray shuffled across to the next delivery and was leg before. More celebrations came from the fielding side as the batsmen took a while to leave the scene.

To receive the hat-trick ball was Carl Hooper, batting at number seven because of his hand injury. An enigmatic batsman, he had frequently disappointed his fans with his lack of consistency, but if he could stay with Lara the game might still take some winning by England. Cork bowled it perfectly, dead straight, and Hooper shuffled across and was struck on the pads. In response to the almost hysterical appeals, umpire Cyril Mitchley slowly raised his finger. Cork sank to his knees, arms raised in triumph, and the crowd roared its approval of England's first Test hat-trick since Peter Loader took one in 1957, the first one at Old Trafford since Australian Jimmy Matthews captured two in a game against South Africa in the Triangular series of 1912, and the 22nd in all Tests.

The Times made this pertinent comment about England's all-rounder: 'Dominic Cork is one of those rare and priceless cricketers who seem forever to be making things happen. Already, in a mere three Test matches, he has achieved more than many pretenders to the all-rounder role have managed in complete careers'. Michael Henderson, writing in the same paper, said, 'England have got themselves a proud, committed and match–winning cricketer'.

With the West Indies 6/161—still 60 behind—the game appeared to belong to England, but Brian Lara—60 not out—had other ideas. He decided to attack, hooking and cutting Cork. With Ian Bishop as his partner, he seemed intent on getting his side in front as soon as possible. Bishop had one lucky escape when the ball rolled into his stumps without dislodging a bail. The fast bowler made just nine in 37 minutes, but he added 30 runs with Lara before a ball from Watkinson went from pad to glove to Crawley.

Now partnered by Kenny Benjamin, Lara produced an assault which was in its own way every bit as dazzling as Cork's hat-trick. Every bad ball seemed to go to the fence, and even some good ones as well, as the left-hander struck a series of fours. He reached his fifth Test century with a sweep to the boundary. It was batting on a different level to anything else seen in the game.

Brain Lara prepares to go on the attack during his breathtaking 145. (Patrick Eagar)

Reaching that milestone did not mean the job was done. An innings defeat was averted, but with the West Indies just 13 in front, Benjamin was caught by Nick Knight at first slip off Angus Fraser.

Joined by Curtly Ambrose, Lara continued to play his strokes, and the pair survived until lunch. If the stand could prosper, England might yet struggle to win. A chase of 150 or so in the last innings would not be welcome.

After a partnership of 49, Lara, on 145, pulled a ball from Fraser cleanly but uppishly, and Knight ran in and dived forward to take the catch. The sigh of relief was there, but it was lost in the roar of the crowd. Lara walked off, disappointed with himself, but to a deserved standing ovation. His 145 was made in 281 minutes off 226 balls and contained 16 memorable boundaries. He had removed the possibilty of play becoming anticlimatic after Cork's hat-trick. Most would agree that the little Trinidadian is the best batsman in the world today.

If Atherton thought the agony was over now with the removal of Lara he was forced to think again. Walsh, a man with an extravagant batting technique, hit Fraser for six, and held out while 31 runs were added for the last wicket before he was bowled, fittingly, by Cork for 16. Ambrose remained 23 not out. Cork had 4/111, Watkinson 3/64 and Fraser 2/53 in an attack that did its best not to wilt under Lara's onslaught.

After such a dreadful start to the day the West Indies had fought back heroically to add 153 runs for the last four wickets. However, a total of 314 meant that England needed only 94 to win. It seemed about 50 runs short of a defendable total, but the batsmen knew that they would be in for a torrid time making them.

The West Indies' only chance was to take some early wickets, so it was

A delivery from Ian Bishop breaks Robin Smith's cheekbone as England falters in its chase for victory. (Patrick Eagar)

vital for captain Atherton and debutant Knight to make a solid start. This they did, scoring 28 in the first eight overs and 39 in 13. Over a third of the way there, and all wickets intact—surely England would cruise to victory.

Following the advent of a streaker, Atherton tried to make two for a shot to third man, but was run out for 22 after a look at the video replay. Tea was taken one run later, with the odds still very much in England's favour.

Any complacency the home side might have felt was quickly shattered after the break. It took 17 minutes to get a run, and that was from a mis-field, then Knight was caught by substitute fieldsman Chanderpaul at slip from the bowling of Ian Bishop for 13.

Crawley almost followed him, but the umpires decided that the ball had not carried to the fieldsman. Graham Thorpe top scored in the first innings, but failed to get off the mark in the second. He hooked Benjamin to Ambrose at fine leg, and England was suddenly 3/45.

Robin Smith had made only a single when a delivery from Bishop beat a hasty defensive parry, hit the shoulder of the bat and smashed the earpiece of his helmet into the side of his face. In a very shaky state, Smith was helped off. A trip to hospital diagnosed a depressed fracture of the cheekbone.

In the next over all-rounder Craig White received another lifter from Benjamin and could only fend it to Chanderpaul in the slips. England was 4/48 (really five with Smith's injury although he remained in the rooms for a while in case he might be needed), and had still nearly half the runs to get. Surely, this game could not be lost, could it?

In the last series between the two countries, England had been bowled out for 46 in Trinidad. Was something similar on the cards? During this period, Atherton, in a masterpiece of understatement, described the situation in the dressing room as 'a little bit tense'. According to Alan Lee in *The Times* getting the runs 'now looked about as straightforward as running through quicksand'.

Into this crucial situation strode keeper Jack Russell—a man with a point to prove. Recalled to the England side because of the injury to Alec Stewart, Russell had an opportunity to prove to the selectors that he could bat. Supposed lack of ability with the bat had been the apparent justification for ignoring Russell's claims to a place in the side. He determined to attack, knowing that a boundary or two would sway the situation.

He cut Benjamin, then hooked Ambrose, and when Bishop bowled, he played him twice to the leg side boundary. Crawley then hit a short ball from Benjamin for four.

At 4/82 Richardson conceded that his team's chance had gone by bringing on Arthurton and Adams to bowl the last few overs. The target was duly achieved without further loss. Russell remained 31 not out, off just 39 balls with five boundaries. He had knocked a large hole in the theory that he wasn't much of a batsman. Crawley held on for just under two hours in making 15 not out, a contribution every bit as important as Russell's, and he had the pleasure of scoring the winning run.

England's six wicket victory was achieved at 5.49 pm, having kept the crowd on the edge of their seats for the best part of six hours. The series was now levelled at 2–2 with two games remaining. Dominic Cork was made the

Man of the Match, although Lara, with 87 and 145, must have pushed him all the way. Russell too, deserved some consideration for excellent keeping and fighting batting. Cork, though, was delighted. 'Everything seems to be working for me. I am just trying to keep going on the crest of the wave.'

Atherton's side had come back again, showing a character that many believed it did not possess. Writing in *Wisden Cricket Monthly*, Jack Bannister said, 'England won because of superior discipline and better-directed cricket... Not often do the opposition outfight them (West Indies). England did at Old Trafford'.

The Times cricket correspondent, Alan Lee, gave his summary: 'Consistency may still be beyond them but the other familiar shortcomings of the England cricket team—courage, character and self-belief—no longer apply. Twice now they have picked themselves up off the floor in this gripping series, yesterday completing a victory in the Fourth Cornhill Test that looked inevitable from the first, sensational over of the morning but was finally achieved amid high tension in the early evening'.

England maintained its resolute play for the remainder of the series, and the last two Tests were drawn, creating a shared series. Much of this was due to Lara, who continued his good form, scoring centuries in both of those games. Perhaps, as at Old Trafford, he alone stood between his side and defeat.

For Mike Atherton the draw in this game and series was a vindication. He led the side well and was its leading batsman. After the tribulations he had suffered in the previous twelve months, few would begrudge him that success.

A day which starts with a hat-trick, contains a classic century from a great player, a collapse when chasing a small target, and then victory achieved by a player, who, according to some, couldn't bat, is something out of the ordinary. It proves once again, as the game seems prone to do, that Test cricket is far from dead. It remains a game capable of high drama, of gut–wrenching tension strung out over hours. Something that produces a day like this must still be the greatest game of all.

ENGLAND v WEST INDIES

Played at Old Trafford, Manchester, on 27, 28, 29, 30 July, 1995.
Toss: West Indies.

WEST INDIES

C. L. Hooper	c Crawley b Cork	16	(7) lbw b Cork	0
S. L. Campbell	c Russell b Fraser	10	(1) c Russell b Watkinson	44
B. C. Lara	lbw b Cork	87	c Knight b Fraser	145
J. C. Adams	c Knight b Fraser	24	c & b Watkinson	1
R. B. Richardson *	c Thorpe b Fraser	2	b Cork	22
K. L. T. Arthurton	c Cork b Watkinson	17	(2) run out	17
J. R. Murray +	c Emburey b Watkinson	13	(6) lbw b Cork	0
I. R. Bishop	c Russell b Cork	9	c Crawley b Watkinson	9
C. E. L. Ambrose	not out	7	(10) not out	23
K. C. G. Benjamin	b Cork	14	(9) c Knight b Fraser	15
C. A. Walsh	c Knight b Fraser	11	b Cork	16
Extras	(LB 1, NB 5)	6	(B 5, LB 9, NB 8)	22
Total		**216**		**314**

Fall: 21, 35, 86, 94, 150, 166, 184, 185, 205, 216.   36, 93, 97, 161, 161, 161, 191, 234, 283, 314.

Bowling

First Innings: Fraser 16.2–5–45–4, Cork 20–1–86–4, White 5–0–23–0, Emburey 10–2–33–0, Watkinson 9–2–28–2.

Second Innings: Fraser 19–5–53–2, Cork 23.5–2–111–4, White 6–0–23–0, Emburey 20–5–49–0, Watkinson 23–4–64–3.

ENGLAND

N. V. Knight	b Walsh	17	c sub b Bishop	13
M. A. Atherton *	c Murray b Ambrose	47	run out	22
J. P. Crawley	b Walsh	8	not out	15
G. P. Thorpe	c Murray b Bishop	94	c Ambrose b Benjamin	0
R. A. Smith	c sub b Ambrose	44	retired hurt	1
C. White	c Murray b Benjamin	23	c sub b Benjamin	1
R. C. Russell +	run out	35	not out	31
M. Watkinson	c sub b Walsh	37		
D. G. Cork	not out	56		
J. E. Emburey	b Bishop	8		
A. R. C. Fraser	c Adams b Walsh	4		
Extras	(B 18, LB 11, W 1, NB 34)	64	(LB 2, W 1, NB 8)	11
Total		**437**		**4/94**

Fall: 45, 65, 122, 226, 264, 293, 337, 378, 418, 437.   39, 41, 45, 48.

Bowling

First Innings: Ambrose 24–2–91–2, Walsh 38–5–92–4, Bishop 29–3–103–2, Benjamin 28–4–83–1, Adams 8–1–21–0, Arthurton 9–2–18–0.

Second Innings: Ambrose 5–1–16–0, Walsh 5–0–17–0, Bishop 12–6–18–1, Benjamin 9–1–29–2, Adams 2–0–7–0, Arthurton 2.5–1–5–0.

England won by 6 wickets

Bibliography

The following were of great assistance in the preparation of this work.

Books

Arlott, John: *Days at the Cricket*, Longmans, 1950.

Bala, Rajan: *The Winning Hand – Biography of B.S. Chandrasekhar*, Rupa, 1993.

Barker, J.S: *Summer Spectacular*, Sportsmans Book Club, 1965.

Barker, Ralph: *Innings of a Lifetime*, Collins, 1982.

Bedser, Alec: *Twin Ambitions*, Stanley Paul, 1986.

Benaud, Richie: *A Tale of Two Tests*, Hodder and Stoughton, 1962.

Bettesworth, W.A: *Chats on the Cricket Field*, Merrit and Hatcher, 1910.

Brearley, Mike: *Phoenix from the Ashes*, Hodder and Stoughton, 1982.

Brodribb, Gerald: *The Croucher*, London Magazine Editions, 1974.

Brogdan, Stanley: *The First Test*, Hawthorn Press, 1946.

Brown, Lionel H: *Victor Trumper and the 1902 Australians*, Secker and Warburg, 1981.

Cashman, Richard: *The Demon Spofforth*, New South Wales University Press, 1990.

Chappell, Ian: *Chappelli*, Hutchinson, 1976.

Coward, Mike: *Cricket Beyond the Bazaar*, Allen and Unwin, 1990.

Cowdrey, Colin: *M.C.C. – The Autobiography of a Cricketer*, Hodder and Stoughton, 1976.

Cozier, Tony: *The West Indies – Fifty Years of Test Cricket*, Angus and Robertson, 1978.

Downer, Sydney: *100 Not Out – A Century of Cricket on the Adelaide Oval*, Rigby, 1972.

Evans, Godfrey: *Behind the Stumps*, Hodder and Stoughton, 1951.

Eytle, Ernest; *Frank Worrell*, Hodder and Stoughton,1963.

Fingleton, J.H: *Brightly Fades the Don*, Collins, 1949.

Fingleton, J.H. *The Greatest Test of All*, Collins, 1961.

Frindall, Bill: *The Wisden Book of Test Cricket*, Queen Anne Press, 1990.

Gavaskar, Sunil: *Sunny Days*, Rupa & Co., 1977.

Guha, Ramachandra & Vaidyanathan, T.G: *An Indian Cricket Omnibus*, Oxford University Press, 1994.

Hadlee, Richard & Brittenden, Dick: *Hadlee*, AH & AW Reed, 1981.

Holmes, Bob & Marks, Vic (eds): *My Greatest Game*, Mainstream, 1994.

Larwood, Harold & Perkins, Kevin: *The Larwood Story*, Bonpara, 1982.

Jaggard, Ed: *Garth*, Fremantle Arts Centre Press, 1993.

Lilley, Arthur A: *Twenty Four Years of Cricket*, Mills and Boon, 1912.

Lindwall, Ray: *The Challenging Tests*, Pelham, 1961.

McGlew, Jackie: *Cricket for South Africa*, Hodder and Stoughton, 1961.

Mason, Ronald: *Ashes in the Mouth*, Penguin, 1984.

May, Peter: *A Game Enjoyed*, Stanley Paul, 1985.

Moyes, A.G. 'Johnnie': *Australian Cricket – a History*, Angus and Robertson, 1959.

Moyes, A.G. 'Johnnie:' *The West Indies in Australia 1960–61*, Angus and Robertson, 1961.

Pardon, Charles Frederick: *The Australians in England 1882*, J.W. McKenzie, 1982.

Pawle, Gerald: *R.E.S. Wyatt – Fighting Cricketer*, George Allen and Unwin, 1985.

Pollock, Graeme: *Down the Wicket*, Pelham, 1968.

Richardson, V.Y: *The Vic Richardson Story*, Rigby, 1969.

Ross, Alan: *The West Indies at Lord's*, Eyre & Spottiswoode, 1963.

Rowan, Lou: *The Umpire's Story*, Jack Pollard Pty Ltd, 1973.

Snow, John: *Cricket Rebel*, Hamlyn, 1976.

Stevenson, Mike: *Illingworth – A Biography*, Ward Lock, 1978.

Sutcliffe, Bert: *Between Overs*, W.H. Allen, 1963.

Swanton, E.W: *As I Said at the Time*, Collins Willow, 1983.

Travers, Ben: *94 Declared – Cricket Reminiscences*, Elm Tree Books, 1981.

Warner, P.F: *The M.C.C. in South Africa 1905–06*, Chapman Hall, 1906.

Webster, Ray & Miller, Allan: *First Class Cricket in Australia Vol. 1*, 1850/51 to 1941/42, Ray Webster, 1991.

Wright, John: *Christmas in Rarotonga – the John Wright Story*, Moa, 1990.

Yallop, Graham: *Lambs to the Slaughter*, Outback Press, 1979.

Zoehrer, Tim: *The Gloves are Off... Now for the Facts*, EMW Publications, 1995.

Magazines

Australian Cricket

Cricket Lore

The Cricketer (Australia)

Cricketer International

The Cricket Player (New Zealand)

Playfair Cricket Monthly

Sportsweek's World of Cricket (India)

Wisden Cricket Monthly

Annuals

The Cricket Almanack of New Zealand 1954, (Arthur Carman, editor), 1954.

DB Cricket Annual 1978, (Don Neely, editor), Moa, 1978.

The Shell Cricket Almanack of New Zealand 1978, (Arthur Carman, editor), 1978.

Newspapers

The Adelaide Advertiser, The Argus, The Australasian, The Courier Mail, The Daily Telegraph, The Evening Post, The Examiner, The Guardian, The Guardian Weekly, The Observer, The Sporting Globe, The Sun, The Sun–Herald, The Times.